Anonymous

Report of the Joint Committee of Investigation

Appointed by the Kansas legislature of 1872: to investigate all charges of bribery and corruption connected with the senatorial elections of 1867 and 1871

Anonymous

Report of the Joint Committee of Investigation
Appointed by the Kansas legislature of 1872: to investigate all charges of bribery and corruption connected with the senatorial elections of 1867 and 1871

ISBN/EAN: 9783337152628

Printed in Europe, USA, Canada, Australia, Japan

Cover: Foto ©Suzi / pixelio.de

REPORT OF THE

JOINT COMMITTEE

OF

INVESTIGATION

APPOINTED BY THE

KANSAS LEGISLATURE OF 1872,

To Investigate all Charges of Bribery and Corruption Connected with the Senatorial Elections of 1867 and 1871.

TOPEKA, KANSAS:
S. S. PROUTY, PUBLIC PRINTER.
PRINTED AT THE "COMMONWEALTH" STATE PRINTING HOUSE,
1872.

CONCURRENT RESOLUTION.

Resolved by the House of Representatives, the Senate Concurring:

That five thousand copies of the report of the testimony taken by the Joint Committee to investigate charges of bribery and corruption in the Senatorial elections of 1867 and 1871, and the Senate Wood Investigating Committee be and the same is hereby ordered to be printed in pamphlet form for the use of the House and Senate: *Provided*, That the report be printed in solid form, and the testimony of each witness shall be printed in a separate paragraph.

That the Joint Committee and Senate Committee be directed to deliver the testimony by them taken to the Secretary of State, who is hereby directed to superintend the printing of said testimony, and to distribute the same to the members of the Legislature, the President of the Senate, the Governor and State Officers.

Adopted by the House February 24, 1872.

ALEX. R. BANKS,
Clerk of the House.

Concurred in by the Senate February 24, 1872.

GEO. C. CROWTHER,
Secretary of State Senate.

REPORT OF THE JOINT COMMITTEE.

The following resolution was adopted by the Kansas Legislature, January 24th, 1872:

Be it resolved by the House of Representatives, the Senate concurring therein:

That a committee consisting of five members of the House of Representatives, and three members of the Senate be appointed to investigate all charges of bribery and corruption connected with the Senatorial elections of 1867 and 1871, with power to send for persons and papers, and report to the Legislature as soon as practicable; and that for the purposes of this investigation each member of the Committee which shall be appointed under this resolution shall have power to administer oaths and affirmations.

On February 24th, 1872, the Committee appointed under the foregoing resolutions made the following

REPORT.

Mr. President of the Senate and Speaker of the House of Representatives: The Committee appointed under the foregoing resolution met on the 26th day of January, 1872, and organized and issued subpœnas for witnesses and ... and on

ERRATA.

Page 100 and 101, *F.* H. Drenning, instead of *T.* H. Drenning.

Page 215 to 217, J. T. La*n*ter, instead of J. T. La*u*ter.

Page 255 to 259, W. S. Burke, instead of W. S. *Banks*.

is herewith submitted, ...

From the testimony taken, your Committee find,

CONCURRENT RESOLUTION.

Resolved by the House of Representatives, the Senate Concurring:

That five thousand copies of the report of the testimony taken by the Joint Committee to investigate charges of bribery and corruption in the Senatorial elections of 1867 and 1871, and the Senate Wood Investigating Committee be and the same is hereby ordered to be printed in pamphlet form for the use of the House and Senate: *Provided*, That the report be printed in solid form, and the testimony of each witness shall be printed in a separate paragraph.

That the Joint Committee and Senate Committee be directed to deliver the testimony by them taken to the Secretary of State, who is hereby directed to superintend the printing of said testimony, and to distribute the same to the members of the Legislature, the President of the Senate, the Governor and State Officers

A[illegible]

Cc[illegible]

REPORT OF THE JOINT COMMITTEE.

The following resolution was adopted by the Kansas Legislature, January 24th, 1872:

Be it resolved by the House of Representatives, the Senate concurring therein:

That a committee consisting of five members of the House of Representatives, and three members of the Senate be appointed to investigate all charges of bribery and corruption connected with the Senatorial elections of 1867 and 1871, with power to send for persons and papers, and report to the Legislature as soon as practicable; and that for the purposes of this investigation each member of the Committee which shall be appointed under this resolution shall have power to administer oaths and affirmations.

On February 24th. 1872, the Committee appointed under the foregoing resolutions made the following

REPORT.

MR. PRESIDENT OF THE SENATE AND SPEAKER OF THE HOUSE OF REPRESENTATIVES: The Committee appointed under the foregoing resolution met on the 26th day of January, 1872, and organized and issued subpœnas for witnesses and adjourned until Tuesday, the 30th day of January, and on that day met and proceeded to take the testimony of witnesses, and continued from day to day, and ceased the taking of testimony on the 23d day of February, 1872. We summoned to appear before us persons within the State of whom it was alleged that they knew something of the subject matter of the inquiry, and the testimony of those who appeared was taken. Under the authority of a concurrent resolution, a committee employed James Chew as their clerk, who reduced to writing all the testimony taken, which testimony is herewith submitted, and made a part of our report.

From the testimony taken, your Committee find,

That, at the Senatorial election of 1867, a large sum of money was used and attempted to be used in bribing and in attempting to bribe and influence the members of the Legislature to secure the election of S. C. Pomeroy, E. G. Ross and Thomas Carney, by S. C. Pomeroy, Thomas Carney, Perry Fuller and others in their employ.

See the report of a committee appointed in 1867, in House Journal of 1867, from page 957 to page 971 inclusive. Also see testimony herewith submitted of Geo. A. Reynolds, I. S. Kalloch, R. D. Mobley, S. D. Macdonald, Thomas A. Osborn, Joshua Wheeler, William Spriggs, D. R. Anthony, Edward Russell, *et al.*

It also appears in reference to that election that S. C. Pomeroy and Sidney Clarke, in March, 1866, jointly paid one thousand dollars, and promised to pay the further sum of two thousand dollars, for which they executed their joint notes to M. W. Reynolds, who has been recently appointed receiver of the land office at Neodesha in consideration that he would use the columns of his paper, the *Journal*, at Lawrence, to secure the election of S. C. Pomeroy to the United States Senate in 1867, and Sidney Clarke to Congress in the fall of 1866. It also appears that S. C. Pomeroy paid in addition the further sum of two hundred and fifty dollars to the said M. W. Reynolds. It further appears that M. W. Reynolds sued upon these notes in the Douglas county district court, and the defendants Pomeroy and Clarke pleaded therein an illegal consideration for the notes, and that the findings of the court upon trial upon the merits were for the defendants and the judgment against the plaintiff Reynolds. That Reynolds had the case prepared for the Supreme Court, and then directed his counsel not to proceed further in the cause, and that shortly thereafter he was appointed to the public office he now holds. From the depositions of Pomeroy and Clarke taken and used in that case it would seem that the payment of the one thousand dollars and the promise of two thousand dollars to M. W. Reynolds, were to advance Republicanism in Kansas and secure a Republican victory at the election of the fall of 1866.

When such testimony as this is viewed in the light of the then well known fact, and the subsequently demonstrated truth that the State was then Republican by a majority of 11,000, without the aid of the Lawrence *Journal*, its falsity is apparent. That the one thousand dollars was paid, and the two thousand dollars promised to be paid, was so paid and promised to be paid to subsidize the *Journal* in the interest of S. C. Pomeroy and Sidney Clarke, personally, is a fair conclusion from the testimony. (See the testimony of George

A. Reynolds, W. W. Nevison, and the depositions of S. C. Pomeroy, Sidney Clarke and George A. Reynolds, and the findings of the court.) As a thorough investigation of the Senatorial election of 1867, by reason of the lapse of time since that date, absolutely required for its preparation and completion, much more time than the ordinary length of a legislative session, the Committee were forced to be content in that regard with what they could glean from the witnesses brought before them for the proof of other facts. Yet, from all the testimony before the Committee on that question, we have no hesitation in recording our well established conclusions, that money was used in a large amount and in a corrupt and criminal way by candidates for United States Senator, and by their friends with their knowledge. In relation to the election of 1871, the Committee find that, the testimony shows that Sidney Clarke was a candidate for election to the office of United States Senator in 1871, and that his friends engaged for him, which act he afterwards ratified, some eighty rooms at the Tefft House; that, in addition thereto he rented and fitted up on the opposite side of the street from the Tefft House, and on the corner of Kansas avenue and Sixth avenue, a suite of five rooms, which was during that canvass designated as "the soup house," and "the bread riot," where refreshments were kept. That he deposited with the Kansas Valley National Bank, when he came here, twenty-five hundred dollars, which were drawn out by Mr. Adams upon authority from Clarke.

That Sidney Clarke overdrew his account about sixteen hundred dollars. (See testimony of Clarke, Adams and Abell, *et al.*) That he offered to members of the Legislature appointments to office and payment of expenses of the election of members of the Legislature, for their votes for himself for United States Senator. (See the testimony of King, Phinney, Bond and Wheeler.) That he told R. S. Stevens to make whatever arrangement he pleased with Caldwell in regard to his (Clarke's) expenses. (See testimony of Clarke.) That Stevens paid out for Sidney Clarke, during that canvass, about twenty six hundred dollars. (See testimony of George A. Reynolds.)

That his friend D. M. Adams, with the knowledge of Clarke, undertook to purchase Senator Wood's vote with the promise of an office, which promise was secured by a certificate of deposit of the Kansas Valley National Bank for the sum of three thousand dollars, actually issued. (See the testimony of King, Abell and Adams.) That Mr. Wheaton, of Fort Scott, a friend of Mr. Clarke's, who was here endeavoring to secure Clark's election, offered to buy the vote of W. C. Webb for Mr. Clarke, for the sum of two thousand dollars, at Fort Scott in December, 1870. (See testimony of Webb.) These things all conspire to place the fact beyond question that Mr. Clark intended to use, used and was endeavoring to use, and with his knowledge permitted his friends to use and endeavor to use money and other valuable considerations in an illegal, corrupt and criminal way, to secure votes for himself for the United States Senate. (See testimony of Clarke, Adams, Phinney, King, P. T. Abell, W. C. Webb and W. Shannon.) It also appears that R. S. Stevens, who is a resident of Attica, New York, and General Manager of the Missouri, Kansas & Texas Railroad, and whose business headquarters were then, as now, in Sedalia, Missouri, was here in the interest of Mr. Clarke, and expended an amount of money for his use in the canvass. Also that P. T. Abell was here and spent a sum of money in the interest of Mr. Clarke, and was at that time in the employment of James F. Joy in his railroad business in this State. (See testimony of George A. Reynolds and P. T. Abell.) Also that John McDonald, a resident of St. Louis, Missouri, (who had a peculiar interest in Mr. Clarke's election, was here in Clarke's interest. It also appears that Adams paid out of Clarke's money the entire expense of "the soup house." That a part of the money paid by Stevens went to pay the expenses of "the soup house." And that Colonel P. T. Abell paid two or three hundred hundred dollars as a part of the expenses of the "soup house." May it not be that the disgraceful "soup house'" is made the *ledger scape-goat* of greater sins of these men? (See testimony of Adams, Abell and Reynolds.) It can hardly be supposed, even by the most verdant, that Mr. Adams would issue the paper of the Kansas Valley National Bank for three thousand dollars, and Mr. Wheaton offer to pay two thousand dollars for a vote for Mr. Clarke, without the authority of Mr. Clarke.

In the case of the certificate for the three thousand dollars, the testimony of Mr. King shows that the transaction, which was a direct attempt to obtain a vote for Mr. Clarke by bribery (the bribe being a mail agency, or its cash equivalent—three thousand dollars) was with the knowledge and consent of Mr. Clarke, if not by his positive direction. The facts that Mr. Wheaton came here and labored for Mr. Clarke, and was at the time he made the offer to Mr. Webb, and had been before the strong friend of Mr. Clarke, leaves but little doubt even with the most skeptical, that was an effort directed and assented to by Clarke, to bribe Webb with two thousand dollars. The offer made to Phinney by Clarke himself and S. C. King, as shown by Wheeler's testimony, are of the same character, except that in the latter it does not appear that any money was to be used in connection with the appointment. (See testimony of Clarke, Wheeler, King, Phinney and Abell.)

In relation to the matters affecting Alexander Caldwell, the testimony shows that Len. T. Smith was his particular friend, and was a Democrat and here working earnestly in the interest of Mr. Caldwell, and recognized by him as his confidential adviser and agent. That J. L. McDowell was here working for and on confidential terms with Alexander Caldwell. in consideration of the promise of Caldwell to remove Mrs. Johnson, a widow, whose husband was killed early in the war, at Morristown, Missouri, from the postofice at Leavenworth. (See testimony of McDowell, Thomas, *et al.*)

That a large lobby of Leavenworth men were here in the interest of Caldwell. That Thomas Carney was here upon confidential relations with Caldwell. That some kind of a written agreement existed between Caldwell and Carney in relation to the senatorial election. (See testimony of McDowell, *et al.*)

That Carney stated, but about two weeks ago, that he was coming before the Committee to testify, and sent such message to the Committee; that he was notified by telegraph as well as by summons to appear; that he was going to tell all he knew, and that he knew that Caldwell and those in his interest had purchased the votes of members of the Legislature to vote for Caldwell, (see the testimony of Osborn,) that a check for *seven thousand* dollars, drawn by Len. T. Smith in favor of Thomas Carney, went into the hands of T. J. Anderson, which was by Mr. Anderson presented and cashed at the Kansas Valley National Bank, on the 23d day of January, 1871, (see testimony of D. M. Adams).

That another check for the sum of *five thousand* dollars, drawn by J. W. Morris, was cashed under very suspicious circumstances by the Topeka Bank, on the night of the 23d day of January, 1871. (See the testimony of Morris, Mulvane and Jacob Smith).

That another check for *one thousand two hundred dollars* was drawn by Robert Crozier, and cashed at the Topeka Bank, on the 24th or 25th day of January, 1871, and the cash delivered to Len. T. Smith. (See testimony of Mulvane and Crozier.) That Len. T. Smith borrowed an amount of money from Thomas A. Osborn to pay his hotel bill. (See testimony of Osborn.) That a draft upon the treasurer of the Kansas Pacific Railway Company for *ten thousand dollars* was presented by T. J. Anderson, and cashed at the Kansas Valley National Bank, on the 23d day of January, 1871. It will be borne in mind that the first vote for United States Senator in 1871, was upon the 24th day of January, 1871, and the joint convention and final vote on the next day, being on the 25th day of January. There is now a note for three thousand five hundred dollars in the Kansas Valley National Bank, made by Anderson, and endorsed by Caldwell, for transactions in this canvass, which note is for the benefit of T. J. Anderson. That Mr. Caldwell claims that the Kansas Pacific Railway Company by its agents, at or about the time of the Senatorial election of 1871, promised to give to him thirty thousand dollars as its share of the election expenses of that election, or as its *bonus* for his influence as United States Senator. That Caldwell demanded of and importuned Mr. Perry, the President of the Kansas Pacific Railway Company to pay to Mr. Caldwell the said sum of $30,000 at Leavenworth, after his election, and that by an arrangement with Mr. Perry, Mr. Caldwell and his faithful friend Len. T. Smith came to Topeka from Leavenworth to see about and settle up this *thirty thousand dollar* transaction, and that the agents of the company here did not admit the promise as alleged by Caldwell, but did not stand as square on the subject as the President of the company wished. (See testimony of J. P. Usher.) That Len. T. Smith wanted to arrange with Jacob Smith, President of the Topeka Bank, to cash checks given in the canvass. (See testimony of Jacob Smith.) That Len. T. Smith wished to be informed of any members of the Legislature who could be bought. (See testimony of Greeno.) That Len. T. Smith said they were dead broke on the morning of the 23d or 24th, but as soon as Major Anderson came they would have plenty of greenbacks again, and that he would be back in a few moments. That Anderson did come back and apparently had something, and went into Caldwell's private room with Caldwell. (See testimony of Raymond.) That W. H. Carson got one thousand dollars of this corruption fund. (See testimony of Shannon and Spriggs.) That money was paid and offered to be paid to various members of the Legislature by Caldwell's agents and friends. (See testimony of Spriggs, Hammond, Greeno, Melville, Neal, Osborn, Thomas, Floyd, Chase, G. W. Wood, Manning, Burke, H. D. Baker, and others.) That George Smith paid out to members of the Legislature, for Mr. Caldwell, and with an understanding that it should be refunded to him by Caldwell, over twenty thousand dollars. (See testimony of Spriggs.) That Caldwell promised appointments to office and other favorable official acts for votes. (See testimony of Bond and others.) That Caldwell said after his election, at different times, that his election cost him more than any one was aware of, and clearly indicated by his conversation, and in fact said, that he paid for his seat in the United States Senate from this State, twice as much as the salary of the office for the full term of six years would amount to, or about *sixty thousand dollars*, and that he paid Carney's election expenses, amounting to more than *ten per cent. of the whole sum*, or over six thousand dollars. (See Burke's testimony, also Adams and Davis.) That Caldwell offered twice or oftener to pay all of Sidney Clarke's election expenses, and that he did agree with R. S. Stevens, to pay them upon consideration of Clarke's withdrawal and Clarke's friends support of Caldwell in the joint convention. From all the testimony your Committee find that Alexander Caldwell used bribery and other corrupt and criminal means, by himself and his friends, with his full knowledge and consent, to secure his election in 1871, to the United States Senate, from the State of Kansas.

Your Committee have also to report that the most important witnesses, Thomas Carney, Len. T. Smith, W. H. Carson, T. J. Anderson are now fugitives from the State, for the purpose of depriving this Committee of their testimony, and that their absence is in contempt of proper processes issued and served upon them, and as your Committee is convinced, from all the circumstances surrounding their sudden and clandestine hegira, for a cash consideration paid to at least two of them (see Burke's and Osborne's testimony.) W. A. Martin and Joel Thomas, important witnesses as we believe, have failed to appear, and we have been unable to learn of their whereabouts since they were served—Thomas being served by copy, Martin twice with personal service, once a subpœna and once with the rule of the Senate. Thomas Moonlight and John Fletcher have failed to appear in obedience to process. Every reasonable effort has been used to get these witnesses. Diligent inquiry does not discover that R. S. Stevens has been in the State during the pendency of this inquiry. Ever since this inquiry began, there has been an organized effort of persons in the interest of Mr. Caldwell, and perhaps others, to keep out of the reach of the Committee wittness whose attendance was greatly desired. Every obstruction that could be has been thrown in our way by these persons.

The secrecy with which the crimes which the testimony

we submit discover, the interest of all concerned to conceal them and the disgrace which attaches to all the parties implicated, even remotely, make the labor of proving them very difficult. Men who have been guilty of giving or taking a bribe, or in anywise connected therewith, as a general rule do not hesitate to hide their own and confederate's infamy behind the less odious crime of perjury.

The time left us after our assignment to this duty before the close of the session was entirely too short to permit us to go entirely through the work we have had in hand, especially when it is remembered that we had our ordinary legislative duties to perform, as well as this extraordinary duty. The magnitude of our labors and of the subject referred to us can be fully appreciated by those, only, who have met the inquiry face to face. When the testimony which we herewith submit is read in the light of the facts that Len. T.Smith left the State about the time this investigation was ordered and remains away; that Carney, Anderson and Carson are fugitives who have sought refuge beyond the territoral limits of the State; that Fletcher, Thomas and Martin are skulking, secreted or absent from the State, there can be but one conclusion, and that is that some person or persons are guilty of the offenses into which we are enquiring; and that they know it. (See testimony of Osborne, Burke, Adams, Spriggs and others.)

From the testimony all will see that the full and complete exposition of these high crimes is the incessant labor of months instead of the few days we have had. As our report must of necessity be made before this session closes, and as adjournment is near at hand, we are compelled to close our labors with the testimony of the sixty-four witnesses which we have examined, and the documents attached to their testimony, all of which we respectfully submit.

J. D. SNODDY,
Chairman on part of Senate.
E. S. STOVER,
H. C. WHITNEY.
WM. H. CLARK,
Chairman on part of House of Rep's
G. W. CLARK,
J. J. WOOD,
J. BOYNTON,
D. H. JOHNSON.

TESTIMONY.

CAPITOL, Jan. 30th, 1872.

Committee met pursuant to adjournment.

The following members of the Committee were present:

Jas. D. Snoddy, *Chairman on part of Senate.*

Wm. H. Clark, *Ch'm. on part of House of Representatives.*

Senate Committee.—Jas. D. Snoddy, E. S. Stover, H. C. Whitney.

House Committee.—Wm. H. Clark, J. J. Wood, G. W. Clark, D. H. Johnson, J. Boynton.

Upon motion, it was ordered that the Committee sit with closed doors:

DR. H. S. GREENO,

Sworn and examined by Chairman, testified as follows:

Q. Where do you reside?

A. In Topeka.

Q. Where did you reside last winter during the Senatorial election?

A. In Topeka, Kansas.

Q. What business was you then engaged in?

A. In the drug and medicine business.

Q. How long after that election did you continue in that business?

A. I continued in that business by myself until about the 27th of April, 1871. Then I sold one-half interest in the business to W. H. Peckham, and sold the balance of my interest in October, to Peckham & White.

Q. For what consideration did you sell the one-half interest to Peckham?

A. For about twenty-two hundred dollars. I have not the papers with me from which I could tell the exact amount.

Q. Was that amount paid by Peckham to you at that time?

A. No sir, it was not.

Q. Did he execute to you any security for that sum?

A. He gave me his notes after the invoice was taken at thirty and sixty days time.

Q. Were the notes paid when due?

A. No, not in full; part of them was paid.

Q. How much?

A. Some time in June he fixed up $1500, and gave me his note for $500.

Q. Did you ever have any conversation with him about his financial affairs between the time of sale and the payment of $1500?

A. I did.

Q. Did he at any time tell you where, or from whom he expected to get money to pay the obligations?

A. Well, yes.

Q. Of whom did he say he expected to receive money?

A. From Mr. Caldwell or the Caldwell party.

Q. When was this conversation with reference to the Senatorial election, before or after the election?

A. This conversation was after the election.

Q. About how long?

A. This was about the time we commenced taking the invoice of the stock.

Q. Can you give the date or about the date you began taking invoice?

A. About the 17th of April, 1871.

Q. Did he tell you when this promise to let him have money was made.

A. He said it was made during the Senatorial contest.

Q. Did he state what the consideration of that promise was?

A. He stated that he had expended a considerable amount of money to secure his election in his own district, and it had cost him a good deal to come up and represent his district; and that he had positive assurance from Mr. Caldwell's friends that they would make it all back to him, and pay him well for his influence in trying to secure the election of Mr. Caldwell. He stated that he was sorry that he had not worked for Sidney Clarke; that Mr. Clarke had promised to buy his farm, and if he had worked for Mr. Clarke he could have sold his farm for all it had cost him. He told me he was afraid Caldwell was going to play off on him. After we had completed the inventory, he went over to Leavenworth to see Caldwell and Len. T. Smith. When he left he said he was going to make them come to time in some shape. He said he was satisfied they had been fooling him, and playing off on him. He came back and then went over again. Once he came in the store about the 1st of May, and said he noticed in the papers that Mr Caldwell had returned from Washington and he was going over to see him again. He said if they did not pay him all they agreed to pay him, that he knew just how much it cost him to secure his election, and he was going to try to get that back anyhow. At the time I first had conversation with him about this, he was to buy my entire stock. This conversation was a short time after the adjournment of the Legislature; he was to pay me two thousand dollars down and give me his notes secured for the balance, whatever it might be, at six, twelve and eighteen months time. After the invoice was completed, he said he had been disappointed in getting his money, and desired me to retain a half interest in the business.

Q. What money did he say he had been disappointed in getting?

A. From his conversation I inferred it was the money he said he was to receive from Mr. Caldwell or the Caldwell party for his support of Mr. Caldwell. At the time of these conversations and sale to Mr. Peckham, Mr. Melville was a partner of mine, and the business was carried on in the name of H. S. Greeno & Co., and Mr. Melville was present at the greater part of these conversations, and knowing to them.

Q. You may state, if at any time in these conversations Mr. Peckham stated how much money he was to get from Caldwell or the Caldwell party.

A. He told me he was to get, or expected to get, two thousand dollars at least, that his services were worth that at least. He said he had worked hard; he had done a good deal of dirty work for them.

Q. Did Mr. Peckham in these conversations say or convey to you the idea that he had been promised money for his support of Mr. Caldwell in the Senatorial election of last winter?

A. Yes, sir.

Q. By whom?

A. T. J. Anderson and Len. T. Smith.

Q. After Mr. Peckham had been to Leavenworth to see Caldwell or Smith, what did he say about having seen either of these gentlemen when he returned?

A. He stated that he had seen Smith, and once that he had seen Caldwell. He said Smith told him he would make it all right with him yet.

Q. About how many times have you heard him speak about getting money from these gentlemen?

A. It was almost a daily occurrence for several weeks.

Q. Did he ever get that money, or any part of it?

A. Not that I know of.

Q. Did you talk with Peckham during the contest about what he was to get?

A. I don't recollect that I did. During the contest he made use of this expression: "I am a Democrat and there is no chance of electing a Democrat; that it cost me a good deal to secure my election and leave my place and come up here, and I believe I will, as long as money is being used, go in and make the most I can out of it." This conversation substantially was had several times.

Q. State whether or not Mr. Peckham had ever denounced Mr. Caldwell, or the Caldwell party, because they had not lived up to their contract with him?

A. Yes, he did on several occasions. He called them villains and rascals, and generally dishonest, and used Mr. Caldwell's name in such denunciations.

Q. What was Len. T. Smith doing here last winter?

[The witness at this point in the examination was called out to see the Sergeant-at-Arms of the House who had fallen and injured himself.]

NOBLE L. PRENTISS,

Sworn by Chairman, testified as follows:

Q. Where were you during the contest for the election of United States Senator last Winter?

A. I was in this city.

Q. What were you doing?

A. I was Local Editor of the *Record*, and Senate Reporter for *Record* and *Commonwealth*.

Q. Do you know or have you heard of any one being purchased to vote for Mr. Caldwell?

A. I don't know anything positively, and have heard the common rumors through the State, except on one occasion.

Q. Do you recollect about the time J. B. Davis's article in reference to that election was published of having conversation or hearing conversation about what members sold their votes in that election?

A. I remember conversation of that kind.

Q. When and where was it, and what was said?

A. The particular conversation I am unable to fix the date; I presume in October or November, 1871, after the publication of Davis's article; the place was the counting-room of the *State Record* in this city; the persons present were: F. P. Baker, Major Thomas J. Anderson, Wm. G. Souther, and myself, were in and about the room. The conversation turned on the Davis's article, and I particularly suggested that the article read very well, and I said if that article was published so as to mention the names where persons were referred to, but not named, it would look better. I then went behind the desk of the counting-room and commenced to write an article on this plan, and when I got down to where the article spoke of the representatives of a certain county getting twelve thousand dollars, I inserted "Doniphan" in brackets; I wrote on till I got down to where a certain class of persons sold, and then there came a discussion, and Anderson said he believed he could give the names of some of the men, and he looked over a memorandum book which he took out of his pocket, but I don't recollect that he gave me any names. He did not specify any amounts. Then we had a talk about what names should be put in, and we said that we would insert there a majority of those who voted for Caldwell.

Q. Since this investigation has been begun, has F. P. Baker written you? If so, what?

A. He has. The substance of the letter is as follows, as near as I can give it: "There is going to be an investigation and we will all be summoned; I shall know nothing about it, neither will Tom Anderson, and I don't want any one else should. Would you take the responsibility of that article, and go and visit your wife?" My wife was then in Missouri and Baker knew it; I suppose the letter referred to an article in which it was said that a gentleman in the city had a memorandum-book with the names of those who sold out in the Senatorial election last winter.

JOSEPH L. SPEER,

Sworn and examined by Chairman, testified as follows:

Q. Were you here last winter during the contest and election of United States Senator?

A. I was, and was a member of the Legislature.

Q. Have you any knowledge of money or other improper means being used to influence votes at that election?

A. I have no direct knowledge of my own.

Q. State what knowledge you have.

A. On the evening after the first ballot was had, a Mr. Walter H. Whitehead, of Jefferson county, came to me in the hall of the Tefft House and said he wanted to see me, and he told me I could make a big pile of money out of the Senatorial election if I would vote for Caldwell. I replied to him that that was all right; that I had not time to talk with him then; afterwards I had a conversation with T. G. Newman, and in one of these conversations I said that I thought I could have had $2,500 for my vote and influence for Caldwell. Whitehead lives the second house east of my house, near Newman's; T. G Newman lives at Newman Station; I went to Caldwell's room; Caldwell and Len. Smith were there, and I then told Caldwell that the probabilities were that I would not support him; that I learned that the Kansas Pacific Railway was in favor of him, and I did not like them; I afterwards voted for Caldwell. I think I went to Caldwell's room before dinner, and immediately after the first ballot I went there without any invitation, and saw Caldwell and Len. Smith, I think.

Q. Did you express to Caldwell at that time your conviction that Clarke was beaten, or would be beaten, and that you would have to look about for some one else to vote for?

A. No, I don't think I did.

Q. Did you go there merely to tell Mr. Caldwell that you could not vote for him?

A. You and most of the Committee, I suppose, know that I am a brother of John Speer, and John was then in rather a difficult place, and I wanted a man who I thought would be friendly to him, and I talked with Mr. Caldwell about that, and with Mr. Len. T. Smith about that; I think I told him that Clarke's chances were not gone; and I told him I thought Carney could be elected; he told me Carney was not a candidate; I told him that made no difference if we gave Carney forty votes, he would be a candidate. I told Caldwell that I wanted a man in the United States Senate who would be friendly to John Speer, and Caldwell said his sympathies were with John; that he thought John had been harshly treated about that matter; and I know that Smith said he had always been friendly to John.

Q. Was there any promise on the part of Caldwell to be friendly to John Speer in case he was elected?

A. Yes, sir, I understand it so.

Q. Was there an understanding between you and Caldwell before his election to the effect that if you supported and voted for him, that he should use his official influence to aid John Speer out of his difficulty?

A. I think there was not such an understanding—but you gentlemen, can readily understand that I would not want a man there who was *unfriendly* to my brother.

Q. How came you to go to Caldwell's the second time?

A. I went there to talk to Caldwell.

Q. About what?

A. About the Senatorial election.

Q. Did he send for you?

A. No, I went voluntarily.

Q Who was present?

A. Caldwell was there; I think, Len. T. Smith, and a man who wore spectacles. I told Caldwell I thought he would be elected. I think I did not commit myself for him till the next morning. At the time of this interview, I thought Caldwell was using money buying votes, and I think so yet. Nothing was said in that interview about the use of money. The next morning of the Joint Convention, Caldwell was sent for, and came to a caucus of Clarke's friends at Clarke's room. Mr. Clarke introduced all the men who were there to Mr. Caldwell, and stated what counties they were from. Caldwell said that was neatly done, and he hoped to be able to do that well himself sometime, and said he was glad to meet us. I think Mr. Bond asked some pledges with reference to public *lands*. Caldwell said his sympathies were with settlers on the public lands.

EVENING SESSION.

WEDNESDAY, January 31, 1872.

Committee met pursuant to adjournment. Full Com mittee.

NATHAN CREE

Having been sworn, testified as follows:

Examined by Chairman.

Q. Where do you reside, and what is your business?

A. I live in the city of Lawrence, and I am Editor of the *Democratic Standard.*

Q. State from whom you derived your information which led you to publish the article which was published in your paper on the 18th of January, in which you gave the names of certain Senators and Representatives of this State, and stated in that connection that they were charged with having sold their votes to Caldwell.

A. From Sidney Clarke, George A. Reynolds and Wilson Shannon, junior.

Q. How long before the publication of that article did you get the information which led you to make the publication?

A. Well, the information I got from Mr. Clarke was on the 16th of January, two days before the publication of that article.

Q. How was that information communicated by Mr. Clarke?

A. Well, I met Mr. Clarke in the Lawrence postoffice. Mr. Clarke and I are acquaintances, and I have been on speaking terms for some years. I jokingly said to him: "Mr. Clarke, why is it Pomeroy has sent Jim Legate to Washington Territory?" Mr. Clarke, jokingly replied: "Because I suppose photographs are not so plenty there as here." General conversation sprung up between Mr. Clarke and myself. We spoke about the Senatorial investigation, and some remarks were made between us about some articles which I had written concerning an investigation of the Senatorial election of last winter. I said I thought there ought to be an investigation of Mr. Caldwell's election, and made some remarks of a general nature to the effect that it was the general belief that it had been carried by fraud—that others said so, and that it ought to be looked into; and I told him that I had the names of parties which had been given to me as having been charged with having voted corruptly. I said I thought I would publish these to stir up the Legislature to do something. Mr. Clarke said if I had the list of the members of the Legislature, he could tell me who voted corruptly last winter, and asked me if I had a list of the members of the Legislature. I told him I had not, but could get one. We had some general remarks about Mr. Caldwell. He said Mr. Caldwell was a very unfit and unworthy representative of the State. He said Mr. Caldwell had gone back on all the engagements he had ever made, he believed, last winter; and he went on to state to me that he had been in Washington not long since, and that he there met Mr. Kalloch. He said he was in Mr. Kalloch's room, and Mr. Kalloch stated to him in a confidential manner how Mr. Caldwell had treated him. He said Mr. Kalloch informed him that he went over to Leavenworth a short time prior to the election of 1871, and that he borrowed some money o Mr. Caldwell, $3,000 I think, and he said that when the transaction was finished, Mr. Caldwell said to him: "Now, Mr. Kalloch, I am going to be a candidate for the United States Senate, and I want you to see me through of this thing, and if you do, it is my calculation to never demand this money of you." Mr. Kalloch went on to state to Mr. Clarke, (so Mr. Clarke informed me.) that since then Mr. Caldwell had been pressing him for the payment of that money.

Q Was there any other conversation between you and Mr. Clarke relative to the last Senatorial election?

A. Well, there was some other conversation of a general nature. He said Mr. Caldwell's own talk was that he wanted of make back what money he had spent in securing his election. He said he often talked just in that way: that is, that he wanted to make back what his election had cost him. I believe that was all of the conversation we then had that is germane to this inquiry. We recurred again to the list which he had spoken of giving me. I forget whether he or I alluded to it. It came up between us; he asked me when I would be in my office; I told him I guessed I would be in all that afternoon; this was about three o'clock in the afternoon; he said: "This is about my dinner hour, or I would go down with you now. I will go up and get dinner, and come down after dinner." But a little before dark, I happened to be in the postoffice again. He was there, and he said to me: "I will go down to your office in a moment," and went on in the postoffice. As he was going past me, I said to him: "I am going up in Governor Shannon's office; cannot you go up there?" He said he would; I went up into Governor Shannon's office, and in a little while he came in; we sat down, Wilson Shannon, junior, being present. I had in the office there this volume, which I hold in my hand. ("Laws of Kansas, 1871",) containing a list of the members of the Legislature of that year. Well, the subject was brought up about the list, and Wilson Shannon took the book and ran over it. Mr. Clarke said in the meantime, he could give us a list of the members, who were sold last winter. Wilson Shannon took the book and said to him: "Take that now and mark the names of the persons. He took the book and had his pencil in his hand. He ran over the list and mentioned the names, commencing with the Senate. The first name he mentioned, was G. W. Hogeboom. Said he: "He sold out." He went on to say, that Mr. Speer slept with him, (that is, Mr. Joseph Speer,) or "roomed" with him. He ran down the list. The next name he mentioned, was that of Sol. Miller; he stated something that had been said about Sol. Miller, which he believed to be true. Then J. Wood was the next name on the Senatorial list, and he said that Mr. Wood offered his vote for $3,000, and told Mr. Dan Adams of Topeka. Dan. wanted Wood to vote for him, (that is, Clarke.) He said Wood wanted $3,000 for his vote. Then passing on down the list, he came to members of the House, and mentioned the name of A. Barber, of Linn county, and stated that Mr. A. P. Clarke, of Black Jack, was acquainted with the facts in the case. This is A. P. Clarke, of Black Jack, Douglas county. He mentioned the name of T. L. Bond, of Montgomery, and said Mr. T. Bond told him that he was offered $3,000 for his vote in Caldwell's room. He did not say who offered it, but that Bond told him that. He stated that the young man seemed very much tempted and looked as though he would like the money, but did not like to give up his integrity. Next, W. C. Butts of Jefferson county, and he alluded to Joe Speer as knowing the facts in the case. C. B. Butler, of Leroy, Coffey county, he said he believed had been bought out. He related some conversation or correspondence that somewhat compromised Mr. Butler, which I cannot detail now, but I have it elsewhere.

Mr. Clarke also said that he thought Rufus E. Cable had sold out too, but did not claim to know anything definite about it. And the name of Felix T. Gandy, of Jewel county, was mentioned. He said that Mr. Downs, of Atchison, told him that Gandy wanted $1,000 for his vote for Mr. Clarke. He marked the name of J. B. Kennedy, of Doniphan county, John G. Lindsay, of Anderson county, he said, had been he believed sold out. He mentioned E. C. Manning, of Cowley county, and narrated some facts with reference to a correspondence that had taken place, in which Mr. Manning had been charged with that by Dan Adams and himself, I think he said too. A. Moore, of Marion county; J. H. Moore, of Doniphan county; J. B. McLaughlin, of Clay county; Jas. Phinney, of Morris county, and S. G. Whittaker, of Doniphan county.

These were all that he marked, and it was growing dark in the office then, and he went out. The next day he came down to my office—the *Democratic Standard* office—and I showed him an article which I had written in which I mentioned some of these names, and I told Mr. Clarke that I wanted him to give me the names of witnesses that could substantiate the assertion that they sold out. I had copied the names off as they are marked down here in this book: that is, such names as I had copied into the article. And Mr. Clarke sat down by my table, and we took first the name of Hogeboom. (Here witness took a paper which he said was in Mr. Clarke's handwriting and said:) I took the list and copied what was written, and running down the names asked him at each name to write down the name of the witness who would substantiate the statements, opposite or against.

Hogeboom—He wrote Abell, of Atchison, and Joe Spear, of Jefferson.

Sol Miller—Abell and Davis.

J. Wood—Dan. M. Adams and Col. Abell.

A. Barber—A. N. Clarke.

Byers—E. C. Beates, of Junction City.

Butts—J. L. Spear.

Mr. Clarke further wrote that C. B. Butler wrote a letter

to a man of the name of Saunders, Avon township, Coffeo county, pledging himself that if elected he would vote for Clarke. Brown, of Burlington *Patriot*, and many others in Coffey county, have seen the letter. He voted for Caldwell

At that point Mr. Clarke laid down his pencil and his handwriting was not very plain. I picked up my pencil and I took the names of the following witnesses as he then gave them to me. I wrote the following as his statement: Gandy offered to sell for $1,000 to F. W. Downs, of Atchison; and he referred to Abell and Dan Adams as authority for his statement about Mr. Gandy, of Jewell county; and to the Thomases, of Topeka, as authority for the statement with reference to A. A. Moore, and to J. Wesley Simcocks, of Council Grove, as authority for his statement with reference to Mr. J. W. Phinney, of Morris county, and also to J. L. Sharp.

Some general conversation was had about the Doniphan delegation, and some remarks were made about the story of the Doniphan delegation selling, and I spoke of Sol Miller, as his name was on the list, and he said he was not certain whether Sol sold out here or before he came over to the Legislature. He said that Mr. Abell had told him that it was his opinion that Sol had sold out before he came over. I asked him about Mr. Wood, of Doniphan county; what he knew; asked him if there could be any mistake about Mr. Wood. No, he said, there could be no mistake about Mr. Wood; he offered "square" to sell to Dan Adams; and he said, "Dan Adams will stand up to that; he told it to me himself." I asked him what Mr. Abell knew about the Doniphan men. He said that Abell talked with all those men to get them to vote for him, and he said they gave Mr. Abell to understand that they wanted money, and said that Mr. Abell had Sol Miller "on the strings" for a long time; and finally Sol voted for Caldwell.

Well, I guess that is all the conversation we had then; but I told Mr. Clarke I would let him see my article before I published it, and he asked me what time I would have it ready. After he went out I considerably modified what I had written before, and he came in again about six o'clock to see the proof of the article. I showed him the proof of the article as it appeared in the paper. He read it over, and I asked him now if that was all right; he said it was.

In all these three conversations that we had, Mr. Clarke stated that he was in favor of this investigation; that he would like to have it go on. And he understood what use I was going to make of the statements he gave me.

I guess that is all with reference to these names.

There are some other statements that Mr. Clarke made. The first conversation that we had in Governor Shannon's office, in the afternoon of the 16th of January, after Mr. Clarke had gone through this list and marked the names and stated certain things with reference to each one, Mr. Clarke says: "Now, in order that you may understand my connection with this matter, I want to tell you what took place between myself and Mr. Caldwell last winter." On the evening before the final ballot for senator, Mr. Clarke said that while at the supper table he received a note from Mr. Caldwell asking him to go to his room. I think that Mr. Clarke said that he sent back a reply that he could not go. I think he said that, but am not certain. Afterwards Mr. Clarke said he was in his room and who should come in but Mr. Caldwell, and he said Mr. Caldwell sat down before him and put his hands on Mr Clarke's knees, and said Mr. Caldwell stated, just begged, as he stated to him, "You know what I have done here, and you see that you cannot be elected. I don't know how this thing is going to go." He then (said Mr. Clarke) offered me (making a slight pause)—money;—my expenses—everything, if I would get out of the way, or "withdraw from the field." He said that Mr. Caldwell said that success would redeem the disgrace of the thing. Mr. Clarke said that he replied that he could not enter into any such arrangement, nor have anything to do with it; that his duty to himself and his friends forbade it. And Mr. Caldwell went away. They had another interview the same night towards morning after "caucussing." Mr. Clarke went on to detail what took place at the caucus, but I don't undertake to give it. He said he and Mr. Caldwell had another interview about two o'clock or towards the morning; (whether in Mr. Caldwell's room or his own I am not positive); and that Mr. Caldwell urged the same thing upon him again, but that he made the same reply as before, and Mr. Caldwell went away. And my recollection is that Robert S. Stevens was present at that conversation, (I mean the Superintendent of the M. R. & T. R. R.) Mr. Caldwell went away, and Mr. Clarke said that after Mr. Caldwell went away Mr. Stevens told him, (Clarke), "You cannot be elected, and," says he, "you may as well have your expenses and save yourself." Clarke said he replied to Mr. Stevens that he could not enter into such an arrangement. "Well," said Mr. Stevens, "I will do it." Mr. Clarke said he told him he might go and do what he pleased; and Stevens went away, and what he did Mr. Clarke said he did not know exactly, but stated that he lately had had a conversation with Mr. Stevens, and that Mr. Stevens told him that in the election last winter he went back to Sedalia, Missouri, and drew on Caldwell for money, and Mr. Caldwell made some excuses and put him off; and (said Mr. Clarke) Mr. Stevens said to me that he had no doubt at all but that Mr. Caldwell intended to entirely repudiate what he had agreed upon. Wilson Shannon was present and heard this conversation. He detailed the same thing again last Saturday in the presence of myself, J. H. Shimmons, Governor Shannon, and Wilson Shannon, junior.

Q. Have you had any other information from any one in regard to these matters?

A. Geo. A. Reynolds, of Lawrence, said that on the night before the election of Mr. Caldwell, J. M. Luce came to him and said to him, that he had been about such places as this (the Legislature,) a good deal, and knew about what he was worth, and said he, "Caldwell's people have offered me $2500, and I am going to vote for him if you cannot do any better." Mr. Reynolds, also stated to me a conversation that he had had with Moses Neal, and he said that Mr. McCartney, of Wilson county, on the evening before Mr. Caldwell's election, stated that Caldwell's people or friends had offered him $1500 for his vote, and gave him to understand that he would vote for Mr. Caldwell if his side would not pay him more. He did not vote for Caldwell. And Mr. Reynolds also related to me a conversation that he had had with Mr. Dan. Adams of Topeka. He said that Dan. Adams told him that he had paid a check for $1,000 to Charlie Columbia, of Council Grove, and said that Columbia told Adams that it was for Phinney's vote. I believe that is all. I don't recollect anything else that is pertinent, except that I want to add that when Mr. Clarke marked the list of those whom he charged with having sold out, he marked the name of I. M. Williams of Jackson county; said he: "Tom Anderson bought him."

Dr. H. S. GREENO

Having been recalled, resumed his testimony, as follows:

Examined by the Chairman.

Q. What was Len. T. Smith doing here last winter?

A. He was here working in the interests of Mr. Cald well to secur e his election.

Q. Do you know what their business relations were at that time, and had been for sometime previous?

A. I don't know anything but from hearsay.

Q. Did you hear either of them say?

A. I heard nothing said with regard to what their business relations were, or had been. I heard Mr. Smith talk with regard to the election of Mr. Caldwell.

Q. Did Mr. Peckham sell his farm?

A. Not that I know of, sir.

Q. Did Peckham say that the promise of Clarke to buy his farm was upon the condition that he should vote for Clarke as United States Senator.

A. He said if he had worked for Mr. Clarke he could have sold his farm to Mr. Clarke for all it had cost him, improvements and all. If he had gone in and used his influence, he could have sold his farm to Mr. Clarke for all it had cost him.

Q. Did he say that Clarke had promised to buy his farm?

A. I am not certain that he said Mr. Clarke promised to buy his farm. The language was that Mr. Clarke would have bought his farm and paid him for what it had cost him and all its improvements. I don't know whether he said Mr. Clarke had told him so personally.

By Mr. Whitney.

Q. You stated last night that you know Dr. McCartney of Wilson.

A. Yes sir, I did.

Q. When did he first commence going to your store?

A. It was the early part of the session of the Legislature, prior to the election.

Q. What did he come there for?

A. Well, he came there to become acquainted with me, and as a physician. I don't know what particularly. He used to come to get a drink of something stimulating.

Q. Did he ever meet any of Caldwell's political friends there by appointment or otherwise?

A. I cannot call to mind any particular person that he met there.

Q. Do you remember his going there immediately after the first ballot for Senator?

A. Yes, sir; he came there several times. There was not a day that he was not there several times during the session.

Q. Do you know of his getting any money there in your store from Caldwell or any one in his behalf?

A. I don't know that he received any money in my store from Caldwell or his friends or anybody in his behalf.

Q. Do you know of his receiving any money anywhere?

A. I don't know positively of his receiving money of any person.

Q. Do you know of his having the promise of money from the Caldwell party for voting for Caldwell?

A. Of my own knowledge, I do not.

Q. Did you ever hear any one say that he did?

A. Yes, sir.

Q. Who?

A. I heard Len. T. Smith say that he had "fixed" McCartney for him.

Q. When was this relatively to the election?

A. It was just on the eve of the first day of the election. I think about the time that the first ballot was taken.

Q. Where?

A. It was in the back part of my store, in the office.

Q. Who did he say this to?

A. To me personally.

Q. Any one else present?

A. I don't know that there was at that time.

Q. Did he communicate to you how he fixed him?

A. Yes.

Q. Please state how.

A. Well, perhaps that ought to have a little explanation. Mr. Smith told me that Dr. McCartney was in debt to a firm at Leavenworth; was behind there; didn't state the name of the firm; but he said they had fixed it with McCartney by liquidating or fixing up the claims of this party at Leavenworth.

Q. Was the amount communicated?

A. He said it was $1,500, or about that.

Q. Do you want to make an explanation now?

A. The only explanation is just this, that Mr. Smith came to me, and said to me in conversation that they were bound to succeed, or make the election of Caldwell sure; that they had money to do it, and they were determined to do it. (This was before any vote.) He had never failed in anything he undertook, and if I knew of any person that could be bought, that was in the market or had votes that could be controlled with money, he wanted that I should make them known to him.

Q. Who else did Smith speak of in your hearing relative to the same or similar transactions?

A. I don't remember any person particularly but Dr. McCartney. There were others talked of that he would like to get, but none that he had fixedor got.

Q. What did he ever say about Peckham?

A. I never had any conversation with Mr. Smith about Peckham.

Q. Did Smith ever deposit any money in your store to pay any members of the Legislature?

A. Not to my personal knowledge.

Q. Did he ever tell you that he did?

A. No, sir.

Q. Was Smith in there every day during the few days anterior to the election?

A. Not every day; but two or three times.

Q. Had he any appointments to meet any one there?

A. Well, he came there to meet me personally once, but I dont't know any one else.

Q. Had he any appointments with you in reference to the election?

A. Not that I am aware of.

Q. Did any one ever tell you that they had money given them by Caldwell during that election?

A. There was a man there frequently of the name of Steele who had received $1,000; not a member of the Legislature. He came from away out west somewhere.

Q. What did he say he got a thousand dollars for?

A. To pay to some person who was a member of the Legislature to vote for Caldwell. I know the person but could not recall his name.

Q. Whom did he get it from?

A. He said it was the Caldwell faction.

Q. Do you know Major Irwin, member for Neosho county.

A. I do.

Q. Did he come to your store with McCartney?

A. He did often.

Q. Do you know of any arrangement having been made whereby Irwin's vote was contracted for?

A. I do not.

Q. Did you see McCartney frequently after the election?

A. I did.

Q. Did he ever say anything to you about this arrangement with Smith in any way?

A. Not after the election.

Q. What did he say before on the subject?

A. I inferred from general conversation that he was going to make Mr. Caldwell come down handsomely for his vote, but I don't remember his words particularly. That was the substance.

Q. That was before the election?

A. Yes, sir.

Q. Did he ever complain after the election that they had gone back on him?

A. No, sir; I don't think he ever did. He seemed very well satisfied.

Q. Did you ever know Gandy, of Jewell county?

A. I don't remember.

By G. W. Clarke.

Q. You stated that Mr. Steele received $1,000 to pay to some member. Will you take this book which contains a list of the members for that year, and say if you recognize the name?

A. He said it was for some member, but I don't remember the person at all. He said he had got $1,000, and was going to put it in his trowser's pocket, and was going home, and they might go to thunder. He said he had got it from Caldwell's party.

DR. H. C. LINN

Having been sworn, testified as follows:

Examined by the Chairman.

Q. Do you know D. R. Anthony?

A. I do.

Q. Did you ever have any conversation with him in regard to the use of money in the Senatorial election last winter?

A. Well, I heard Anthony make a good many remarks. It was in the morning after the election, with a number of gentlemen in one of Crawford's rooms; some fifteen or twenty; Anthony came and made the remark, as well as I remember, that he knew of $3,000 that had been given two men to control three votes. While those parties were trying to control one vote, they bought up the other two for $500 apiece, and I remarked to him "stop!" and I asked him if he would swear to it, and he said he would swear to it, as I understood him. Crawford and Jenkins were present. This is pretty much all that I remember, though I have heard Anthony say a great deal.

Q. Do you know of any money being used in the Senatorial election by Caldwell or any other persons?

A. I didn't see any used. A man who was in Thad. Walker's office said that he knew where I could get $5,000 for my vote; Walker knows the man, and he said that he was a man who had been defeated for the Legislature, and had come down to work in Mr. Walker's interest.

R. W. JENKINS

Was sworn and testified as follows:

Examined by the Chairman.

Q. Did you hear Mr. D. R. Anthony make any remarks about the Senatorial election of last winter immediately after that election or next morning?

A. Yes, sir; I did. Not the next morning, but immediately after the election.

Q. Where were you when those remarks were made?

A. In Mr. Sam Crawford's room while the vote was being taken here, and immediately after the election there was a number of gentlemen gathered in there, and were talking about the election, and what brought about the result and some gentlmen remarked that it was no use for a man to make a dash for the United States Senate here unless he had sufficient money to control votes enough to secure his election or words to that effect, and Dr. Linn was there, who was our representative, and was very indignant. He remarked that he was in favor of a thorough investigation of the matter, and belived that it had been by fraud or done bribery, or something that way. And Anthony remarked that he knew of two men that had got $3,000 for their vote, and Dr. Linn got up and says to Anthony, "Will you swear to that?" and Anthony said, "I will." Well they went on to considerable talk among them about this matter, and urging that they needed to investigate, or something of that character; I don't know how the conversation terminated, but that was about the last that was said.

Q. Have you any knowledge of any person giving or offering to give money in exchange for votes in that election?

A. I have not.

SIDNEY CLARKE,

Having been sworn, testified as follows:

Examined by the Chairman.

Q. Where do you reside?

A. In Lawrence, Kansas.

Q. Were you here during the contest for the election of United States Senator last winter?

A. Yes, sir.

Q. Do you know whether or not in that contest, any money or other valuable considerations were offered or used by Mr. Caldwell or his friends to secure votes for Mr. Caldwell?

A. I know it only as it was communicated to me by other persons.

Well, sir, by whom were such facts communicated to you?

A. On the day following the election, just about as I was leaving the Tefft House at Topeka to proceed to my home at Lawrence, I was met, I think in the hall, between the room that I occupied and the office, by four gentlemen whose names, as near as I can recollect are: G. W. Wood, member of the House of Representatives from Cherokee; Wm. Peckham, member of the House of Representatives from Douglas county; I think a Mr. Rucker, from the Cherokee Neutral Lands, and by Dr. O'Connor, (I think) from Baxter Springs. One of those gentlemen, I don't remember which, handed to me a written instrument setting forth in substance, as I now remember it, that Mr. Wood, (G. W. Wood) had been offered a sum of money to vote for Mr. Caldwell. I think I had packed up my trunk to leave the city; was in a great hurry; remarked to the gentlemen that I was about leaving town; that it was a matter that I knew nothing about, and handed back the paper.

Q. Did you receive such or similar information from any other persons.

A. Yes, sir.

Q. From what other persons?

A. From, (I think,) Mr. T. L. Bond, member of the House of Representatives from Montgomery county.

Q. Any other?

A. I don't remember any other at this time. Mr. Bond, being a member of the Legislature from Montgomery county, was a stranger to me at the time of this election. I received a letter from him soon after the election, saying, in substance, that he had been elected by the people of Montgomery to vote for myself as United States Senator; that he was in favor of my election. On my arrival at Topeka, Mr. Bond was in frequent conversation with myself in reference to the Senatorial contest. He reported to me at different times that he was offered a money consideration by persons "up stairs," giving me to understand Caldwell's rooms. A short time before the election took place he came into my room one day and reported to me that he had been offered the sum of $3000, if I recollect correctly, to vote for Mr. Caldwell, and that the money, or a portion of the money, had been shown him. I said to Mr. Bond, that he was a young man, that he had just commenced in Kansas, that we were all young men together, and that he could not afford, if he expected to live in the future, to take the money. Mr. Bond did not take the money so far as I know and believe. He voted on the first ballot for myself. That was the substance of the transaction. I have never seen Mr. Bond since I left Topeka, nor had any subsequent conversation with him. Daniel M. Adams reminded me to-day that he was present and heard this conversation, though I did not remember his presence myself.

Q. Did you know Mr. Phinney, member of the House, from Morris county?

A. Yes, sir.

Q. Did you have any conversation with him last winter, or at any time since then, with regard to this election?

A. I think I had several conversations with him as with other members of the Legislature.

Q. In any of these conversations did you hear him say anything about wanting money for his vote?

A. I remember having a conversation with Mr. Phinney in his room at the Tefft House, where he mentioned to me the fact that he had been an old friend of mine; had attended several political conventions at his own expense for my political interest, and that he had been elected to the Legislature to vote for me, and that his expenses ought to be paid. I told Mr. Phinney that I was there without money; that I was comparatively poor; that I was not able, nor was I trying to fish for votes by the use of money; and had a general conversation of that tenor with him. At the conclusion of the conversation he said, "I am all right any way, but I have telegraphed to Council Grove for my brother-in-law, Mr. Columbia. He will be up here very soon, and we will come and see you." That is the last I saw of him, only I saw him as I saw other gentlemen.

By Senator Stover.

Q. Did he indicate about how much money he ought to have?

A. I don't remember that any sum was named. The sum and substance was that he had been elected, and was poor, and wanted his expenses, and that it was all right; that Mr. Columbia, whom he had telegraphed for, would come, and they would come and see me.

By the Chairman.

Q. Have you any information as to whether Mr. Phinney obtained any money for his vote; if so, state it.

A. Mr. Simcock stated to me that he was informed by Mr. Withington, I think, of Lyon county, that Mr. Phinney had had deposited in Mr. Swallow's bank at Emporia a sum of money during the past summer, and deposited sometime since the senatorial election. Mr. Simcock also informed me that Jonathan Hammond, of Morris county, made the statement to Mr. W. F. Shamleffer that he, Hammond, made $200 out of Phinney's vote. I think Mr. Simcock also stated to me that L. McKenzie, of Parkerville, Morris county, heard Hammond state that he had helped to negotiate Phinney's vote, and received his share: $200. Mr. Simcock also stated to me that he was under the impression that J. L. Sharpe and Isaac Sharpe, both of Council Grove, had heard Hammond make the same statement.

By Senator Stover.

Q. Did you infer from conversations with Mr. Phinney that he wanted money for his vote?

A. I am free to confess that I did; that my suspicions on the money question were actively aroused, and that was my feeling in reference to the subject. I don't think that he stated his wants to me in any other form than that he thought his expenses in the campaign ought to be paid.

Q. Did you have any conversation with Mr. Columbia on the subject?

A. No, sir; I don't think I did. I have no recollection of it.

By Senator Whitney.

Q. Had you a conversation with Dr. McCartney? If you had, state what it was.

A. I had one, and I think, two interviews with Dr. McCartney with reference to the question of voting for Senator. I had been informed, and that information has been since confirmed, that he was elected with the distinct understanding on the part of his constituents that he would vote for me for Senator. I met and consulted with him with that expectation. I found him somewhat reserved in his conversation, and failed to obtain from him any positive declaration as to the way he would vote. I was frequently consulted, however, by other parties, among whom I remember a Mr. McClure, of Tioga, and by a gentleman in Pottawatomie county, whose name I don't now remember. They represented to me—in fact it was a general representation by persons most familiar with the position of Dr. McCartney—that he wanted money for his vote. After the first vote had been taken, the two gentlemen to whom I have referred called at my room, and requested to see me outside of my door in the entry. I stepped out and they handed to me a note written in pencil, signed by Mr. McClure and his associate, stating in substance, as I now remember it, that they were authorized to say that I could have Dr. McCartney's vote for the sum of $1,000. I replied: "Give my compliments to Dr. McCartney, and tell him that he stands a better chance of going to the penitentiary than he does of getting $1,000 out of me." I kept the note, and Mr. McClure and his associate departed, (myself remarking to them as they left, that of course I meant no insult to them.) Since that time I handed the note to Senator Whitney, and he has never returned the note to me. Now I am reminded of it; it was headed or directed to Mr. Ross, as Senator Whitney says.

By the Chairman.

Q. Do you know Luce, of Franklin?

A. Yes, sir, I do.

Q. Do you know whether or not he received any money for his vote?

A. No, sir. I only know what his public declarations were—such as were known to everybody.

Q. Well, go on and state what they were.

A. That he would vote for whoever would give him the most money.

By Mr. Johnson.

Q. Are you acquainted with Lindsay, of Garnett?

A. Yes, sir; very well.

Q. Do you know anything of his transactions?

A. No, sir, I do not.

By the Chairman.

Q. What do you know of the transaction of Mr. E. C. Manning, of Cowley county?

A. I know him. He was a member of the House of Representatives, and had rooms in the Tefft House during the Senatorial election. As I understood it, previous to my arrival at Topeka, from some of the citizens of Cowley county and others whom I deemed well informed on the subject, Mr. Manning had been elected with the distinct understanding on the part of those voting for him as well as those voting against him, that he would vote for me for U. S. Senator. One evening during the progress of the canvass Mr. F. W. Potter, of Coffey county, came into my room and said I had better see Manning; that something was the matter with him. I called upon him in a room occupied by himself and Mr. Potter, if I remember rightly, and had a conversation with him in reference to his vote for Senator. Mr. Manning demanded of me peremptorily that I should pay him the sum of $1,000 before he would take any part in the canvass in my favor for Senator. He said: "It is reported that you fellows have got the money here, and nearly everybody is getting money for their vote, and I am in financial distress and have spent a great deal of money in politics; was a member of the first State Convention, and was a friend of yours when you were first nominated for Congress, and I think you ought to reciprocate now and give me $1,000." I told Mr. Manning that I could not and would not do it; that I had not got the money, and that if I failed in my election for want of money I must simply take the consequences. My impression is that I had two conversations with Mr. Manning of a general character.

In our last conversation I said to him: "Mr. Manning, you were elected to the House of Representatives from Cowley upon the distinct pledge, and with the expectation on the part of your constituents that you would vote for me as United States Senator. Every foot of the land upon which your constituents tread were saved to them by the fight I have made, running through a period of three years, against the Osage Treaty; and if you vote against me I will never go back to Washington until I go down to Winfield in Cowley county, where you reside, and call a meeting of your constituents and state to them the demand you have made upon me. If I must lose your vote for want of money, so be it." In one of the previous conversations referred to, feeling very doubtful whether he would vote for me or not, I referred him to Major D. M. Adams, or got him to talk with Major Adams.

By Senator Stover.

Q. Did any other parties, members of the Legislature, except Mr. Phinney, Mr. Manning and Mr. McCartney, intimate personally or by their friends to you that they wanted money for their vote?

A. I don't recollect any individual cases.

By Rev. Mr. Boynton.

Q. Did Mr. Caldwell ever before the election, through his friends or otherwise, make any offer to you to withdraw from the field?

A. After the first vote was taken, and while I was at supper in the Tefft House, about dusk, I received a note from Mr. Caldwell, or from some of his immediate friends, but my conviction is that it was from Mr. Caldwell himself, asking me to meet him in an upper room of the Tefft House. I finished my supper and went to my room, and consulted with friends who happened to be present (I don't remember their names: the room was full,) as to the propriety of having a personal interview with Mr. Caldwell in compliance with his request. It was thought best that I should see him, and

I went up and found him in an upper room—I don't remember the number—of the Tefft House. Mr. Caldwell said to me in substance: "It is in the power of your friends to decide the contest in my favor in Joint Convention to-morrow. He went on to say that if the election went over another day he might be beaten, but that a coalition between his friends and my friends would certainly decide the result in his favor. I said to him: "Mr. Caldwell, so far as personal political feeling is concerned, I would much prefer to see you elected to ex-Governor Crawford, from the fact that you and your friends have never abused me personally to any considerable extent, while I have been followed for eight months or more with bitter denunciation by those who seem at this time to be the special friends of Mr. Crawford. But I cannot give you my support for Senator." I said to him: "You have obtained your strength by the use of money. I think you have bought twelve or fourteen of my men who were elected to vote for me, and thus got the advantage." In general terms I declined the request to go into Joint Convention and aid in his election, saying to him that I was fearful, if either myself or my friends decided to do so, we should be held responsible by the people of the State for the manner in which he obtained his election. Mr. Caldwell said to me that my friends could decide the result, and make the contest certain for him, and proposed to me that if I would do so he would pay or cause to be paid the legitimate expenses that I had incurred in the canvass.

The interview terminated with this declaration. Mr Caldwell making, however, an earnest request that I would agree to see him sometime during the night. I said to him that I was going to a caucus of my friends, (in my political headquarters,) at the caucus room across the street, and did not make any definite agreement as to any other meeting. I proceeded to attend the caucus, and was engaged until past twelve o'clock. I think it was two o'clock before I returned to the hotel. Sometime after my return to my rooms at the hotel I learned that the Atchison delegation, consisting of the members of the House and Senate, and many leading men from Atchison, of both political parties, were in consultation in Colonel Abell's room almost opposite mine I think this was from two to three o'clock in the morning I was sent for by the delegation, and went into the room; Colonel Abell presided, and the room was in a crowded condition. I was the only one present at that time residing outside the city and county of Atchison. The delegation had under discussion the course they should pursue in Jont Convention on the following day, and decided—if I remember rightly—first by a vote of the members, and secondly, by a vote of those not members, after a full discussion, to support Mr. Caldwell in preference to Governor Crawford. Previous, however, to this I was requested by the president or by the vote of the meeting to go to Mr. Caldwell's room and ask him to go down. I went to his room; found him in bed with Mr. Purcell of Manhattan, and communicated to him the request of the delegation from Atchison. He got up, dressed, and I walked with him down to the room of the Atchison delegation. Certain questions, relating to local measures, were propounded to him by different persons of the Atchison delegation. He answered them, and the vote was taken, as I have before said. My recollection is that after the Atchison delegation had decided to support Mr. Caldwell, and before retiring to bed, I walked into the room occupied by R. S. Stevens, on the same floor of the Teft House. Previous to going to Mr. Stevens' room it had been mentioned to me by several parties; I think now by J. H. Shimmons of Lawrence; by Senator Worden, I think, although I would not be positive; and by Col. Murphy of Atchison; that if my friend supported Mr. Caldwell, it would be nothing more than fair that the expenses which had been incurred at the hotel, should be paid. I uniformly declined these propositions, and remember now of speaking very emphatically upon the subject to a party of friends in a room adjoining my caucus room. There were several present, but I only remember the name of Mr. Shimmons. As I have stated before, after leaving the meeting of the Atchison delegation, and before retiring to rest, I went into Mr. Stevens' room. Mr. Stevens said to me in substance, and to others who were present, that I was a fool not to allow Caldwell to pay my expenses. I declined to Mr. Stevens, saying, I would have nothing to do with the matter. Mr. Stevens' room was quite full of people at that time. Before I left, Mr. Caldwell came in, and something was again said on the subject, but I declined to be a party to the transaction, and left, and went to my own room. I subsequently learned that Mr. Caldwell did make an arrangement with Mr. Stevens, agreeing to pay Mr. Stevens the expenses that had been incurred.

At this stage, the Committee adjourned until seven o'clock the following evening.

EVENING SESSION.

THURSDAY, February 1, 1871.

The Committee met pursuant to adjournment.

All the members present, except Senator Stover.

Senator Snoddy in the Chair.

The following resolution was moved and carried unanimously:

"*Resolved*, That each witness produced before the Committee shall be notified that his entire evidence, whether direct or explanatory, will be recorded, and it shall be the duty of the Committee to cause to be recorded every interrogatory propounded, and everything which a witness testifies to in his examination."

SIDNEY CLARKE

Resumed his testimony.

Examined by the Chairman.

Q. From whom did you get the information that Caldwell agreed with Stevens to pay the expenses as you stated last evening, in your examination?

A. My recollection is that on the day after the election Mr. Stevens had a conversation with me about the payment of the hotel bills, etc., (expenses that had been incurred,) and said that he had an understanding with Mr. Caldwell about it.

Q. When did Mr. Stevens say those expenses were to be paid?

A. I don't remember that he informed me as to the time.

Q. What was the amount of those expenses?

A. I don't know.

Q. Did Stevens say when the understanding between him and Caldwell was made?

A. I don't think he stated specifically, but I can give you my understanding if it is proper to give it in reply to the question. My understanding is that he made it after the remark was made to me in reference to which I have heretofore testified.

Q. Was it your understanding that that arrangement between Caldwell and Stevens was before the election of Mr. Caldwell?

A. I don't remember that Mr. Stevens spoke to me after the time to which I have referred until the day after the election, just as we were about leaving Topeka. I had no positive understanding as to the time when the arrangement was made.

Q. When Mr. Stevens spoke to you and said that you were a fool for not allowing Caldwell to pay the expenses, what reply, if any, did you make to Stevens?

A. I think, as I already testified, I said I would have nothing to do with the matter, and went to my own room.

Q. Did you at that time, or at any other time, in conversation with Mr. Stevens upon that subject of Ca'dwell's paying the expenses of your campaign; tell Mr. Stevens that he could do as he pleased about it?

A. I don't remember what remark I made to Mr. Stevens other than that I have stated.

Q. What was Mr. Stevens business at that time?

A. I have always understood him to be the General Manager of the M. K. & T. Railroad.

Q. State if you know in whose interests R. S. Stevens came to Topeka last winter, and labored in the Senatorial contest.

A. I understood him to be friendly to my own election.

Q. Was there any understanding between you and R. S. Stevens, that he should come and assist in procuring your election?

A. No, sir; no more than among my friends generally.

Q. Did you at any time before the Senatorial contest last winter, have a conversation with R. S. Stevens, the subject of which was the Senatorial election, and his connection with it?

A. I don't remember now, whether I met Mr. Stevens during the winter and previous to the Senatorial election or not.

Q. Question repeated.

A. My recollection is that I met Mr. Stevens two or three times during the summer and fall, but I don't think I saw him after going to Washington in November, up to the time of the election. I might, but cannot remember. It is quite possible he may have come to Washington, but I have no recollection of it.

Q. Did you at any of these times during the summer or fall of 1870, when you met Mr. Stevens, have any conversation with him, the subject of which was the then approaching election, and his connection with it?

A. It is quite likely, I might have talked with Mr. Stevens on the subject; I presume I did.

Q. Do you not recollect any conversation you had with Mr. Stevens during that summer or fall in relation to the then approaching Senatorial election?

A. I have no recollection of any specific conversation with Mr. Stevens; but presume I talked with him generally on the subject of the Senatorial election.

Q. Do you recollect where you saw him last, before you went to Washington in November?

A. I do not.

Q. Where did Mr. Stevens reside?

A. I think he resides at Attica, N. Y.; his business is in Kansas.

Q. His office is in Sedalia, Mo., is it not?

A. I think it is; his headquarters are there.

Q. How many rooms had you at the Tefft House, during that canvass?

A. I cannot answer the question, but understood from my friends who engaged the rooms, that there were about—well, I cannot answer that question. I don't know how many were engaged.

Q. Who engaged the rooms for you?

A. I think the room that I occupied myself, and one or two rooms adjoining, were engaged by Daniel M. Adams, A. S. Thomas, and perhaps T. N. James, all of Topeka, although I am not positive as to the last.

Q. Did they make the arrangements for your canvass for United States Senator for you?

A. I think that before any steps were taken to procure rooms, Mr. Adams informed me at Washington that he had made arrangements at the Tefft House.

Q. For whom?

A. For myself.

Q. Did he do that without authority from you?

A. My recollection is that he did it of his own volition, although it was entirely satisfactory to me.

Q. How many rooms did he report to you that he had engaged for your headquarters?

A. I don't remember; it has passed out of my mind. I don't remember that he named the number of rooms. I think, however, it was in the neighborhood of fifty, although I am not positive.

Q. Did he state the amount that was to be paid for the use of these rooms and other expenses at the hotel per day, per week, or otherwise?

A. No, sir.

Q. Have you settled and paid for the rooms that were engaged for you by Mr. Adams as your headquarters?

A. I never attended to the matter myself. Mr. Adams gave me to understand that a final settlement was effected with Mr. McMecken. On visiting Topeka, however, last summer, a suit was instituted against me to recover the sum of $400 or $500 additional.

Q. Additional to what?

A. Additional to what Mr. Adams had paid, as I understand.

Q. How much did Mr. Adams say that he had paid?

A. I don't remember the sum. I think I can remember by refreshing my recollection. I can only state from memory, as I have no memoranda on the subject, and am liable to be mistaken. I think Mr. McMeckin was paid by Mr. Adams $1,000 for the hotel bill during the canvass and previous to the election. I think subsequent to that time Mr. Adams effected what he claimed to be a settlement with Mr. McMeckin for $1,500 additional.

Q. How many days were you at the Tefft House at that time?

A. I don't remember. The reason that it is so large is that he charged me at the rate of six or eight persons for the room I occupied. I feel certain that it was six.

Q. In these bills, amounting in all to $2,500 as you have stated, were any other hotel bills included except those which accrued during the Senatorial contest?

A. I don't know, but I think not.

Q. Had you any bank account here during that time?

A. I think I had an account with Mr. Adams. (I had.)

Q. Did you pay any part of this $1,000 payment or the $1,500 payment?

A. I am not certain, but think it quite probable I gave a check for the $1,000 which was paid to Mr. McMeekin first.

Q. Had you money deposited in this bank before the beginning of the session of the Legislature in 1871, and within a short time before?

A. I had not.,

Q. At the time that you say you drew the $1,000 check on Mr. Adams' bank, how much money had you deposited there to draw against?

A. My recollection is I deposited between $2,000 and $3,000 when I first came to Topeka for the purpose of defraying my expenses.

Q. When was that deposit made; about what date?

A. At the time I came—I think it was the time I came to Topeka to attend the canvass. I don't remember the date.

Q. Was it before or after the Legislature convened, and if after, how long?

A. I don't remember the date.

Q. Did you draw any other check against that amount of money in the bank?

A. I don't remember whether I did or not.

Q. Do you recollect which way the balance was at the time you left this city immediately after the Senatorial contest, in your banking account with that bank?

A. My recollection is that after arriving at Washington Mr. Adams informed me that he had settled up the hotel expenses, and that they amounted in all to about some $1,800 or $1,900, including the $1,500 of which I have already spoken. I am not sure but that a portion of this money was paid for the rent of rooms on the opposite side of the street, and for stoves and fitting up of the room, the weather being quite cold.

Q. The question is, Mr. Clarke, whether or not you now recollect which way the balance in that bank was at the time you left Topeka.

A. I don't remember, but think I can recollect if you

will give me a moment. I think I was owing Mr. Adams on the final settlement some $1,700 or $1,800, but am not positive. Mr. Adams will know more distinctly himself.

Q. Then I understand you to state that you overdrew your account at Mr. Adams's bank to the amount, as you now recollect, of some $1,700 or $1,800: Do I understand you correctly?

A. Well, I am not positive. I cannot be positive in my statements because I myself did not have any charge of the expenses which were incurred at the hotels and at the rooms to which I referred on the opposite side of the street. My recollection is that I overdrew my account to about $1,500, but Mr. Adams will be able to be more positive.

Q. What amount did you say that Mr. McMeekin is now prosecuting the suit for?

A. Somewhere from $400 to $500.

Q. Are you not able to state the number of days or about the number of days that you were at McMeekin's hotel at that time?

A. On reflection, I should think the record would show that we were there about three weeks, and that eighty rooms were originally engaged to accommodate myself and friends.

Q. Was it the agreement between Mr. Adams and Mr. McMeekin, as you were informed by Mr. Adams, that you were to pay for the eighty rooms engaged, and for the persons who occupied them?

A. I cannot say how that was. I understood that a dispute arose sometime during the occupancy of the rooms, as to the bargains, but don't know how it was settled.

Q. At that time that Mr. Adams informed you, when you were in the city of Washington, that he had engaged headquarters for you at the Tefft House, did he inform you that he had engaged eighty rooms for you and your friends, and that you were to pay the expenses for those rooms and your friends who occupied them according to the terms of the agreement between himself and McMeekin, the proprietor of the hotel?

A. Mr. Adams simply communicated to me the information that he had engaged the rooms.

Q. Did he not then say anything about who was to pay the bill for the rooms, and for the persons who occupied them?

A. I have already said in answer to the former question that he simply informed me that he had engaged the rooms.

Q. Did he say nothing about how much was to be paid for the rooms or who was to pay for them?

A. As I remember, the information came by telegraphic despatch, and as I have stated in the two preceding answers, no other information was communicated, as I now remember.

Q. Did you at any time authorize Mr. Adams to settle with Mr. McMeekin for the use of the rooms that he said he had engaged at the Tefft House for that occasion?

A. I think I told him before I left Topeka that I should depend upon him to effect a settlement, as I had nothing to do with making the bargain for the rooms, and I knew nothing about the terms myself.

Q. Before you left for Washington, after the contest was over, had you any conversation with Mr. McMeekin in regard to the settlement of the bill?

A. I have no distinct recollection; but I presume that Mr. McMeekin spoke to me about it, or I spoke to him, and if so, told him that Mr. Adams would arrange the matter.

Q. Well, sir, what other expenses were there on your part settled by Mr. Adams other than this hotel bill?

A. My understanding was there were general expenses incurred; for instance, the living and fitting up of rooms outside the hotel, putting up of stoves, purchase of some furniture for the rooms, and, I think, some refreshments were provided at the headquarters across the street. In fact, I know there were.

Q. Do you know how much was paid for those expenses across the street?

A. I do not, sir.

By W. M. Clarke.

Q. Did you have a conversation with Mr. Kalloch during last summer or fall in Washington city in regard to the Senatorial election?

A. I did.

Q. Will you state that conversation as near as you can?

A. The conversation which took place between myself and Mr. Kalloch was, if I remember right, accompanied with a request that I should treat it as confidential, and I decline to give it.

[It was moved by a member of the Committee, and carried unanimously: "That Mr. Clarke be required to give that conversation in full."]

Q. Was there anything stated in that conversation about a promissory note that Mr. Kalloch had given to any person before or during the Senatorial campaign of 1872?

A. Yes, sir.

Q. What was said?

A. Mr. Kalloch said to me that he supposed I must have heard that there had been some difficulty or there had been a transaction between himself and Mr. Caldwell, and that for the purpose of letting me know exactly how it was, he would state to me the facts. He said that after Mr. Caldwell had announced himself as a candidate for Senator he was hard up for money, as he almost always was, and that he went over to Leavenworth and borrowed of Mr. Caldwell the sum of $3,000, and executed his note, as I understood him, for the sum. I ought to say, perhaps, that Mr. Kalloch said to me that looking over all the candidates he had made up his mind previous to that time to give Mr. Caldwell his support for Senator. After the vote was executed and the money borrowed of Mr. Caldwell, Mr. Kalloch said that Mr. Caldwell said to him: "Now, Kalloch, I want to be elected Senator, and you are in a position to do me a great deal of good," or something to that effect. "If I am elected I shall not collect of you this note. If I am not, I shall expect you to pay it." This is the substance of the conversation, as I now remember it, related to me by Mr. Kalloch.

Q. Did Mr. Kalloch inform you whether he had paid that note or not?

A. He informed me that—I think he said—the note was put in bank, and protested, and that he paid it, or that some kind of compromise was effected. I don't remember distinctly about this conversation.

Q. How did he say he had paid it?

A. I understood him to say that he sold to Mr. Caldwell a pair of fancy ponies in part payment.

Q. Had you any conversation with him about any other parties obtaining money of Mr. Caldwell?

A. Yes, sir.

Q. Who was that?

A. I decline to answer, this being also confidential.

[It was moved and carried unanimously by the Committee: "That Mr. Clarke be required to answer."]

Q. What was that transaction as related by Mr. Kalloch, and who was it between?

A. Between Mr. Geo. Noble, Assistant Superintendent of the K. P. P. R., and Mr. Caldwell.

Q. Go on and state what it was.

A: Mr. Kalloch said that after he had borrowed this money from Mr. Caldwell, George Noble wanted some money for his own personal use and went over to Leavenworth and also borrowed (as I understood him to say,) the sum of $3,000, or thereabouts; that Mr. Noble gave to Mr. Caldwell his note for the money, and that Mr. Caldwell repeated the same conversation to Mr. Noble in reference to collecting the note, in substance, that he had had with Mr. Kalloch, namely; that if he was elected he did not expect to collect the note. If he was not elected, he should expect Mr. Noble to pay it.

Q. Did Mr. Kalloch state whether Mr. Noble had paid that note or not?

A. Mr. Kalloch stated that Mr. Caldwell was pressing Mr. Noble to pay it.

Q. Did Mr. Kalloch state to you whether he paid his (Kalloch's) note to Mr. Caldwell before or after Mr. Caldwell's election to the United States Senate?

A. He did not state to me the date when the payment was made.

B. F. SIMPSON

Having been sworn, testified as follows:

Examined by the Chairman.

Q. Where do you reside?

A. At Paola, Miami county, Kansas.

Q. Were you here during the Senatorial contest last winter, which resulted in the election of A. Caldwell; and, if so, in what capacity?

A. I was here as member of the House of Representatives.

Q. Have you any knowledge of the use of money or of any improper means being used by Mr. Caldwell or any other candidate for the United States Senate to secure his election or advance his interests in that direction?

A. I have no personal knowledge.

Q. Have you any information derived from any source of such a state of facts as I have indicated?

A. The most direct information I have is, that a night or two previous to the election, I had a conversation with James F. Legate of Leavenworth to this effect, substantially: I met Mr. Legate in one of the halls of the Tefft House, and he inquired where I was going. I replied, I was going to attend a caucus whereby I hoped we could beat him and Caldwell for the Senate. Mr. Legate said I was foolish, for there was no use of trying that, and used substantially this language: "My judgment is, or my information is, that Caldwell has already secured votes enough to elect him, having been buying up men all day." This is substantially what he said. The substance of this conversation was repeated by James F. Legate on another occasion in the presence of Col. Sells, of Douglas county. I understood Mr. Legate to be a prominent supporter of Mr. Caldwell for the Senate. He voted for him and urged his election. I have heard, and I think I had it from a young man by the name of Johnson, who was Assistant Sergeant of the House, who was a brother of D. B. Johnson, a member of the House from Johnson county, that the Johnson county delegation, consisting of one Senator and three members, were taken into a room, and offered $10,000 for their vote, and the conversation in which this statement was made was in relation to the election of Caldwell. It was after the election. I don't swear that I heard this from young Johnson, but I had it from some source. But the information comes from young Johnson. He was in the room and heard this offer.

Q. Where is this young man Johnson?

A. Well, I suppose he lives in Shawnee township, Johnson county.

By J. Boynton.

Q. Do you know G. W. Wood, of Cherokee county?

A. I do.

Q. Have you at any time had any conversation with him in regard to the Senatorial election of 1871?

A. I have.

Q. State when and where.

A. I had a conversation with G. W. Wood on last Monday. The conversation was on the Missouri & Fort Scott R. R. on my way from Paola to Kansas City.

Q. Please give that conversation.

A. Mr. Wood said in that conversation to me that he had been offered, I think, it was two thousand dollars for his vote upon the Senatorial question. He said that they were "very good men" who offered him that money to control his vote, but did not state to me the name of the men who offered, nor for whom he was to vote for this money, but left me to infer that from previous remarks.

By the Chairman.

Q. Have you any other knowledge or information in regard to this matter, Mr. Simpson?

A. I have no knowledge. I have heard a great deal of talk on this subject, but what was said and by whom I cannot remember or repeat.

W. W. NEVISON.

Having been sworn, testified thus:

Examined by the Chairman.

Q. Where do you reside?

A. I live in Lawrence, Kansas.

Q. Do you know of a man by the name of M. W. Reynolds?

A. Yes, sir, I do.

Q. Do you know of any business transaction between him and S. C. Pomeroy?

A. I know this, that two notes were placed in our hands—Mr. Rigg's and mine—signed by S. C. Pomeroy and Sidney Clarke for $1,000, each payable to George A. Reynolds, or order, or bearer, and these two notes were handed to us by Milton W. Reynolds. We commenced a suit in Douglas county against Pomeroy and Mr. Clarke to collect these two notes.

Q. Have they been collected?

A. They have not been collected.

Q. Is the suit still pending?

A. The suit was tried in the District Court, and I prepared a case for the Supreme Court. I had instructions from M. W. Reynolds not to proceed any further with the case.

Q. When did you receive those instructions?

A. I think perhaps six months ago. It must have been so long. It was about the time he first went to Parsons.

Q. What defense was made in the action?

A. The defense was that the notes were given for the purpose of influencing votes, and they were, therefore, void as against public policy.

Q. Influencing votes when?

A. In 1867.

Q. In what kind of an election?

A. It was the influencing of the election of Senator Pomeroy, and also Mr. Clarke and the Republican nominee of the State Convention.

Q. That was the defense?

A. It was, sir.

Q. Have you any papers in your possession in relation to that defense which were signed by the defendants?

A. I have in our possession at Lawrence. A subpœna was served on me a day or two since by this Committee while here, and I sent for them from here. We had a deposition of Senator Pomeroy and Sidney Clarke as to the condition and circumstances in which these notes were given. The depositions were taken in their behalf in Washington, signed by each of them.

Q. At the time that M. W. Reynolds directed you not to prosecute that case any further, did he assign any reason, if so, what?

A. He gave no reasons.

Q. What was the judgment of the court below?

A. It was for the defendants, upon special findings of the court.

Q. When was that judgment?

A. It was, I think, sir, perhaps the spring of 1870—no, the fall of 1870—it may have been the spring of 1871.

Q. Was it before or after M. W. Reynolds directed you not to prosecute the suit?

A. It was before.

Q. What business is M. W. Reynolds engaged in now?

A. I don't know, but understand he is editor of a paper.

Q. Has he any public office?

A. Don't know, sir.

Q. Have you any information from M. W. Reynolds as to what these notes were received for?

A. Yes, I have information from Milton and George both.

Q. What is that information?

A. George and Milton told me that the agreement was that they should support Pomeroy and Clarke; Pomeroy for Senator and Clarke for Representative; that Mr. Reynolds was to support with his paper the re-election of Senator Pomeroy for the Senate, and Clarke for Congress.

Q. What Mr. Reynolds?

A. M. W. Reynolds.

Q. To whom were the notes payable?

A. They said they were payable to George, but they were designed for Milton Reynolds.

Q. State what M. W. Reynolds said in relation to the performance of the services directed to be performed and in consideration of which the notes were given.

A. He said he supported Mr. Sidney Clarke for Congress and Senator Pomeroy for Senator, and that he had expended money when Pomeroy was elected for the reception at Lawrence, and that he had spent a great deal of time in assisting to procure his re-election; that after the Convention at Topeka he made an arrangement with Mr. Sidney Clarke by which Sidney Clarke should be released from his obligation to pay his part of the two one thousand dollar notes; that Milton Reynolds and George Reynolds called at the house of Sidney Clarke after the Convention, at which Convention Sidney Clarke was nominated for Congress; that it was then agreed between Milton and George Reynolds and Sidney Clarke that Clarke should not pay any part of the two one thousand dollar bills or notes, for the reason that the paper which Reynolds published was going to support Andrew Johnson's policy, and that would not be a detriment to Sidney Clarke because he was already nominated, and therefore Sidney Clarke was to be released from paying his payment or part of the note.

Q. Is that all the information you have in regard to this matter?

A. That is all. As to the giving of the notes, it was thus: George Reynolds said that Mr. Clarke and Mr. Pomeroy wanted Milton to support them for re-election with his paper, and that Mr. Pomeroy and Sidney Clarke agreed with him, that is, with George, that it Milton did so support them they would give to George, for Milton, their joint notes of $1,000 each, and that that was the only consideration for the notes, and that the notes were signed at the same time—I think in the room of Senator Pomeroy at Washington—by Sidney Clarke and Senator Pomeroy.

Q. Was the suit tried on its merits before the court below?

A. It was tried in the District Court, county of Douglas, Kansas, and was tried upon its merits, and was a very full trial Judge Horton, of Atchison, Mr. A. S. Aiken also, appeared for the defendants, and I tried the case for M. W. Reynolds, and it was tried by the court, and special findings were made by the court in favor of the defendants.

S. J. CRAWFORD.

Was sworn and testified thus:

Examined by the Chairman

Q. Where do you live?

A. At Emporia, Kansas.

Q. Were you at Topeka during the Senatorial contest a year ago this winter, which resulted in the election of A. Caldwell to the United States Senate?

A. I was.

Q. State, if you know, whether or not any money or other improper consideration, or influence, or appliances were used by any person who was a candidate for the United States Senate at that time, or by any persons employed or working in his interests, to influence votes of members of the Legislature for such candidate?

A. Only from hearsay.

Q. Well, sir, you may state what you have heard in that respect, and of whom you have heard it?

A. I heard, on the day of the election, Mr. D. R. Anthony make this statement, that he knew of two men, members of the Legislature, who had received $3,000 each—I think it was $3,000—for their support of Mr. Caldwell. That was the understanding. I don't know that those were the exact words, but that was the substance of his remark. He also stated at the same time that he could prove his statement I heard Mr. Atherley, who was, I think, mayor of Burlington at that time—at any rate a citizen of Burlington—make this statement, in a room where a number of gentlemen were immediately after the election, that he and some of his friends had traced two checks, given by Mr. Len. T. Smith, in some way through one of the Lawrence banks, to the amount of, I think, $2,900. That was about the substance of his statement. And I don't recollect of his stating that it was for the support of Caldwell, but that was the subject of the conversation, and the general impression left on the minds of all present at that time. The checks in question were given to Mr. Butler, Representative, from Leroy district, Coffey county. Mr. Busick, of Lincoln county, told me, in the presence of others, I believe, that he had information to the effect that a Mr. Campbell, of Ottawa county, had received $2,000; that the money was in four five hundred dollar bills; and that the man had it in his possession. He said, at the same time, that on their way down here he had loaned this man $100, that is, this man Campbell; and that after he was here and before the election he went to Campbell and asked him for the money he had loaned him, and that he could not pay him until he got one of those five hundred dollar bills changed, and that at that time he saw the other three, making $2,000, and that, in substance, he knew that Campbell had no money when they were coming to Topeka. I recollect that during the contest Mr. Stotler informed me that he had been in conversation with Mr. Len. T. Smith, and that Smith had informed him that Caldwell and his friends had $75,000 in money to use in securing Mr. Caldwell's election. Mr. Stotler, at the time he gave me this information, had just walked immediately out of Mr. Caldwell and Mr. Smith's room. Mr. Steele, of Sedgwick county, member, at that time, of the House, owed me $200; money that I had paid upon a note which I had endorsed for him before he was elected or nominated as Representative. After the Senatorial election, the note being due, I handed it to Mr. Chase for collection—to present to Mr. Steele for payment. He, Mr. Chase, informed me that he presented the note to Mr. Steele, and Mr. Steele first told him that he had no money. The note was presented a few days after the Senatorial election. Mr. Chase told him that the note was due, and that he wanted to have the money, or needed it, or something to that effect, and rather insisted upon payment. After some hesitation and more or less confusion, he told Mr. Chase to wait a moment and he would go upstairs and get the money. He went up and brought down a pocket-book containing money, and handed Mr. Chase two one hundred dollar bills, and at the same time Mr. Chase saw that he had a number of other bills in the same pocket-book, indicating that there was a considerable amount of money.

Q. What is Mr. Steele's full name?

A. J. M. Steele.

Q. Had you any conversation before the vote was taken with Mr. Steele, and, if so, did you learn from that conversation who he was going to vote for?

A. Yes, sir, I had, and he gave me to understand that he would support me. He, himself, and his friends also, assured me of his support.

Q. Did you know at the time of the election, that is, at he time of his election, who he professed to be for the United States Senate, and what was the sentiment of his district upon that question?

A I was told that it was favorable to myself, and was also informed that my friends aided in securing his nomination and election.

Q. Was there any understanding or agreement between yourself and Mr. Steele at the tfme of his nomination whom he should support for the United States Senate in case he was elected?

A. No, sir; I don't think that I had seen Mr. Steele at any time during, or immediately preceding his nomination, or between his nomination and election.

Q. Where does this gentleman, Mr. Chase, reside?

A. In this city.

Q. What is his first name?

A. Enoch.

Q, State who Mr. Steele voted for on the first vote.

A. Well, I know that from the record and from hearsay, that he voted for me on the first ballot, and for Mr. Caldwell on the second.

Q. Do you know or have you ever heard of the reason he assigned for changing his vote for Caldwell on the second ballot?

A. I do not. I never heard him say anything on the subject. I learned outside, but don't know from whom, that they were to have the United States Land Office removed from Augusta to Wichita. The Rev. Mr. Perkins, of Marion county, a Presbyterian minister, informed me that he had ascertained the fact that Mr. A. A. Moore, member from Marion county at that time, had received $5,000 for his vote, and that the money was deposited in the Junction City Bank.

Q. What is Mr. Perkins' address?

A. Florence, Marion county, Kansas.

Q. Well, sir, have you any other information in regard to any such transactions or circumstances that might lead to the conclusion of unfair means being used?

A. I have such information as the public generally had; I heard and saw what was going on generally.

Q. Do you know of Mr. Clarke using any money or other means of that character; I mean, Mr. Sidney Clarke, or any one in his interest?

A. Mr. Stotler informed me that a friend of Mr. Clarke's, Mr. Schuyler of Burlingame—tried for one day to get Mr. Stotler to fix the price or state the amount that he would ask to support Mr. Clarke.

Q. What, Mr. Stotler!

A. Mr. Jacob Stotler.

Q. Do you know what house Mr. Caldwell stopped at?

A. The Tefft House.

Q. Do you know what part of that house he occupied on that occasion for himself and persons in his interest?

A. I don't recollect the numbers of the rooms, but one of the rooms that he occupied was one of the front rooms up stairs that had previously been used as the parlor, with rooms joining that. His friends occupied other rooms on the left of the stairway, as you go up stairs.

Q. Do you know what part of the house Mr. Clarke and his friends occupied, and how much?

A. The occupied rooms; I don't know how many—on the lower floor—on the second floor, possibly to the left, what might properly be termed the rear part of the building.

Q. State whether or not you had any conversations with Len. T. Smith during the Senatorial contest, and if so, state the substance of those conversations.

A. I did, and the impression left on my mind from what

he said was, that they had a large amount of money to use in securing Mr. Caldwell's election.

WILLIAM MELVILLE

Having been sworn, testified as follows:

Examined by Chairman.

Q. Where do you reside?

A. I reside at Topeka.

Q. Do you know Mr. Peckham?

A. Yes sir.

Q. When did you first get acquainted with him?

A. Last winter.

Q. Where?

A. At the drug store of H. S. Geeno & Co., Topeka.

Q. What time did you get acquainted with him?

A. During the session of the Legislature.

Q. What was you doing?

A. I was in the drug store; engaged in it.

Q. Did your hear Mr. Peckham make any statement any time during the Senatorial contest last winter, in regard to that contest?

A. Yes, sir.

Q. Well, sir, you may state what he said about it.

A. It was just before—the night before the election; he was in the store, and he said that he was going to vote for Mr. Caldwell for a consideration of $2,000.

Q. Anything more?

A. There was a great deal of conversation going on, but I could not state what.

Q. Well, after that, did you hear any conversation with regard to the matter?

A. Yes, sir.

Q. When and what?

A. It was at different times. We had sold out to Mr. Peckham, and this money was to have been paid over, and he failed to get it after going for it two or three different times.

Q. Where did he go for it?

A. To Leavenworth.

Q. Did you have any conversation with him after his return from any of those Leavenworth trips?

A. No, sir, not myself. Dr. Greeno did all the business; but I heard it.

Q. State what he said on his return from Leavenworth.

A. He said he failed to get the money, and at one time I heard him say that he wished he had saved his money and stayed at home instead of going to the Legislature this winter; and another time he said that he wished he had voted for Mr. Clarke. because Mr. Clarke would have bought his farm and paid him for his improvements.

Q. Any other or different conversations?

A. Well, I don't know. He was always dissatisfied when he came home.

By J. Boynton.

Q. Did you ever hear Mr. Peckham say that he saw Mr Caldwell and talked with him about the money?

A. I did, sir. At one time he waited for one or two days to wait until Mr. Caldwell got home from Washington, because we were needing the money, and that was the way we came to know about it.

By G. W. Clarke.

Q. On what terms did you you sell to Mr. Peckham?

A. He was to take the whole store, but could not raise the money, and he took the half. At first, it was to be so much cash and balance in notes, but he could not raise the cash and we took his notes at thirty and sixty days for the half interest upon the store.

Q. Has he paid those notes?

A. No sir.

Q. Do you know the reason why?

A. Well, he claims that he advanced more money after he went into the business than the notes amounted to, and the reason it was not paid when it was due was because he did not have the money to pay it.

Q. Did he give any reason why he could not get the money?

A. At that particular time—no, sir.

Q. At the time he bought into the business, did he tell you that he expected money from any source in particular?

A. No, sir, he did not tell me.

By Mr. W. H. Clarke.

Q. Do you know how often Mr. Peckham went to Leavenworth to see Mr. Caldwell about this money?

A. I think three times, but I will not be certain.

Q. Do you know from anything that Mr. Peckham told you of any other person going to Mr. Caldwell for money about the same time Mr. Peckham did?

A. Yes, sir.

Q. Who was it?

A. Mr. H. C. Vannatta.

Q. Did Mr. Peckham tell you how much Mr. Vannata was to get from Caldwell?

A. No, sir.

Q. Did Mr. Peckham ever in your presence talk rather harshly of Mr. Caldwell, and give you the reason why?

A. Yes; he talked against him because he had gone back on him as he claimed.

Q. Can you give us any of his expressions?

A. No, sir, I don't think I can.

Q. Mr. Melville, did you hear any other persons state that they had received any money out of the Senatorial election?

A. Yes, I did. Mr. Steele, Minneapolis, Ottawa county. I heard him and Mr. Redfield state that he had got two five hundred dollar bills. He said it was to procure a vote, and he put the money in his pocket and went away the next morning by the train.

Q. Are you and Mr. Peckham on good terms at present—friendly terms?

A. We are not.

Q. What is the cause?

A. He hid an invoice of goods; I accused him of it, and he slapped my face, and I slapped him back.

MONDAY, February 5, 1872.

THOMAS L. BOND,

Having been sworn, testified as follows:

Examined by the Chairman.

Q. Where do you reside?

A. I live in Saline, Saline county.

Q. What business are you engaged in?

A. At present I am Regisser of the United States Land Office, Western District, Kansas.

Q. How long have you been in that position?

A. I have been in that position since the 8th day of last May.

Q. Where did you reside before that time?

A. In Elk City, Montgomery county.

Q. Were you here in Topeka last winter, and, if so, in what capacity?

A. I was representing Montgomery county in the House of Representatives.

Q. Were you present at the election of the senator for U. S. Senate, last winter?

A. I was.

Q. In whose favor for U. S. Senator were you elected?

A. There was not any immediate issue at stake in our

county; but both were supposed to be Clarke men, and I guess we both were.

Q. Did you support Mr. Clarke in that entire campaign?

A. I did as long as he was a candidate.

Q. When did he cease to be a candidate?

A. I don't remember the exact hour. Sometime late on Tuesday night or early on Wednesday morning. Wednesday morning I guess it was, when he really ceased to be a candidate for United States Senate.

Q. Who was present beside his friends at that interview?

A. I guess not any beside his friends.

Q. Was Bob Stevens present?

A. I don't remember.

Q. In whose interests was he engaged in the campaign?

A. I have not had sufficient conversation with him to know. He was ostensibly there in the interests of Sidney Clarke.

Q. Where did you go from that consultation with Sidney Clarke?

A. I don't know particularly; I dont' remember; I guess I went down to the hotel, near the office.

Q. Were you in Caldwell's room?

A. I don't remember being in Caldwell's room that morning.

Q. Were you in his room the night before?

A. I was in his room during the morning. It was after the adjournment of the caucus.

Q. What time did the caucus adjourn?

A. To the best of my recollection it was between one and two o'clock.

Q. How long was it after that before you went into Caldwell's room?

A. It was directly after the adjournment of the caucus.

Q. How long did you stay?

A. I stayed there, to the best of my recollection, about two or three minutes.

Q. Were you there any more between that time and daylight?

A. I don't remember being there after that time.

Q. Were you in consultation with Mr. Caldwell at that time?

A. I had a short consultation with him.

Q. Was anything said with regard to supporting him?

A. I did say something about that.

Q. State what that consultation was.

A. I said to him that I was there representing the interests of the settlers, and that, as I understood, Mr. Clarke was about to withdraw from the field, it would be necessary for his friends to look for another candidate whom they should support. I told him that before I could support him for the United State Senate, I would ask—oh, no, this in a subsequent conversation—at the first conversation I simply told him that in connection with one or two others I wanted to speak to him. I wanted to see him in connection with Mr. Manning and Mr. Reynolds', of Howard county. He met us then in, I think, Mr Reynolds or Mr. Manning's room, I don't remember which; and then I had the conversation mentioned above. I told him that before I could support him for the United States Senate, it was necessary that he promise to look to the interest of the settlers on the Osage Reservation more especially. We had an instrument which I gave him, or Mr. Reynolds did, which he signed.

Q. A written instrument.

A. Yes, sir.

Q. Where is that instrument?

A. Well, I guess I have a copy of it in Montgomery, but have not one with me.

Q. What was the substance of it?

A. The substance of it was that he would protect the interest of the settler as far as lay in his power.

Q. Was that all?

A. I guess that was about all.

There might be a little more in it, but that was the main thing. The object was to get him to protect our interests; there being much trouble then about our land, some danger of loosing it entirely in fact.

Q. Had you any other conversation with him?

A. I had not.

Q. You never spoke to him but these three times?

A. I did not.

Q. What during the whole campaign?

A. Yes, sir. Well, nothing more than to pass a few words with him. He wanted me to support him, and I told him that I wanted to support Sidney Clarke, and meant to do so; that I was favorable to Leavenworth; that I knew him, and was favorable to him too, but did not expect to support him for the United States Senate.

Q. Did you have any conversation with any of his friends during the canvass upon the subject of supporting Mr. Caldwell?

A. I had conversations with a great many of his friends, and told them all about the same thing.

Q. Did you ever make any arrangement to support him until that morning?

A. I did not.

Q. Did you make any contingent arrangement, or have any contingent understanding with any one?

A. I had not.

Q. Do you know whether any money was used by Caldwell?

A. I do not.

Q. Did any one say to you that he knew anything to that effect?

A. I never heard any person particularly. I have heard that sort of thing rumored all over the state, but never heard any positive charges, giving instances.

Q. Was anything said between you and Caldwell, or his friends, in reference to any appointment to office?

A. Mr. Caldwell and his friends frequently told me that I could have anything I wanted if I would support him.

Q. What did Caldwell himself say?

A. I told Mr. Caldwell—I don't remember of ever Mr. Caldwell promising me any position positively, before he was elected.

Q. Did he at any time before he was elected offer to appoint you to any position?

A. He did in this way: He told me that if there was any position that I wanted, to let him know.

Q. That was before his election?

A. Yes, sir.

Q. And after his election too?

A. Yes, sir.

Q. Well, sir, what position did you ask him for?

A. I asked him for a position in the land office at Humboldt.

Q. Did you get it?

A. I did not.

Q. Did you get any position from him?

A. I did.

Q. What position?

A. The position I now occupy I got through his influence.

Q. Had you any conversation with Manning in regard to his election?

A. None, except what I have already stated.

Q. State if Mr. Clark at any time during that campaign made any offers or promises of appointments to you?

A. Mr. Clarke offered me a position in the U. S. land office at Humboldt.

Q. Was that promise made before the vote was taken?

A. Before the vote was taken.

Q. Well, did any one else offer you any position?

A. Mr. Crawford told me if I would come to him and support him and work for him, he would give me any position I wanted.

Q. Before or after the first ballot?

A. Before and after the first ballot.

Q. Well, sir, did any other persons make any such offer?

A. I don't remember whether the Senator from the 16th district, Allen county, made that proposition or not.

Q. Did Mr. Ross?

A. I had no conversation with Mr. Ross at all.

Q. Had you ever any conversation with me?

A. No, sir, I guess you thought it was not worth while trying to get or talk me over.

Q. Did Crawford make any approaches or advances to you with money or other valuable consideration.

A. Only as I told you; not with money.

Q. Did any other candidate?

A. No, sir.

Q. Do you know anything about what was called the "Soup House?"

A. I don't remember positively, but think that was the name given by some members to Clarke's caucus rooms.

Q. Where were they?

A. They were on the southeast corner of Kansas avenue and Sixth street.

Q. Up-stairs?

A. Yes, sir, on the second floor.

Q. How many rooms had he there?

A. To the best of my recollection there were five. I think it was the whole second floor or story.

Q. The corner building?

A. Yes, I think, but don't remember positively.

Q. Well, sir, suppose you commence at the east end of these rooms and describe the order in which they come.

A. I could not do it; all I remember is that there were such rooms, and that there were eatables and drinkables there.

Q. Well, that is just what I was asking for.

A. Well, beginning in the east—

Q. You can begin in the west if you prefer it.

A. In the extreme west I believe they had a kitchen, connected with the main room, or rather an ante-room than a main room.

Q. What was there in that ante-room or kitchen?

A. There they had the food part of the time.

Q. Cook stove?

A. I believe they had a stove, but don't remember whether they had a stove in there or not. Then in the next room, that is, in the extreme west room of the building, second floor, with which this ante-room was connected, they had a table set when I was there. I never was in there but that the table was set.

Q. Were you in there frequently?

A. I don't remember being in there but three times: twice one evening and once another evening.

Q. Well, how many persons would that table seat?

A. I could not say.

Q. What was the capacity of it? How long was it?

A. I am not able to say exactly, but think it was as long as this room.

Q. This room is about twenty-four feet.

A. Well, I think that would be about twenty feet then.

Q. How was that table supplied?

A. Supplied with chicken, bread, butter and coffee—what one generally gets for supper.

Q. Oysters?

A. I don't remember oysters.

Q. Cold or hot supper?

A. What we call a cold supper.

Q. But there was coffee?

A. Yes.

Q. Well, what is the next room going east?

A. I don't remember, being in the next room. In fact, I don't remember ever seeing any one in it.

Q. The next room?

A. I think in the next room they had liquer and cigars.

Q. What kind of liquors?

A. Principally whisky.

Q. Well, sir, was that sold?

A. I never saw it sold.

Q. How was it disposed of?

A. Every man helped himself.

Q. The same with cigars?

A. Yes, sir.

Q. These were free to everybody that came in?

A. Yes; I saw that even the anti-Clarke men were allowed to drink the whisky and smoke the cigars if they saw fit.

Q. Well, sir, in the next room?

A. In the next room there was nothing but a table, which was used really as a caucus room. In the next room there were a couple of beds. (There is some mistake; this I think, must be the room where I have put the table, or where the whisky was.)

Q. Have you any idea what it would cost to run such an institution as that?

A. I don't know; I never tried it, and don't suppose I ever shall.

Q. Well, sir, you have read this article in the "*Lawrence Standard?*"

A. Yes, sir, I have.

Q. Your name is mentioned here in connection with the transaction; have you any idea what transaction that language referred to, if there was any transaction?

A. There was no such transaction; I was told since I came here that Mr. Clarke said I told him that I had been offered $3,000 for my vote, if I would sell. The statement is untrue, if made.

By Senator Stover.

Q. Did you ever have any conversation with Mr. Clarke in reference to any one offering you a certain sum of money for your vote?

A. I don't remember ever having anything of the kind.

Q. Did you ever advise with him on the subject as to whether you could take it or not?

A. I never did.

By W. H. Clark.

Q. Did any one ever offer you any sum of money during than campaign?

A. No, sir.

Q. Did any one tell you you could get any money for your vote?

A. I was told that by a good many people. The first man that told me that was Col. D. R. Anthony. He told me I could get three to five thousand dollars if I would promise to vote for Mr. Caldwell; that I was foolish if I did not take the money, and keep it, and vote for whom I pleased.

By J. J. Wood.

Q. Was D. R. Anthony canvassing in favor of any one of the candidates?

A. I had heard him express his preference for Thad. Walker. He was rather against Caldwell than for any one.

JOSHUA WHEELER,

Having been sworn, testified as follows:

Examined by the Chairman.

Q. Where do you live?

A. Atchison county, Kansas.

Q. Where were you during the Senatorial contest last winter?

A. I came here two days before the election took place.

Q. Were you in the contest?

A. Yes, sir, I might be considered so. I was sent for by Governor Carney.

Q. Did you see him when you came?

A. I did, sir.

Q. What did he want?

A. He understood that I was opposed to the election of Mr. Clarke. It was understood that Governor Carney was out of the field, and being opposed to Sidney Clarke, I was in favor of Mr. Caldwell.

Q. Did you take any part in the canvass?

A. Yes, sir, I did what I could to get Mr. Caldwell elected.

Q. What did you do?

A. My ground was that I was opposed to Mr. Clarke, believing him to be corrupt.

Q. But what did you do?

A. I talked with members of the Legislature.

Q. Any one in particular?

A. I talked with Mr. Bennett, of Doniphan county, Sol. Miller and the members from Atchison county.

Q. Is that all you did?

A. Yes, sir, that is all I did.

Q. Did any of those persons you talked to change their position?

A. Well, our entire county changed their position the night before the election took place.

Q. Do you know the reason?

A. Well, I understood the reason to be just this: they found Mr. Caldwell sufficiently strong to elect him, and they thought it was no use to stand out against him.

Q. Is that all?

A. Yes, sir, that is all.

Q. Is that all the reason why they changed?

A. That is all the reason they assigned to me.

Q. Did any one else change that you know of after you came down?

A. I don't know that I could put my mind upon any individual. I only know that the gentlemen I have referred to did between supper time and the next morning.

Q. Were you with them during the night?

A. I was not, sir.

Q. Where were you that night?

A. I remained in Mr. Caldwell's room until probably eleven o'clock, at the Tefft House.

Q. Well, where then did you go?

A. I went to bed.

Q. Do you know of any money being used, or offered to be used, by any person to secure votes for any person for the United States Senate?

A. Well, I know that there were propositions made to some of our men by Sidney Clarke. I understood that Mr. King should get the position of Consul to Europe in consideration for his vote.

Q. What place in Europe?

A. Well, several places were in view. If I had a letter

here that was written, I could tell. I would state that after Mr. Clarke failed, efforts were made to secure the position for Mr. King from Mr. Caldwell.

Q. Was this before or after the election of Caldwell?

A. After.

Q. Did Mr. King support Mr. Clarke?

A. He did, sir.

Q. In consideration of that promise?

A. Well, that is what I understood. I had some conversation with Mr. King myself, before I came down here, and stated why I should oppose Clarke, and he stated that if he had known what I had told him he would not have committed himself to Mr. Clarke; and he talked to me as though he would not support Mr. Clarke, but when I came I found he was in earnest for Clarke, who had promised him that position.

Q. Did he vote for Caldwell?

A. He did, sir.

Q. Was there any promise from Caldwell to him in regard to that place?

A. I think not, sir.

Q. Anything more of that kind do you know of?

A. Well, not as direct as that. I have indirect knowledge.

By G. W. Clark.

Q. Do you know of any man being offered $100 for his vote at the last election, or any other Senatorial election?

A. I know during the campaign when Mr. Pomeroy was in the field, there was a member of the House, whose seat was contested, and Mr. Pomeroy gave A. H. Horton $100 to secure his seat, with the understanding that he should vote for Mr. Pomeroy.

Q. Was that in 1867?

A. Yes, sir.

Q. Do you know who it was?

A. I cannot give the name; it has slipped my mind entirely.

Q. Do you know any other case?

A. No, sir, I do not.

By J. Boynton.

Q. You say Mr. Pomeroy gave $100—by whom?

A. To the lawyer to secure the seat.

By the Chairman.

Q. Did that man secure his seat?

A. He did.

Q. How did he vote?

A. For Pomeroy.

F. P. BAKER,

Having been sworn, testified as follows:

Examined by Mr. W. H. Clark.

Q. Where were you last winter during the Senatorial campaign?

A. I was in Topeka.

Q. What were you doing there?

A. Publishing a newspaper.

Q. How long afterwards did you continue to publish it?

A. Up to 7th of December, 1871.

Q. Had you ever any conversation with any parties about money being used in that campaign to elect any person?

A. Yes, sir.

Q. With whom?

A. It is pretty hard to say. I have talked almost with everybody about it.

Q. Did you have any conversation with Major Anderson?

A. Yes, sir.

Q. What was the subject of that conversation?

A. Well, I have talked with him I suppose twenty times.

Q. Will you give the subject?

A. Well, I have heard him say that it cost $8,000—I think that was the sum—to get the vote of Doniphan county. It was divided among all the delegation, except one.

Q. Who was that one?

A. He did not say. I don't mean that he paid the money, but that he said it cost so much.

Q. Did he state whom the money was paid to?

A. No, sir.

Q. Did he state who paid it?

A. Well, the impression was carried that it was paid for the votes for Caldwell; but I can't say that he said that; that was the impression.

Q. Did he name any one of the delegation from Doniphan county as having received money?

A. I don't think he did.

Q. Did he name any other persons that got money from parties?

A. No, I don't think he ever named any person direct.

Q. Did you have a conversation with Major Anderson in the *Record* office, Topeka, sometime last fall about making out a list of the names of the parties who sold out during the Senatorial campaign of 1871.

A. I did.

Q. What was that?

A. Perhaps I could get at it by telling the whole story. We had been reading an article from the Augusta *Republican* which set forth that a great deal of bribery had been committed; that a whole delegation had peen bought up, and I had stated to Prentis, who was associated with me, that something ought to be said about that. The question arose between us that an article would look well taking part of the article from the Augusta *Republican*, and incorporated in it—as, for instance, Mr. Such-a-man, and Mr. Such-a-man sold out, how it would look. About that time Tom Anderson came in, and either Mr. Prentis or myself said, "Here's a man who can tell us how we can get that information; and we explained to Tom what we were talking about. He said, pulling a pocket-book out, "I have got it right here." He began to look and said: "I don't find it; give me a House and Senate roll." I took it for granted he was going to give me the names. He took the roll and said: "Commence at the top, and go right down the whole of them." Well, that was about the gist of it. I was expecting that he would give the men—name them, but he did not do it.

Q. Was this remark made by Anderson: "Put that name down; I bought him myself."

A. I dont think it was. If I it had been, I think I should have remembered it, for I was anxious to get names.

Q. Has he at any time given you any names of men?

A. No, I don't believe he has—only by inuendo.

Q. Did he ever name a man?

Q. Well, I will explain: The question was up once when Senator Wood was out at Washington asking for the Land Office at Concordia or Salina, and talking about it, he said: "He ought not to have it, for he has got his pay already."

Q. Had you ever any conversation about any financial difficulty between Mr. Anderson and Mr. Caldwell?

A. Yes, I have.

Q. What was Mr. Anderson's statement of that difficulty?

A. Well, that Mr. Caldwell owed him for money expended last winter, and that he had not paid him.

Q. Did he say how much?

A. My impression is $3,500.

Q. Did Mr. Anderson ever explain to you how he spent that money or how Mr. Caldwell came to owe him so much?

A. Well, in connection with the Senatorial election.

Q. Did Mr. Anderson ever state how much Mr. Caldwell had paid him?

A. I don't think he did.

Q. Do you know from any conversation how much Mr. Caldwell has paid Mr. Anderson?

A. No, I do not.

Q. Was there any offer of money made to you during the Senatorial campaign?

A. No, there was not.

Q. Did you write a letter to Mr. Prentis of Lawrence?

A. Yes.

Q. Do you remember what was in that letter?

A. Well, I had written a good many, but the one which I supposed you referred to is one in which I suggested the idea that he would leave the State for two or three weeks.

Q. Did you suggest anything else in that letter?

A. Yes, I guess I did, namely: that I should throw the onus of that article upon him.

Q. Anything further?

A. Not that I remember. When the matter first came up, a good deal was said about the investigating matter, and rather hastily I wrote that letter, but as he has got the letter, I am perfectly willing you should have a copy.

Q. Did not you state in that letter to Mr. Prentis that if he would leave the State you and Tom Anderson would not know anything?

A. I won't deny it, but if I did; I presume I did.

Q. What did you mean?

A. Simply, that when this matter was talked of a good deal was said, and I very foolishly wrote that letter. What I meant was that in that case it would not come out about that conversation.

Q. No other object in that view?

A. No, sir, that is all.

Q. Did you have any consultation with any one before you wrote it?

A. Not that I remember.

Q. Are you in the habit of writing such letters without an object?

A. Well, my object was that this thing might not get out; that was all. If he were gone, that matter would not get out.

Q. Had you any conversation with Mr. Anderson about Mr. Prentis leaving the State?

A. I don't remember; I might, but can't tell.

Q. Or Mr. Legate?

A. I don't remember that I have talked with Mr. Legate at all.

By Mr. Wood.

Q. Why did you not want that conversation to get out?

A. I have already said it was a foolish thing. It was written on the spur of the moment, and I ought not to have done it.

Q. I suppose you had some reason at the time for not wanting it to get out?

A. Well, it was that nothing might be said that would reflect on Tom who is a personal friend. If there is a reason I presume that that was really it.

By G. W. Clark.

Q. You say you are a warm personal friend of Tom Anderson's?

A. Yes, sir.

Q. You and he have had very frequent conversations over the Caldwell election?

A. Yes, sir.

Q. Has he never told you about any single person who he knew had been bought out?

A. Only in that general way; never to say that such or such a man got so much or so much money.

Q. Do you know of any one getting money last winter?

A. I do not.

Q. Do you know from hearsay, or from any reliable authority?

A. I know it is the common talk among people generally, but not whether it is reliable as a matter of judgment.

Q. I ask, have you heard it from any particular person?

A. I cannot say, only as I heard about Senator Wood.

By the Chairman.

Q. During the canvass of last winter, did you have any conversation with Bob Stevens?

A. I had, but don't remember that it had any relation to the Senatorial election.

Q. Were you in Sidney Clarke's banquet hall, or soup room, or caucus room?

A. I was occasionally; perhaps two or three times.

Q. What kind of a thing or place was kept there?

A. Free eating and free cigars, and it may have been there were free liquors.

Q. How many times were you there?

A. I don't remember of being there but once?

Q. How long was that machine running?

A. About ten days, I judge.

Q. Do you know what it would cost to run such an establishment—what it would cost a day?

A. It would be guess work entirely. I don't know. It might be three or five hundred dollars a day. I went in once and got a supper, and told them I was foraging on the enemy.

By Mr. Wood.

Q. Who did you hear, by inuendo or otherwise, had received money or other consideration for their vote?

A. I stated Senator Wood.

Q. Is that the only one?

A. No; by inuendo I learned that all but one, as I said, of the members from Doniphan county.

D. R. ANTHONY,

Having been sworn, testified thus:

Examined by the Chairman.

Q. Where were you residing in January last, at the time of the Senatorial election?

A. In Leavenworth.

Q. What is your business?

A. Engaged in the insurance business.

Q. Was you here at Topeka any time during the canvass?

A. I was.

Q. About what time?

A. From the 15th of January to the date of the election, about a week or ten days.

Q. Were you here working in the interest of any person working for his election?

A. I was not.

Q. Were you working here in opposition to any one?

A. I was opposed to the election of Mr. Caldwell and Mr. Clarke both.

Q. Have you any knowledge, or any means of getting any knowledge, of the appliances that were used by any person that was a candidate for election at that time, to secure votes?

A. I had general knowledge.

Q. Well, sir, you may state what knowledge you had.

A. I could hardly state what that general knowledge is. It is simply the general belief and talk in the streets, the opinion being so general and extended that it could hardly be stated.

Q. Had you any information of any means being used from any person at that time, that are usually denominated improper, to secure votes?

A. I believe there were.

Q. Had you any information that there were such means used?

A. Nothing more than the rumors. I had no knowledge of any one using them except the talk among parties of the amounts that were offered for votes.

Q. Have you since that time—that is, since the election—learned anything or been informed of any transactions of that kind?

A. No, sir, except on rumor.

Q. Did you have any conversation with Mr. Caldwell's friends during that canvass about such transactions, or with regard to the manner and mode of his making that canvass?

A. I did.

Q. Well, sir, state what they said about that.

A. The general talk at that time was that they were buying Caldwell through; that money was his strength.

Q. You had such talk with them?

A. I did.

Q. What did they say?

A. I think some of them said he had money and was buying votes, and some said he was not.

Q. Did you ever have any conversation with James F. Legate in regard to the matter?

A. I did.

Q. More than one conversation.

A. Yes, a dozen.

Q. Can you state the substance of those conversations, so far as they related to the means used to procure votes?

A. Well, my conversations with Legate were more of this character: I found fault with Legate for supporting Caldwell; I said it was not the Caldwell influence that elected him to the Legislature; and his reply was that he was going in for Caldwell for the purpose of getting rid of Mr. Carney, though he had no expectation of electing him. This was the subject of the conversation until toward the last. He had, he said, "got into the boat" then, and he had gone so far that he was going through with it. That was the substance of the conversation.

Q. Did you have any other talk with any other friends of Mr. Caldwell than these you have mentioned in reference to the mode and manner of his election?

A. I think I did with perhaps half the Leavenworth men.

Q. Did you know anything about the plan of Mr. Clarke's canvass?

A. I did not.

Q. Or Crawford's?

A. I did not; only what was general.

Q. Do you recollect a man by the name of Dr. Linn, of Pottawotamie county.

A. I do, sir.

Q. Did you have any conversation with him during the canvass, or immediately after its close?

A. I did.

Q. Where at?

A. I think in the Tefft House. I talked to him a good many times.

Q. I call your attention to a particular conversation in the room of Governor Crawford, immediately after election; do you recollect of him being there when several others were present?

A. I do not particularly.

Q. At the time when the conversation turned upon the way that Caldwell had secured his election, do you recollect of saying that you knew two men that were bought?

A. I may have said so. I heard of two men that were

bought; also of the whole of the Doniphan delegation being bought; but it was only street rumor.

Q. Do you recollect of saying that you knew of two men that had been bought, and that you were willing to swear to that fact?

A. No, sir.

Q. Do you know Mr. Peckham?

A. Yes, sir.

Q. Did you ever see him in Leavenworth along in April or May last?

A. I did, I presume.

Q. Had you any conversation with him there about the Senatorial election?

A. I had.

Q. Do you know what it was?

A. I do not.

Q. Do you know whether he was there at any time to see Caldwell?

A. I do not;—let's see,—I won't be positive. There have been so many to see Caldwell that I would not say whether he was there or not. He may have been there for that purpose, and may have told me so, but I don't remember.

By Senator Whitney.

Q. Did you not state in Governor Crawford's room, immediately after the Senatorial election, that you knew of two members of the Legislature, who were bought, and that Caldwell or the Caldwell party gave $3,000, and that they only got $500 of it, or words to that effect?

A. I stated that I was told that.

Q. Who were the two members referred to?

A. The two members of the lower House from Nemaha county. They were telling as a joke that they sold for $500 when they were willing to pay a thousand.

Q. Who told you this in reference to these men.

A. Well, I cannot say who told me, but I either heard it in Walker's room or in Crawford's room. The two Murdocks were in the room more than anybody else, and I presume they heard it.

By G. W. Clark.

Q. I believe you referred to the amount that was offered for votes; will you state what amounts they were paying?

A. I don't remember of stating that. The conversation that I had was that I recollect telling several people that they were buying. I told several members that they were, and not to take less than $5,000; that they ought not to take less when they could get that.

Q. Did you hear that there was $5,000 offered?

A. No, I don't know as I did in any one case. I was not in a position to get the facts. The Caldwell party were not very confidential with me, though I was, and am, well satisfied that the means that secured the election was money.

By Mr. Wood.

Q. Upon what ground did you believe that money or other corrupt influences were used to secure the election of Mr. Caldwell?

A. Because Mr. Caldwell had no other influences to rely upon except his money both at home and here. He was not known as a politician.

By Senator Whitney.

Q. Now, Mr. Anthony, where did Mr. Caldwell keep his bank account in Leavenworth?

A. I was told, in the First National Bank in Leavenworth and in Philadelphia.

Q. How much money did Mr. Caldwell or Len. Smith, either or both, bring up to use in that Senatorial election?

A. I don't know.

Q. Did they use money directly in your opinion—I mean money in kind,—or did they draw against some fund somewhere?

A. They did both; I think they did. That is my opinion.

Q. What bank or house did they draw on?

A. I don't know.

Q. Did you ever hear any of Caldwell's immediate friends say how much money it took to secure Caldwell's election?

A. I have heard, but can't say it was from his immediate friends.

Q. What was Caldwell's politics in 1864?

A. As I understand it he had no politics.

Q. Do you know how he voted in 1864?

A. I do not.

Q. You knew him in '64?

A. I did, sir.

Q. Do you know the first time when he took sides in politics?

A. It was three years ago, when he made a speech in a small meeting he had.

Q. Was that a Republican meeting?

A. Yes, sir.

Q. Was Caldwell started out as Senatorial candidate by the substantial people of Leavenworth?

A. I don't think he was started in that way—yes, by a few substantial men, but not by the popular will of the people, but eventually a very large majority supported him.

Q. Well, who started him?

A. Jim Legate started him.

Q. When was he first spoken of as candidate for Senator relative to the election?

A. I think it was after the election of members of the Legislature.

W. S. VAN DOREN,

Having been sworn, testified as follows:

Examined by Chairman.

Q. Where do you live?

A. In the city of Leavenworth.

Q. Were you in Topeka during the Senatorial contest in 1871?

A. Yes, sir, I was.

Q. In what capacity?

A. I was in the Senate represenating the 23d district, Leavenworth.

Q. Do you know Caldwell?

A. Yes, sir.

Q. Sidney Clarke?

A. Yes, sir.

Q. Crawford?

A. Yes, sir.

Q. Do you know of either of these three gentlemen or any other gentleman using any money or pledging any office to secure votes for United States Senator?

A. I do not.

Q. Have you at any time heard of such a proceeding?

A. I may have heard rumors on the street and seen newspaper articles about it, but nothing definite.

Q. Did you ever have any conversation with Mr. McDowell on the subject?

A. No, sir.

Q. Where did you board during the time?

A. I had a room with Mr. Fenlon over a hardware store, and took my meals at the Tefft House.

Q. Where did Caldwell stop?

A. At the Tefft House.

Q. Where did Clarke and Crawford stop?

A. All at the same place.

Q. You say you don't know of Caldwell offering any money or promising any offices to any one to get him to support him?

A. No, sir.

Q. Did you never him say anything about it?

A. No, sir.

Q. Had you ever had any conversation with Caldwell about his election prior to it?

A. Yes, sir.

Q. Did he never say in such conversation how many votes he had?

A. No, sir. I never talked with him much about the election.

Q. Do you know how much money Caldwell brought here to use?

A. I have not the slightest idea.

Q. You saw a good deal of that contest, didn't you?

A. I expect I saw very little of it, sir. We generally kept our own rooms or were in the Senate.

Q. Were you not at the caucuses?

A. I was not.

Q. How often were you with Mr. Caldwell?

A. I did not see Mr. Caldwell more than ten minutes altogether last winter here at Topeka.

Q. What was Len Smith doing here?

A. He was here attending the election, assisting Caldwell.

Q Was he doing anything else than assisting Caldwell?

A. Not that I know of, sir.

Q. What is his politics?

A. Democratic; same as I am.

Q. How long was Smith here?

A. I cannot tell.

Q. Do you know whether he had any money here?

A. I don't. He must have had some, but I don't know how much.

Q. Do you know whether there was any arrangement between Mr. Caldwell and Mr. Clarke in relation to Mr. Clarke's withdrawal?

A. I have heard rumors of an arrangement between them?

Q. Can you tell what the rumors were?

A. I heard it rumored that Mr. Sidney Clarke had withdrawn from the contest and thrown his strength in favor of Mr. Caldwell.

Q. Upon what arrangement or basis?

A. I never heard any particulars of the arrangement.

Q. When did you learn that in relation to the Senatorial election of Mr. Caldwell?

A. I first heard it early in the morning of the day upon which Mr. Caldwell was elected.

Q. Do you know from whom you learned it?

A. Yes, sir.

Q. Will you state?

A. Mr. Len Smith came into my room very early in the morning—probably 3 o'clock—2 or 3 o'clock, and seemed to be in a very fine humor about something. I asked him what was the matter, and he said, "We have seventy votes for Caldwell to-morrow, and it may be eighty." That is all he said; he passed out of the door in a hurry. I then got out of bed, and went over to the Tefft House; met Mr. J. L. McDowell and asked him the cause of Len Smith's good humor, or why it was about the votes; how it was settled. I don't recollect my language, but went over to see about it any way.

Q. What information did you get from him?

A. He told me that Clarke's forces had come over to Caldwell.

Q. Did he state on what terms?

A. He did not, sir.

By Senator Whitney.

Q. What was Caldwell's politics in the general election of 1864?

A. I don't know, sir.

Q. Did you know him at that time?

A. I may have known him then very slightly.

Q. You both lived in Leavenworth then?

A. Yes.

The witness then said: If this testimony is to be published, I want to add a little more. It is only a personal explanation that I want to make. It is, that neither Mr. Caldwell, nor Mr. Len Smith, nor any of their immediate friends ever asked me to vote for Caldwell. That is all.

TUESDAY, February 6, 1872.

DR. J. W. MORRIS,

Having been sworn, testified as follows:

Examined by Mr. W. H. Clark.

Q. Where do you reside?

A. At Leavenworth city, Kansas.

Q. Were you in Topeka during the Senatorial contest of last winter?

A. Yes, sir, part of the time.

Q. Do you know Mr. Caldwell?

A. Yes, sir.

Q. Do you know Mr. T. F. Darling, of Leavenworth?

A. Yes, sir.

Q. Was he a member of the Legislature last winter?

A. Yes, sir.

Q. Did you have any conversation with him in regard to his supporting Mr. Caldwell for United States Senator?

A. Yes, sir.

Q. What was that conversation?

A. I called to see Mr. Darling after the first vote had been taken, and stated to him that I called in to see him because our people at Leavenworth felt very anxious that there should be a united vote from Leavenworth for Caldwell. I asked him if there were any reasons why he should not support Mr. Caldwell, and if there were I should like to know them; and said that if I could give any good reasons or explanations to satisfy him that he ought to vote for Mr. Caldwell—I was anxious to do so in order to get that united vote from Leavenworth. He said that no one knew how he was going to vote previous to his vote the day before, and no one knew how he was going to vote on the next time, nor they would not know.

Q. Did you say anything to him in that conversation, or in any other conversation, that he could have any consideration for his vote, if he wished it, or words to that effect?

A No, sir.

Q. Did you have any authority to hold out any inducements to him, or did you hold out any inducements to him?

A. I had no authority to hold out inducements, and I did hold out no inducements, except to try and satisfy him that whatever his objections were to Mr. Caldwell they were either unfounded or could be removed.

Q. Do you know Mr. Colley, of Leavenworth?

A. Yes, sir.

Q. Did you offer any inducements to him at any time to vote for Mr. Caldwell?

A. I don't think I had any conversation with him in reference to his vote, but in answer to your question I will say I did not.

Q. Were you a director in a bank at Leavenworth at that time?

A. Yes, sir.

Q. What bank?

A. The First National bank, Leavenworth.

Q Had you any knowledge at that time of the deposits of Alexander Caldwell in that bank?

A. I have not a very distinct recollection about the deposits. I have a knowledge that there was a deposit on the books in his name for a considerable amount.

Q. How much?

A. Some seven or eight thousand dollars. That deposit was unchanged for a year. There were some conditions connected with it on account of which it remained there without any change.

Q. Was that deposit made before or after the Senatorial election?

A. Before; and remains there yet.

Q. Had he any other deposits?

A. Not that I know of.

Q. Do you know what deposits L. T. Smith had there at that time?

A. I don't exactly, but they were small, if any.

Q. Was his deposit drawn out during the Senatorial campaign?

A. I don't know whether it was or not.

Q. Was there any money deposited there to your knowledge in the name of any person, for the benefit of Mr. Caldwell or Mr. Smith?

A. Not to my knowledge.

Q. Were there any checks or drafts made on that bank by either Mr. Caldwell or Mr. Smith, during the Senatorial campaign?

A. Not that I know of, sir. I may state here that I was Vice President of the bank, and was not always present at the bank, as a cashier would be. Some checks may have been made, many are made, without my knowledge.

Q. Do you know of any money, or other valuable consideration, being offered to a member of the Legislature by Mr. Caldwell, or any one in his interest, for his vote?

A. I do not.

Q. Do you know of any money, or other valuable consideration, being offered to any one for his influence?

A. No, sir, I don't recollect of any.

Q. Do you know of any money being offered to induce any one to assist in the election of Mr. Caldwell.

A. No, sir.

Q Do you know of any money being used at all during the Senatorial campaign, to secure the election of Mr. Caldwell?

A. There was money used by some parties in his interest to send a large lobby from Leavenworth up here; either passes or money. Some got free passes, but whether or not, I don't know whether it was paid by the citizens of Leavenworth in free railroad passes, or otherwise.

Q. Have you ever heard the statement made that it cost Mr. Caldwell $60,000 to secure his election to the United States Senate?

A. Well, I don't know that I have heard just that statement, but I have heard it stated that it cost him that amount or more.

Q. Who did you derive that information from?

A. I don't now recollect. I did not derive the information; that was the statement of a mere opinion or supposition.

Q. Had you ever any conversation with Mr. Caldwell in regard to the matter of expenses during the Senatorial election?

A. I don't recollect that I have. I had a conversation with somebody with regard to what the bill was at the hotel, but don't think it was Mr. Caldwell.

Q. Was it with any one working in his interest?

A. I don't know that they were. It was some person from Leavenworth who was speaking in general terms of the expenses at the hotel, such as the cigars and the like.

Q. After the Senatorial election, do you know whether Mr. Caldwell was indebted to your bank or not.

A. I do not know; but if he was, it was to a very small amount, or I should otherwise have noticed it.

Q. Do you know what his deposit was on the first of December, 1870?

A. No, sir; I would have means of knowing by referring to the balance book; that is, if it was deposited in the bank in the usual way; there may have been a special deposit.

Q. Do you know whether it was more or less than this $8,000?

A. I don't know. Mr. Caldwell did not keep his regular banking account with us.

Examined by the Chairman.

Q. You state that $8,000 were deposited on certain conditions; were those conditions connected with the Senatorial election?

A. No, sir.

Q. Do you know how many came over here to lobby in the interests of Mr. Caldwell?

A. I don't, sir.

Q. Are you able to state an approximate number from your own knowledge?

A. I would suppose there were seventy-five from Leavenworth, and nine-tenths of them were friends of Mr. Caldwell; but whether they were absolutely working in his interest I do not know.

Q. Did all those friends of Mr. Caldwell have free passes by rail?

A. No, sir, not all. I came over twice or three times myself, and had a pass once, and others I know paid their way.

Q. When you went back over there during the contest did you go over and return in the interest of Mr. Caldwell?

A. No, sir.

Q. Do you know what his hotel bill was?

A. No, sir, I don't recollect having had any conversation with him about his hotel bill?

Q. Have you any knowledge whether Mr. Clarke offered any money, or other valuable influence to procure his election at that time?

A. I have not. There were persons who came from Leavenworth with free passes, who were friends of Mr. Clarke, but whether they got them from Mr. Clarke I don't know. The same remark applies as that I made in reference to Mr. Caldwell.

Q. Do you know whether Mr. Caldwell promised to any member of the Legislature any appointment in case he should be elected?

A. I do not, sir.

Q. What was Len Smith doing here?

A. Well, I expect he could answer that question better than I could.

Q. Are you able to state what he was doing?

A. Only what he appeared to be doing. He appeared to be electioneering—trying to convince people they ought to vote for Mr. Caldwell, as near as I can judge.

Q. Do you know what his politics are?

A. Only by reputation; Democratic.

Q. What business relation, if any, existed between him and Mr. Caldwell at that time?

A. I am unable to say.

Q. Well, sir, do you know what business relations existed between them for a year, two years, or three years prior to that time?

A. They had formerly been engaged together in firm that freighted for the government.

Q. How long had they been engaged in that business together prior to this election, and how long prior?

A. It was several years previous that they were together, and when engaged their company lasted several years; three or four years, or five years, I think.

Q. How long before this election did they cease to be connected in a business way?

A. It had been three or four years since they had been connected in that freighting business.

Q. Had there not been some railroad speculations which they had together?

A. Yes, sir; they were both stockholders and directors in the Missouri River Railroad, and in the Atchison & North Western Railway.

Q. Was that at the time of the election?

A. I believe so, and think they are yet.

Q. Don't they own together a considerable portion of franchises in those roads?

A. I do not know.

Q. Are they not reputed to own a considerable portion of the franchises of those roads?

A. They are reputed to own about one-sixth of the Missouri River Railroad, and about the same amount in the Atchison & Northwestern Railroad; each one-twelfth, not jointly, but as individuals.

Q. Do you know where Robert Crozier is?

A. I believe he is at Clay Center at present. I think he will pass down the road to morrow. He left Leavenworth on Saturday to go to Clay Center.

By Senator Stover.

Q. From your knowledge of the circumstances of the campaign, what in your opinion were the expenses incurred during Mr. Caldwell's campaign?

A. Well, I don't know the exact amount, but can judge from what I saw. For instance: I might estimate the amount of the cigars, and I might an account of what other things had cost—things of which I was observant.

Q. Well, how much?

A. I think that his hotel bill and his other expenses connected with the getting persons here, probably cost him $2,500 or about that amount. Some of his friends, I know, paid their own expenses. I was there as one of the party working for Mr. Caldwell, and I paid my own.

Q. From your knowledge, what do you think it cost Mr. Caldwell in dollars and cents, to secure his seat for United States Senator.

A. Sometimes I think one thing, and sometimes I think another. I don't think I am called upon to make a guess of that kind.

Q. Well, just in your opinion now, how much did it cost him to secure his seat in the United States Senate?

Q. I don't feel that I am called upon to guess about it.

Examined by the Chairman.

Q. Have you a belief, from all that you observed during that canvass in regard to the amount that it cost Mr. Caldwell to secure his election?

A. I would answer that as I did the other question: a belief without knowledge—I don't think I have a right to communicate. I have no knowledge upon which to base such a belief.

Q. Have you a belief?

A. Of course I have formed some opinion in regard to it; but, as I said, it is sometimes one opinion, and sometimes another.

Q. From what sources of information are those various opinions formed?

A. From statements I hear made here and there, and elsewhere; or rather, I may say, from opinions I heard expressed here and there and elsewhere.

Q. Are those opinions which you hear expressed in regard to this matter similar to opinions that you hear expressed in relation to other business matters, and upon which, as a business man, you act?

A. The opinions I hear as I do upon other matters that I am not familiar with. They are not sufficiently definite to form a basis of action in business matters that are of any importance.

Q. Will you state what those opinions are—those of yours?

A. No, sir.

By Mr. Johnson.

Q. Through the diversified reports that you have heard, your opinion has been fluctuating; you have sometimes a settled opinion, you have a settled opinion now, and that settled opinion is formed from the different stories you have heard of to-day; and I would like to know what your opinion is to-night.

A. After hearing different statements made, I have come to the conclusion that neither they who made the statements nor myself, know anything about what it did cost.

By Senator Stover.

Q. You were here a long time during the Senatorial campaign: Do you know yourself or from any reliable source of any improper means being used by any of the candidates for the United States Senate to secure votes or influence?

A. I know only what I have spoken of.

Q. Do you know of any of the candidates engaging rooms here?

A. It was understood that Mr. Clarke had secured a large number of rooms, and that Mr. Caldwell had done the same.

Q. And were paying for them?

A. It was a general impression. I was put in one of Mr. Caldwell's, and my experience is that I paid my own bill. I believe that some of Mr. Caldwell's friends, and some of Mr. Clarke's friends, did not pay for their rooms. I paid for mine.

By J. Boynton.

Q. Were you here when the election took place?

A. Yes, sir.

Q. Do you know what arrangement was made before the election between Mr. Caldwell and Mr. Clark?

A. I do not.

S. C. KING,

Was sworn and testified thus:

Examined by the Chairman.

Q. Where do you live?

A. Atchison, adjoining the city of Atchison.

Q. Were you a member of the Legislature last winter?

A. I was.

Q. Did you take any special interest in the Senatorial election?

A. I did.

Q. In whose favor?

A. Sidney Clarke's.

Q. Did you have any conversation with him referring to his election, after the meeting of the Legislature?

A. Yes, sir.

Q. Did you have any conversation with him at any time, in relation to the mode or means of securing votes in order to procure his election?

A. I don't think I had.

Q. Were you ever in caucus with him?

A. Yes, sir.

Q. Did you ever hear anything at all during that campaign about how any particular man was going to vote?

A. I did.

Q. Do you know who?

A. Well, I could mention some; there were many.

Q. Will you mention some—I mean of those who were not originally Clarke's friends?

A. I don't know any.

Q. Did you ever hear any one say how Senator Wood, of Doniphan covnty, was going to vote?

A. I don't remember of hearing him say so.

Q. Did you ever have any conversation with him in regard to how Mr. Wood was going to vote?

A. I did.

Q. What was that conversation?

A. It was that Wood would not support him?

Q. Was that all of it?

A. That is about all of the conversation; I could not remember distinctly the whole of the conversation.

Q. Anything said about an effort being made to secure his vote?

A. Not in that conversation.

Q. In any conversation with him? With any one?

A. At the caucus, at which I was not present, parties were selected to work upon the opposition members, that is, those known to be opposed to Clarke, and as the majority of the Doniphan delegation boarded at the same place I did, I received a slip of paper just as I went into the hall, from some of the members who had been at the caucus, with the names of two or three of the Doniphan delegation, on which I was told to work; that is, to use my best endeavors to induce them to support Clarke.

Q. Did you do so?

A. Yes, sir.

Q. What did you say to them?

A. I cannot remember particularly.

Q. Can you remember anything that you stated to any of them?

A. I applauded up Clarke—lauded him as a great and good man.

Q. What else did you say?

A. Well, sir, I cannot think of anything else.

Q. Did you have any conversation with Senator Wood, of Doniphan?

A. Yes, sir.

Q. Do you remember any of those conversations with him?

A. Some of them.

Q. Do you remember any conversation in which there was something said about a check of $3,000?

A. Yes, sir.

Q. State what that conversation was.

A, You mentioned the word "check;" it was a certificate of deposit.

Q. What was said about it?

A. It was mentioned by me to Dr. Wood as a bond to be held by me as a trustee upon condition that Dr. Wood received the appointment of mail agent, and in case he was not appointed the certificate was to be drawn by me and paid over to Dr. Wood. The only conversation was representing the conditions of this certificate to Wood, and his refusal to accept.

Q. In consideration of the promise of the appointment of mail agent, or in default of getting that appointment and the payment of $3,000, what was Mr. Wood to do?

A. Nothing that he said he would do.

Q. Why was this presented to Mr. Wood for his acceptance, accompanied with those conditions?

A. I had asked Mr. Wood, in my zeal for the election of Clarke, if he would like to have a position. He said he would. I asked him what position he would like; he said he would like to have the "old man Lowe's position." I reported that desire of Dr. Wood to Mr. Clarke. I don't know whether he told me he could have it or not. The result was that I went back with the statement of some one in authority, and told Wood he could have it, implying conditions.

A. What conditions?

Q. That he must vote for Clarke. He said he would not take Sidney Clarke's word for anything of that kind. He would like to have some assurance that he would get the position. I then went and stated what I understood Mr. Wood to mean—that he would need some bond to secure the place; that is, I went back to Mr. Clarke, I think.

Q. What did Mr. Clarke say then?

A. He asked me what I thought would be necessary, and left me in his room, and he came back, and on my per, suasion to make a bond of $3,000, payable to my order, that the appointment should be made in three months. I was then told, but by whom I don't know, to go to Mr. Dan Adams and the thing would be "fixed up." In connection with the certificate of deposit was a sheet of paper that Dr. Wood must sign, agreeing to support Mr. Clrrke. I didn't read the document over to understand the paper, but I knew that was the tenor of it. I went back to visit Mr. Wood, and told him that I could accommodate him with a position on these conditions, and handed him the paper—that he should support Mr. Clarke if he got the position or appointment. He looked at it, handed it back, and told me: "No, sir." I then went, put the paper in an envelope, handed it back to Colonel Abell, telling him I had failed in the negotiation, with a request that he would give it to Dan Adams. That is all.

Q. Well, I understand you that you were authorized to see Mr. Wood in relation to this matter by Mr. Clarke, and that this promise to appoint him mail agent in the place of Mr. Lowe in three months, and to hold the certificate of deposit for security for the performance of that promise, and to pay to Mr. Wood the $3,000 in the event of a failure of that promise, were upon the condition that Mr. Wood should vote for Sidney Clarke?

A. Well, there were some other conditions, but I have forgotten them.

Q. That was the principal condition, was it?

A. Well, there was something said about his influencing the remainder of the Doniphan delegation. I think it was one of the conditions in the paper.

Q. State what the conditions were, if you can.

A. That he should vote for Mr. Clarke; that was the object of the whole thing. In addition, he was to influence as far as he could the remainder of the Doniphan delegation.

Q. Was there any other similar transaction that you know of in the interest of Mr. Clarke?

A. I don't know of any.

Q. Do you know how many rooms Mr. Clarke had at the Tefft House?

A. I know he had three; no, sir, two; I don't know how many more.

Q. Who was Colonel Abell working for?

A. Clarke, as I understand.

Q. What is Colonel Abell's politics?

A. As long as I have known him—Democratic.

Q. Do you know whether he was at that time connected with or working in the interest of any railroad?

A. Not to my knowledge; only by public repute. He was well known as the agent of J. F. Joy—agent or attorney.

Q. Was he one of Clarke's confidential advisers?

A. I surmised so.

Q. Did he act as an adviser?

A. I cannot tell, but think he did.

Q. Did you have frequent conversation with him with regard to how the canvass was going?

A. I did.

Q. Did you advise with him in regard to men whom you were to see?

A. I believe I did on some occasions.

Q. Did you have conversations with him and Mr. Clarke in reference to how things were proceeding?

A. I think not.

Q. What other persons were there in the immediate confidence of Mr. Clarke.

A. I cannot answer that question intelligently.

Q. Do you know whether Dan Adams was or not?

A. I would judge he was; he was very often there.

Q. There most of the time?

A. I don't know.

Q. Do you know of any improper influences being used by any other candidate than Mr. Clarke?

A. No, I have no knowledge of it, except rumors, which said they were buying—I mean that they all were. It became a staple joke that they were buying.

By Senator Stover.

Q. Did Senator Wood inform you, or intimate, that he would vote for Sidney Clarke for United States Senator, if he (Clarke) would get for him the office of mail agent, or any other office?

A. I had nothing but intimations that he might change his views. He had been at all times steadfast for Caldwell in any conversations I had with him, and acting upon them I went to work to see if his views could be changed in the manner I have said.

Q. What were the contents of the paper above referred to?

A. I cannot tell the contents except the general tenor. It was to the effect of the conditions being that Dr. Wood, in view of getting this appointment should vote for Sidney Clarke. That was about the general tenor of the paper.

Q. What did Senator Wood say when you presented the paper to him to sign and the bond securing it?

A. He said he would not do that thing; he would not accept the proposition and vote for Clarke. I made the proposition to him verbally.

Q. What was his answer.

A. He would not accept.

Q. What was his reason?

A. He did not give it, except something to the effect of saying it would be dishonorable. He would like the position, but it would be dishonorable to sell his vote. He looked upon his vote as his honor.

Q. What did the bond or check contain?

A. It was a clean, clear certificate of deposit without any conditions, drawn in my favor.

Q. By whom?

A. By Daniel Adams.

Q. And you had full discretionary power to use that?

A. I had.

Q. And you returned it to Dan Adams?

A. I returned it to Col. Abell for him to give it to Dan. Adams because I had failed in the negotiation.

Q. About what date was that?

A. I could not give a definite answer.

Q. About what date?

A. It was, think, about two days previous to the election.

By the Chairman.

Q. Did you say that you had full discretionary power to use that certificate as you thought best?

A. Subject to those verbal conditions. It was payable to me alone. I had it to pay over or to return it according to circumstances.

Q How long was Mr. Clarke gone from the room at the time he left you there when you went back and returned to him in regard to this appointment?

A. Probably ten or fifteen minutes.

Q. How far was it from his room down to Dan Adams' bank.

A. Something less than five minutes' walk.

By Senator Stover.

Q. You have stated that Dr. Wood told you he would like to have the office, and what security he would have if he voted for Mr. Clarke. Did he state what security he would require?

A. I don't think he did.

Q. Did he intimate to you what security he would require?

A. It was an intimation that he would like to have security, but I don't remember at any time that he mentioned any amount or what kind of security.

By Senator Whitney.

Q. When did you commence rooming or sleeping with Dr. Wood?

A. From the day he arrived in Topeka until he went away at the end of the session.

Q. When you first commenced rooming together, whose preference for United States Senator was Wood's then?

A. Caldwell's.

Q. He stated so.

A. Often and often.

Q. What was the reason stated by him for supporting Caldwell?

A. That his constituents required him to do so.

By Senator Stover.

Q. Did you state to Sidney Clarke that you had offered to secure Senator Wood's vote by the use of money or this check?

A. No, sir, not subsequent to the failure of the arrangement.

Q. Who handed the certificate of deposit to you?

A. Mr. Dan Adams.

By Senator Whitney.

Q. What was you to do with that certificate of deposit in case Wood failed to get that appointment within three months?

A. Pay the money to Wood.

Q. And there was no other condition in which you were to use that certificate of deposit?

A. No, I think not.

Q. This was a guaranty then proposed by yourself to satisfy Wood that he should get that appointment?

A. Yes, sir.

By Senator Stover.

Q. Is this certificate of deposit that you have reference to the only one you know of issued by Dan Adams to secure the votes of any party?

A. The only one I know of.

Q. From remarks made by Clarke before the Atchison delegation, did you understand that he was in favor of supporting Mr. Caldwell?

A. I did.

8

Q. Did he state that of all the candidates in the field he preferred Mr. Caldwell?

A. I don't think he said it in that manner.

Q. About what did he state?

A. He expressed a sort of preference, not particularly strong, for Mr. Caldwell, and that his friends could not do better than support him; that if they had any terms or concilations to make, that was the time.

J. HOPKINS,

Having been sworn, testified as follows:

Examined by the Chairman.

Q. Where do you live?

A. Leavenworth, Kansas.

Q. What business are you in?

A. I am general agent for the Connecticut Mutual Life Insurance Company.

Q. Were you in the city of Topeka last winter at the election of United States Senator?

A. Yes, sir.

Q. What were you doing here?

A. I was up here in the interests of the Company I represent and politics generally, I suppose.

Q. Were you in the interests of Alexander Caldwell?

A. I was anxious to see Mr. Caldwell elected, being a Leavenworth man.

Q. Did you engage in the canvass?

A. Yes, sir, a little.

Q. What did you do?

A. Talked loud and drank a little.

Q. Do you know of any promises being made by Mr. Caldwell to any person of an appointment?

A. I do not.

Q. Do you know whether any money was used to secure any votes?

A. I do not.

Q. Do you know whether any money was used to secure the influence of any person?

A. I do not.

Q. Do you know what the arrangement was between Caldwell and Thomas Carney?

A. No, sir.

Q. Do you know what, if any, arrangement was made between Caldwell and Clarke?

A. No, sir.

Q. Do you know anything about it?

A. I do not know anything about it. My interest was in the insurance business more than anything else during last session.

Q. How many gentlemen were here from Leavenworth in the interests of Caldwell?

A. I do not know, but suppose there were a hundred from the city of Leavenworth.

Q. Do you know who paid their expenses?

A. I do not.

Q. Have you heard whether Mr. Caldwell, or Mr. Clarke, or any other of the candidates for the United States Senate, offered any money, or made promises of office, to secure or to aid in securing their election?

A. I never heard of any money being used, but of some offices being promised.

Q. Where and what offices?

A. I don't remember now.

Q. By whom was the promise made?

A. I don't know that I can state that.

Q. Cannot you recollect?

A. It was rumor around the Teff't House and on the street. I do not recollect who they were.

Q. Have you had any conversation with any one who claims to know that any money was used?

A. No, sir.

T. H. DRENNING,

Having been sworn, testified thus:

Examined by the Chairman.

Q. Where do you reside?

A. I reside at Wathena, Doniphan county.

Q. Were you here during the Senatorial election last winter?

A. Yes, sir.

Q. How long?

A. I don't remember; a week perhaps, more or less.

Q. Did you take any part in the canvass?

A. I believe some.

Q. For whom?

A. Well, I supported Caldwell.

Q. Had you any conversation with Mr. Caldwell?

A. I believe I talked to him once about two or three minutes.

Q. Do you know Len Smith.

A. Yes, sir.

Q. Did you have any conversation with him?

A. Yes, sir, many.

Q. In relation to the election of Mr. Caldwell?

A. Yes, sir.

Q. In any of these conversations did he say anything to you about the use of money in the election?

A. No, sir.

Q. Did Caldwell say anything about it?

A. No, sir.

Q. Did he say anything about promising any offices?

A. No, sir, he did not.

Q. Do you know whether any money was used by Caldwell or any one else?

A. I don't know except from general rumor.

Q. Where were you stopping during the time?

A. I stopped at the Capital House.

Q. You say that by rumor you know a little money was used. What kind of rumor did you hear?

A. I don't know how to answer that question except in this way: that it was the general talk. In fact, at every Senatorial election that I have been at, it has been the general talk among all that there was more or less money used.

Q. Do you know whether there has been or not?

A. I do not, sir.

Q. Did Mr. Smith say anything about using money. Is that what you mean?

A. Yes, sir.

Q. Do you know a man by the name of Bennett?

A. Yes, sir.

Q. T. H. Moore?

A. Yes, sir.

Q. Where does Mr. Moore live?

A. At Iowa Point, Doniphan county.

Q. Were they both members of that House?

A. Yes, sir.

Q. Had you any conversation with them with regard to their vote?

A. Yes. I did with Mr. Bennett?

Q. Before or after the election?

A. Before.

Q. What did he say?

A. He had not made up his mind whom to vote for. He was talking about voting for Mr. Walker, and I told him I thought Mr. Walker had no chance in the world, and I urged him to vote for Caldwell; the principal argument I used being that Caldwell was going to be. elected, he being the strongest man.

JAMES L. McDOWELL,

Having been sworn, testified as follows:

Examined by Chairman.

Q. Where do you reside.

A. At Leavenworth.

Q. Were you here last winter during the canvass for United States Senator.

A. A portion of the time I was.

Q. What portion of the time?

A. I can hardly remember how long I was here during the canvass. I was here at the time of the organization; went home; think I was home about a week, and came back.

Q. Were you here the remaining portion of the time then?

A. I suppose I was here the remaining portion of the time of what was called the canvass.

Q. In whose behalf?

A. The candidate from our own city, Mr. Caldwell.

Q. Where did Mr. Caldwell stop while here?

A. At the Tefft House.

Q. How many rooms had he there for himself and his friends?

A. Two or three is what he claimed, I think. They may have had a great many more.

Q. Did you stop there yourself?

A. I did not.

Q. What motive had you for coming up and engaging in the canvass?

A. I suppose the same motive that every independent citizen has in the election of a Senator for his State.

Q. State what it was, can you?

A. I certainly can; I have come some four or five times previous to this, and taken an active part in every way to secure the election of a Senator from our own county.

Q. Were you here at the time Mr. Carney withdrew?

A. I was not, sir.

Q. Do you know what, if any, arrangements were made between him and Mr. Caldwell?

A. I do not; I never made any inquiry.

Q. Do you know whether any promises were made by Mr. Caldwell, or any of his friends, to members of the Legislature in the event of his election?

A. I do not, sir.

Q. Do you know whether he used any money or not in that relation?

A. I do not.

Q. Do you know what arrangement was made between him and Mr. Clarke?

A. I don't know that there was any arrangement between him and Sidney Clarke. I certainly advised him never to make any.

Q. Do you know whether Mr. Clarke used any money in that canvass?

A. Of my own knowledge I do not.

Q. Ever hear that he did?

A. I have heard several persons say that they did know of his using money.

Q. Can you give me any names?

A. Some two or three parties. A Mr. Mowry, of Doniphan county, incidentally mentioned it in the midst of a conversation. I heard many rumors during the canvass.

Q. Are you able to state the names of any other persons who are said to know?

A. I am not.

Q. Had you any conversation with Tom Darling last winter about supporting Caldwell?

A. The only conversation I had with Mr. Darling was the night after the first vote.

Q. How many men came over here from Leavenworth?

A. Most of our leading citizens.

Q. About how many?

A. I don't know; a very large number.

Q. What is a fair estimate of the number?

A. I don't know that I could approximate to the number.

Q. Two hundred?

A. I suppose there were two hundred here during the canvass.

Q. Do you know who paid their expenses?

A. I don't.

Q. Do you know Colonel Abell, of Atchison?

A. I do.

Q. Do you know what his politics are?

A. He has always passed for a Democrat?

Q. Do you know what business he was engaged in about the time of Caldwell's election?

A. I don't.

Q. Are you able to give us any information—or do I understand you to say that Mr. Caldwell had used money to secure his election?

A. I have heard enemies of Mr. Caldwell say so; every person who was opposed to his election claimed that he did. I don't know that there was one who knew anything about it.

Q. Do you know Len Smith?

A. I do.

Q. What was he doing here?

A. He was helping Mr. Caldwell.

Q. What were his politics?

A. I believe he was a Democrat.

Q. Do you know what he is to-day?

A. I did not.

Q. Were he and Mr. Caldwell engaged at that time in business together?

A. Not that I know of; I think not.

Q. Had they been previously?

A. I believe they had.

Q. What connection had they with the Missouri River Railway at that time—that is, a year ago.

A. I am unable to say what connection they had with it at that time. They were a portion of the railway parties who built the road. Whether they still retained their interest in it at that time I cannot tell.

Q. Did you have any conversation with Len Smith about the election, before it occurred?

A. Frequently.

Q. Did he ever say anything about the use of money?

A. He did not.

Q. Did he ever say anything about an arrangement between Carney and Caldwell?

A. He did not, except that he said that Carney had agreed to withdraw.

Q. Did he give any reason?

A. He did not.

Q. Had you been residing in Leavenworth previously?

A. I had; fifteen years.

Q. Had you been in the city sometime previous, within a short time?

A. Not within two months.

Q. You know of no instances at all in which Mr. Caldwell, Mr. Crawford, Mr. Clarke, or any of the candidates for United States Senator, gave money or offered to give money, or promised any appointment to office in the event of election, to members of the Legislature or other persons, for votes or in order to secure votes?

A. Personally, I do not.

Q. From any other means do you know?

A. Only own obseruation of the manner in which the canvass was conducted, and that I heard rumors from all sources. I was very frequently invited, to go to a house of public entertainment by different parties, of which I inquired the character, and they stated that it was—well, that there was plenty of food and liquors of choice kinds and free of charge. I never went to it. I made inquiries as to who was furnishing the entertainment. Of my own knowledge I cannot say who provided it, but it was said to be by Mr. Clarke.

Q. Did Mr. Caldwell mrke any such provision for his friends?

A. Only with regard to cigars; I never saw anything else.

Q. You know, then, of no use of money or promise of office on the part of Mr. Caldwell at all?

A. I do not, sir, except of common rumor.

Q. What was that common rumor?

A. One of the common rumors was that McDonald, and a party with him, had deposited some thirty or forty thousand dollars in one of the banks at Topeka. Another, that Mr. Robert Stevens had deposited forty odd thousand dollars in one of the banks for a similar purpose. They came some time after the opening of the canvass; and I was frequently told afterwards that Mr. Clarke was certain to be elected, for they would back him. It was simply a common rumor banded about during the canvass.

Q. Was McDonald here?

A. He was; I don't know whether he was here until the election. He, and this other gentleman that passed for his private secretary, were both here for quite a time.

Q. Did you hear any conversation about Mr. Caldwell using money?

A. I did not, except after the election was over.

Q. Did you never hear any one say that he was running upon his money?

A. I believe I heard you say it; I believe you were one of the candidates.

Q. Was I one of the candidates at that time?

A. I believe you were.

Q. Was not the discussion after the election?

A. It might have been after, but I remember we did have a conversation one night before.

Q. At the Fifth Avenue?

A. I think so.

By Senator Whitney.

Q. When did you first know of Caldwell being a candidate?

A. Sometime previous to the general election.

Q. When was it you ran as the Democratic candidate for Governor?

A In 1866. I ran as the National Union candidate.

Q. You did not run after that did you?

A. I believe not.

Q. Did not the Democratic party support you?

A. There was no such organization known at that time. There was an orgaization composed of Republicans and Democrats, called the National Union, and I presume I had the most of the votes of that organization.

Q. Whom did Caldwell vote for for Governor at that election?

A. I do not know, sir.

Q. What are Caldwell's politics now, if you know?

A. Ever since I knew him, his politics were Republican.

Q. Who first started Caldwell out to run for the United States Senate?

A. I am not able to say.

Q. Was not Caldwell last winter reputed to be the wealthiest man in Leavenworth?

A. He was not.

Q. Who was wealthier—reputed to be?

A. Mr. Scott is reputed to be the wealthiest man in the city.

Q. Was not Caldwell reputed to be one of the wealthiest men in Leavenworth?

A. He is reputed to be one of the wealthy men of Leavenworth. There is quite a number of them.

Q. And was not Len. Smith reputed to be one of the wealthy men of the city?

A. He has been for years so reputed.

Q. Did Caldwell prior to the general election of 1870 have any prominence or significance whatever in the political world?

A. As much as any other man of the party who was not pushing himself into position.

Q. What office did he ever run for before he ran for that of United States Senator?

A. Not any that I remember of.

Q. Was he not distinguished by the mass of people there by reason of his wealth?

A. He was one of the most active, energetic and thorough business men of the city—always so distinguished.

Q. It was not his especial characteristic as being a successful man in the pursuit or accumulation of wealth that distinguished him?

A. His especial distinction was being successful in the channel in which I described him in my last answer.

Q. Did his wealth or his active business habits give him that distinction; which was it?

A. I am unable to separate; the two combine.

Q. Well, sir, what do you think he was worth last winter?

A. I have no idea.

Q. What did he have the representation in the community of being worth?

A. I am unable to say. I have no data to judge from.

By Senator Stover.

Q. Were you here in Topeka during the Senatorial campaign of 1867?

Q. I was a portion of the time.

Q. Do you know of any money or any other improper consideration being used in that election?

A. I was then the lately defeated candidate of the National Union party. I sympathized with or wished for the election of Thomas Carney at that time; but not co operating fully with the party, I went about his quarters very little. I heard any amount of rumors. To-day, in this city, Colonel Anthony stated to me that he had been examined by your committee; that you had not asked him any question relative to 1867. He said he knew that, I know he was an active, stirring friend of Pomeroy's, and afterwards of Ross'; that after the election closed Perry Fuller, in talking over the matter with him, had pulled out his check book, showed him the stumps of his checks for $11,000, a portion of which he said he had drawn on the floor of the House during the balloting. They purported to be drawn on Leavenworth and New York. He said that at the same time he had exhibited to him a list of the names of the members in whose favor those checks had been drawn, that he had paid out some $25,000 in money, and that Mr. Pomeroy had told him shortly after the close of the canvass that he had paid out some twenty-five or twenty-six thousand dollars; and, says I, he was imprudent, was he not Colonel? He says, he told me some two or three times. There was no secret in the matter that it cost him that amount. And I think he told me that Mr. Fuller had told him that his money had been used for both Pomeroy and Ross.

Q. About what did it cost Mr. Caldwell to secure his seat?

A. I don't know. I have no data to fix an intelligent opinion upon.

Q. Did you hear it stated during the campaign that Mr. Carney was paid $10,000 to withdraw?

A. I heard rumors, different rumors.

Q. You know nothing of the transaction yourself?

A. I do not.

Q. Have you any reliable information?

A. I have not. I had worked twice to secure the election of Mr. Carney previous to this; called on him at his room; asked him if it was true he had withdrawn, and if he desired his friends to vote in the same way.

Q. Did you hear any one say that Mr. Clarke was using money to secure his election?

A. I did, but could not tell who said it.

By W. H. Clark.

Q. Did you hear of any money being bet last winter on Caldwell?

A. I did hear of various bets. I never made a bet on any event in my life.

Q. Do you know of any bets being made?

A. I heard of bets being made that he would not be elected. Of my own knowledge I do not know of any such bets.

By the Chairman.

Q. Did you have a paper in your possession relating to the Senatorial election last winter which was signed by Mr. Caldwell?

A. I believe I did sometime after the election.

Q. When did that paper come into your possession?

A. I don't know how long, but some time after the election.

Q. For what purpose was it placed in your possession?

A. I don't remember why it was placed in my possession.

Q. Of whom did you get it?

A. I think of Mr. Len. T. Smith.

Q. What did you do with it?

A. I think I returned it to him.

Q. Are you not able to state the purpose for which Mr. Smith gave it to you?

A. I think he mentioned several reasons.

Q. Do you remember any of those reasons?

A. I think he wanted me to copy it.

Q. Did you copy it?

A. I think I did.

Q. What did you do with the copy?

A. I gave it to him.

Q. And the original?

A. And the original.

Q. Are you able to state the contents or substance of that paper?

A. The substance, as near as I can remember, was this: Mr. Carney stated that he hereby agreed not to become a candidate during the session of the Legislature, or if he did to forfeit his word or pledge of honor.

Q. Who was it addressed to?

A. I don't remember that it was addressed to any person.

Q. Where did Smith say he got it?

A. I don't remember that he told me where he got it.

Q. Did you know the signature to it?

A. I think I did.

Q. Whose was it?

A. I think it was Mr. Carney's.

Q. Any other forfeiture than his word of honor?

A. Not that I remember.

Q. Was there any other reason why he delivered it to you, except to copy it?

A. I don't remember; I think there were several reasons at the time.

Q. Did he say at that time what that piece of paper had cost him?

A. He did not.

Q. Did you learn from any source whatever anything in relation to any other consideration for that?

A. None, except common rumor.

Q. When was this that you had that paper?

A. After the Senatorial election; how long I cannot say.

Q. What business—general business—were you engaged in at that time?

A. I was for four months engaged in getting the right of way for the Kansas Central Railroad; I don't remember whether I had then commenced or no.

Q. Where was this?

A. Don't remember whether in the city of Leavenworth or not.

Q. Where did you make the copy? Did you have an office?

A. I did not; have not for some years.

Q. Were you not at that time engaged as a lawyer or clerk?

A. I was not.

Q. Do you write an excellent hand?

A. Never famed for it.

By G. W. Clark.

Q. Did Jim Legate ever tell you how much he got for bringing out Mr. Caldwell as a candidate for United States Senator?

A. He never told me he got anything. I believe he has frequently told me he never did get anything.

Q. Did not you hold other agreements or papers beside the one spoken of?

A. None other of any kind.

Examined by Chairman.

Q. Did you have any conversation with Mr. Caldwell in relation to the appointment of any person to any office, in the event of his election, at any time during that canvass?

A. Nothing, except as general policy.

Q. Did you have any conversation with him in regard to the general policy that he would pursue in relation to removals from office?

A. I did not. I suggested to him that if elected to office the best policy he could pursue when he made removals was to take the safest and best men in the party to fill the places, provided they were not directly hostile to him.

Q. Was there any other conversation between you and him in relation to any particular office or officer to be removed?

A. Before he or myself came to Topeka, I had a conversation with him relative to one person holding office in this State, and asked him, if elected, whether he proposed to change him. He said he did.

Q. What office was that?

A. That was the post-office in our own city.

Q. Who was the incumbent then?

A. The same as now.

Q. Who?

A. Mrs. Johnson.

Q. Has there been any appointment made since that?

A. A telegraphic despatch states there has been an appointment, but there has been no action taken upon that yet.

Q. Was that conversation between you and Caldwell in relation to the post-office, in the nature of a promise?

A. I asked him if he intended to make a change, if elected, within a reasonable time. He said he did. I believed at the time he intended doing it and would do it.

Q. Suppose that he had stated then that he would not make that change, would you have come to Topeka and worked for his election?

A. I might have come at a later date, but not at that time.

Q. Is it not a fact that that was part of the motive that induced you to work for Caldwell?

A. I don't think it is right to ask me my motives.

Q. Was not that promise on the part of Mr. Caldwell to remove Mrs. Johnson from the postoffice, if he were elected, the inducement which caused you to come here when you did and work for Mr. Caldwell's election?

Mr. Caldwell's statement that he purposed within a reasonable time, if elected, to make a change in the post-office at Leavenworth, I confess, was one of the motives that induced me to come at that time.

Q. Would you have come at that time at all if Mr. Caldwell had not made that promise or statement?

A. If Mr. Caldwell had not made that statement at that time, it is doubtful, I think, whether I should then have come up. I before stated that I had a conversation with Mr. Darling. He stated to me that he had always been in favor of Colonel Vaughan for the Senate. I did not ask him who he intended voting for the next day—nor did I at any time during that canvass ask him how he intended voting. That is all I wished to add.

WEDNESDAY, February 7, 1872.

J. E. SMITH,

Having been sworn, testified as follows:

Examined by the Chairman.

Q. Where do you live?

A. Seneca, Nemaha county, Kansas.

Q. Were you at Topeka last winter during the Senatorial election?

A. I was.

Q. Take any part in that election?

A. Very little.

Q. Were you here all the time?

A Yes, sir.

Q. For whom did you work in that election?

A. My preferences were for Thos. Carney.

Q. Did you assist in promoting his chances of election

A. I think I did not.

Q. Was he a candidate through the whole campaign?

A. I think he was not.

Q. Were you here when he withdrew?

A. I was not.

Q. Was he a candidate at any time when you were here last winter?

A. I did not hear of his withdrawal until I arrived last winter.

Q. Well, then, in whose interest did you work after you came?

A. I had no particular interest in that election at all. My sympathies were rather with Mr. Walker.

Q. Do you know anything about the manner in which that canvass was conducted by Mr Clarke, Mr. Caldwell or Mr. Crawford?

A. My opinion was that it was conducted with a good deal of vim.

Q. Do you knew whether any money was used by these gentlemen?

A. I do not.

Q. Or by any person working in their interest?

A. I do not, sir.

Q. Do you know whether promises of office were made in case of success, by any candidate?

A. Not to me.

Q. To any one?

A. Not to my knowledge.

Q. Do you know it at all, or anything about it?

A. Only by current rumor.

Q. What did you hear?

A. I don't know that I could state.

Q. Can you state any of the rumors?

A. There were some in relation to this Land Office being removed west; and some few post-office changes were contemplated.

Q. Do you recollect any particular one now?

A. I have forgotten them, and have not recalled them since. I presume I could call them up.

Q. Did you ever hear any rumor, or remark, or statement, or promise, in regard to the change of the Leavenworth post-office?

A. I did not.

Q. What did you hear in regard to the Junction City Land Office?

A. I am not acquainted with the districts out there. I think I heard nothing in relation to the Junction City Land Office.

Q. Did you hear anything in relation to the district north of Junction City?

A. I think I heard some rumors of a proposed change.

Q. Are you able to state what those rumors were?

A. I think one gentleman told on the floor of the House that if Mr. Caldwell were elected it would be removed to Concordia.

Q. Well, did that gentleman say that any one had promised to remove it there in consequence of his election?

A. I didn't understand him so.

Q. Who was that man that made that remark?

A. I don't know him; he was member for one of those western districts.

Q. Is that all you know in regard to offices?

A. I think it was.

Q. Where did you stop during the time you were here?

A. The Fifth Avenue Hotel.

Q. Were you about the Tefft House a good deal?

A. I was there occasionally; yes, sir.

Q. Were you engaged in any business while that canvass was going on?

A. Very little.

Q. Any other engagements to look after?

A. I was getting some copies of some papers in the Secretary of States' office.

Q. Did it take the length of time you state to copy them?

A. No, sir.

Q. Do you desire us to understand, Mr. Smith, that you were here merely as a spectator during that time?

A. Yes, sir.

Q. Had you no interest in the result of the election at all?

A. I had no interest in the election of Mr. Caldwell?

Q. Or any other one?

A. No more than what a man would naturally have in the election of an United States Senator for his own State.

Q. Ever have any talk with members as to how they were going to vote?

A. I had a talk with our own members of the House, and the Senator from the county of Nemaha.

Q. Was that conversation in relation to the Senatorial election?

A. Yes, sir.

Q. Was it merely an inquiry on your part, and a statement on theirs as to the manner they were going to vote?

A. It was more a consultation with me after Mr. Carney had withdrawn, whether Mr. Walker, or Mr. Crawford, or Mr. Caldwell, would be the most acceptable.

Q. What did you advise them?

A. I told them that as far as my particular preference went that Mr. Walker would be the least objectionable.

Q. Well, what further did you say to them?

A. They thought that Mr. Walker would do, if he had any show of election, and decided to vote for Mr. Walker on the first ballot.

Q. Did they so vote?

A They did not; Mr. Walker withdrew, I think, before the first ballot was taken.

Q. Well, did you advise them what to do in regard to the matter at that time?

A. No, sir; I told them they could act on their own responsibility afterwards.

Q. Do you know whether Sidney Clarke made any offer to any person of an office for their support?

A. No, sir.

Q. Or Mr. Crawford?

A. No, sir.

Q. Do you know what Caldwell paid or agreed to pay Carney for giving up?

A. I don't know anything about it; never heard anything about it.

Q. Well, then, you don't know much about the election?

A. You have got all I know about it.

Q. Do you know whether Caldwell kept any cigars in the room for his friends?

A. There were some there, but I never smoke.

Q. Anything to drink?

Q. Yes, I think.

Q. Do you know Len Smith?

A. I do.

Q. What was he doing?

A. He was an active member in the third House.

Q. In whose favor?

A. I should judge in the interests of Caldwell.

Q. Do you know of his using any money?

A. I do not.

Q. Had you any conversation with him in regard to this election?

A. Not any private conversation.

By Senator Stover.

Q. How long were you here after the election for United States Senator?

A. No longer than till the train went to Lawrence; about two hours.

Q. Did you return home from here?

A. Yes, sir.

Q. Did you at any time while here, or when you left, have any money in your possession given to or belonging to any member of the Kansas Legislature?

A. Not a cent.

By W. H. Clark.

Q. Did you have any checks?

A. No, sir, no checks.

Q. Notes, or anything of that kind, or other valuables?

A. Nothing of the kind except my own money. Mr. Carney offered to pay my expenses while I was here, but I refused and paid my own.

Q. When did he make that offer?

A. The day I was leaving.

Q. What was his object for making that offer?

A. He was a very particular friend of mine, and thought I came over here for him, and he therefore offered me a fifty dollar bill to pay my expenses at the hotel.

By Mr. Johnson.

Q. Did he ever make any similar offer before?

A. No, sir.

Q. When was the notice served on you to appear before this Committee?

A. To-day.

Q. How long have you been in this city?

A. I came here yesterday morning—no, I came in the night before last.

Q. Do you know Mr. Cobb, Speaker of the House of Representatives?

A. I had an introduction to him last evening for the first time.

Q. Did you see him last night?

A. I saw him; yes, sir.

Q. Where did you see Mr. Cobb last night?

A. I saw him in Mr. Schofield's room in the Tefft House.

Q. What were you doing when Mr. Cobb came into Mr. Schofield's room?

A. I was sitting, reading or talking with Mr. Schofield.

Q. Did you still remain reading or sitting when Mr. Cobb came in?

A. I remained in the room while Mr. Cobb was there. Mr. Cobb came in twice while I was sitting.

Q. Did you speak to Mr. Cobb when he came in?

A. Yes, sir, I did. Mr. Schofield introduced me.

Q. How far were you from the door when Mr. Cobb went into the room?

A. Which door do you mean?

Q. That which Mr. Cobb went in at. When Mr. Cobb came in that room were you mistaken in the gentleman?

A. I didn't know him.

Q. Had you any idea who was coming?

A. I did not. Of course I could not have, because I did not know him.

Q. Did you manifest any uneasiness about that time?

A. I think not, sir.

Q. Now, sir, will you state whether you did not jump behind the door when Mr. Cobb came in?

A. I did not. I think perhaps I might have been in Mr. Schofield's bed-room when Mr. Cobb came in the second time. I won't say that I was not. I was sitting in the chair when Mr. Cobb came in the first time, and the second time I might have been in the bed-room.

Q. Was it the first time that you was in the room that you received an introduction to Mr. Cobb?

A. It was.

Q. Was there anything stated at that time about the Sergeant-at-Arms.

A. No, sir.

Q. You didn't say you thought that was the Sergeant-at-Arms coming after you?

A. I don't recollect saying anything of that kind.

Q. At any time when Mr. Cobb was in?

A. I don't remember of saying anything of the kind.

By the Chairman.

Q. Did you see the Sergeant-at-Arms in the Tefft House last night?

A. I saw a man in the Tefft House that afterwards told me he was the Sergeant-at-Arms.

Q. Did he not come to your room and inquire for you?

A. He did.

Q. Now what did you tell him?

A. I told him that Smith had just stepped out.

Q. What further.

A. I told him if he waited there he would return.

Q. What did the Sergeant do?

A. I don't know whether he stepped into the room; don't remember exactly what he did. I walked down stairs and left him there.

Q. What time during the night was that?

A. It might have been seven o'clock perhaps.

Q. Did you see the Sergeant any more last night at the Tefft House?

A. I saw a man who said he was the Sergeant-at-Arms.

Q. Where?

A. I saw a man at the Tefft House, who I afterwards learned was the Sergeant-at-Arms.

Q. In conversation with whom?

A. He asked me if my name was Smith, and I told him my name was Edward.

Q. At that time did you know who it was that was talking with you?

A. No, sir, I did not know who he was, but I had a suspicion.

Q. Who did you suspect he was?

A. Well, I was under the suspicion that he was the Sergeant-at-Aams, or some officer connected with the body here.

Q. At that time did you know a subpœna had been issued for you?

A. No, sir.

Q. Did you hear that there was likely to be?

A. No, sir.

Q. How came you to suspect as you did then, that he was the Sergeant-at-Arms or some other officer of the Legislature.

A. Well, from the number of invitations that had been sent to gentlemen in the country.

Q. Is that all the ground for your suspicion that he was an officer and had a subpœna for you?,

A. Well, I knew there was an investigation going on, and so came to think of that.

Q. Where were you served with this subpœna to come here?

A. At Lawrence.

Q. By whom?

A. I suppose the same man that came into my room, and asked if my name was Smith, though I could not swear it was the same.

Q. Did you notice whether he had but one arm or not?

A. I don't think I noticed that until he went to write his name on the summons or to hand me the summons. I think now it was when he was getting the papers out of his pocket.

H. P. WELSH,

Having been sworn, testified as follows:

Examined by the Chairman.

Q. Were you here, Mr. Welsh, last Winter during the Senatorial election?

A. I was.

Q. In what capacity?

A. I was a member of the House.

Q. Do you know whether or not Mr. Clarke or any other person made any promise of appointments to offices to secure votes in that election?

A. No, sir, I do not.

Q. Did you hear of any such transaction?

A. I did not.

Q: Do you know whether Mr. Clarke used any money or not?

A. I do not.

Q. Do you know whether he hired any rooms at hotels for the accommodation of members?

A. Only what I heard.

Q. Do you know whether he purchased any cigars or whisky for free use?

A. I don't know who furnished cigars, but one might go into any room and find cigars; but I didn't smoke much myself.

Q. Have you any knowledge of the use of money or other valuable things, either paid or promised to be paid, by any of the candidates for votes or influence to secure election to the United States Senate?

A. I have not.

Q. What was Len Smith doing here?

A. I suppose he was working for Caldwell.

Q. Do you know whether he was or not?

A. I should say he was.

Q. Did Sidney Clarke ever make any offers to you?

A. No, sir.

Q. Any of his friends?

A. No, sir; Mr. Clarke solicited my vote many times, but never made any offers of any kind. Mr. Clarke knew I was opposed to him; he knew that quite well.

By Senator Whitney.

Q. Do you know of Governor Carney having advanced any money to any member of the Legislature, at any time before the meeting of the Legislature or after the same?

A. No, sir.

Q. Did you ever hear of such a transaction?

A. No, sir, I never did.

Q. Did you talk with Carney about the Senatorial election?

A. I did.

Q. Did you talk with him about transferring any of his friends to Caldwell?

A. No, sir, I never had any conversation with Mr. Carney about transferring his friends; no, I never did.

Q. Did you know of Carney influencing any of his friends to vote for Caldwell?

A. I did not—well, I might qualify that; I don't know what you mean exactly. I would correct that answer and say that as far as my knowledge goes Mr. Carney was urging his friends to vote for Mr. Caldwell, but not employing any improper influences.

Q. Do you know of any members of the Legislature that owed Carney?

A. No, sir.

Q. Do you know what induced Governer Carney to come off the track?

A. I do not; at the time he wrote his letter I was at home.

Q. Did you never hear any of Caldwell's friends say why Carney came off the track?

A. No, sir.

Q. Were you in Caldwell's rooms frequently?

A. Only three times in my life.

Q. Who did you see?

A. The first time I was in, there was Mr. Osborn, Dr.

Morris (I think his name is), and—well, there was a good many men there; some Senators and members were there.

Q. Did you ever see Caldwell and Len Smith there alone?

A. No, sir.

Q. Did you ever hear of any betting of money, with great odds on the subject of the Senatorial election?

A. No, sir.

By Senator Stover.

Q. Were you here during the Senatorial campaign of 1867?

A. I was up here, not during the whole campaign, however, but the day before the election. I was here one or two days before the election.

Q. Do you know of any money being used at that time to influence votes?

A. I do not.

Q. Did you hear anything of it from a reliable source?

A. I heard, but who said so I do not know.

Q. Do you know of anybody that does know?

A. I do not; it was common talk.

By Mr. Wood.

Q. Do you believe that any corrupt influences were used in connection with the Senatorial caucus, last year?

A. Well, if I based my belief on rumor, I might have a belief about it—and a belief that there was, but parties I have heard talk about it gave it merely as a belief, or supposition; it was mere assertion.

THURSDAY EVENING, February 8, 1872.

P. T. ABELL,

Having been sworn, testified thus:

Examined by Mr. W. H. Clark.

Q. Where do you reside?

A. Atchison, Kansas.

Q. Were you present at Topeka during the Senatorial campaign of 1871?

A. Most of the time.

Q. Were you acquainted with the different candidates for United States Senator.

A. I think I was acquainted with all of them.

Q. Were you in the interest of any particular candidate?

A. I do not know exactly how to answer that question; I was friendly to one of the candidates; I had my choice, but was here specially in the interest of Mr. Clarke.

Q. Have you any knowledge of how the campaign was conducted by the candidates?

A. Well, I have some knowledge of the canvass. The candidates were electioneering; friends met and enemies too, I suppose. They had their rooms at hotels.

Q. Do you know whether any of the candidates, or any one acting for them, made use of money, promises, or other inducements, to secure votes?

A. Well, part of that question I can answer. I know of none of them using money, or any influence of that nature. As a matter of course I know of their using influences that were proper; none of them, to my knowledge, used improper influences.

Q. Do you know of any members of the Legislature getting money for their vote or influence?

A. I do not.

Q. Did you know of any betting, during the campaign of last winter, on the election of any of the candidates?

A. I have no recollection of any bet. There may have been, and I may have heard of it then, but don't recollect.

Q. Have you heard from any reliable source of money being used in that campaign?

A. Well, sir, that is a very hard question to answer; I heard so much and paid so little attention to a great deal of it, that it is hard for me to say whether my information on on those subjects were reliable. I cannot say that it fixed it in my mind that money was used; still, there were so many rumors at that time of the sort, that I was led to suspect—though I had no fixed noti on of any particular case.

Q. Well, have you heard since the election, from a reliable source, that any member of the Legislature did get money.

A. I don't know that I could say that anybody told me that he knew it. I have heard members of the Legislature say that they were satisfied that money had been used, but do not remember who they were.

Q. Do you know whether Mr. Clarke had any money here for the purpose of buying votes?

A. If he did, I never heard of it.

Q. Do you know whether any of the candidates had money for that purpose?

A. No, sir, I did not.

Q. Just state how you came to be here.

A. My county, (as some of them say that I had some influence with the members from it,) being all Clarke men, I came here because the people of my immediate neighborhood, and the members of the Legislature all wanted me to come. I had been in Atchison from the beginning, and taken part in all public affairs, and generally went wherever I was sent, and they wished me to come and do what I could for the election of Mr. Clarke. We had just had a very bitter quarrel at Washingtion (in Congress) over the A. T. & S. F. R. R. in which it was thought that an effort was being made by the Railway Company, and the people of Leavenworth, to steal our road, and Mr. Clarke took very decided grounds on our side in that controversy, and the people of Atchison in that way, myself too, being at Washington, became friendly to Clarke. Perhaps there were other considerations also—perhaps that was the principal cause, before the election.

Q. Colonel, were you, during the Senatorial campaign of 1867, in Topeka?

A. I was not. I was sick. I believe I was in St. Louis

at the time, and sick. I went there about that time, and was taken sick there, and did not get back before the Legislature was over.

Q. Had you any knowledge of money being used in that election?

A. I have not, sir; none in the world.

Q. Have you heard any person say there was or that they knew of money being used in that campaign?

A. I must answer that just as I did the other. I have heard reports, but none in any particular case that I remember.

Q. Did you ever see a three thousand dollar certificate of deposit last winter payable to S. C. King?

A. I don't think I ever saw it.

Q. Please narrate the whole of the circumstances attending the $3,000 check or certificate of deposit said to have been given to S. C. King, having some reference to influencing the vote of Senator Wood?

A. Well, sir, early in the canvass for Senator in 1871 considerable talk was had with an Atchison delegation with some members of the Donighan county delegation with reference to a joint caucus of the two delegations, for the purpose of uniting, and in a body going for one of the candidates. Mr. King, I think, boarded at the same house with a portion of Doniphan county delegation, including Senator Wood, and in talking over and planning for the purpose of this joint caucus, Mr. King, on one occasion, reported, I think, to perhaps the entire delegation, (but I am not certain, though all were present), that he believed he could secure a majority of the Doniphan county delegation if he could be permitted to promise to Dr. Wood (I think) the appointment of mail agent in place of Mr. Low, who then held it, and who was also a resident of Doniphan county. Some of us saw Mr. Clarke on the subject. Mr. Clarke said he had been instrumental in getting Mr. Low this appointment, and he would see Mr. Low, and if Mr. Low would consent to give it up he thought he could promise it to Dr. Wood, another man, of Doniphan county. Mr. Low was seen, and he told Mr. Clarke that he was becoming infirm, and would about as soon give it up as not, and if it would answer any purpose of the kind he would agree to give it up to Dr. Wood. Soon after, perhaps the same day, or the next, the matter was talked again, and Mr. King stated that while he did not believe a joint caucus could be had with the Atchison and Doniphan delegations, that he believed a caucus could be had of the Doniphan county delegation by which they would agree that a majority should control the whole vote for Senator, and that he was satisfied that four of them would go for Clarke out of the seven, and thereby control the vote. I think some time after—that day or the next—Mr. King stated that some influences had been brought to bear, by which Dr. Wood doubted the good faith of Mr. Clarke in promising him the mail agency, and that he (Wood) wanted security. Mr. Adams (Dan Adams) asked King if he wanted money, and King replied that he wanted money as security. Clarke was not present at this conversation. Adams stated at the time that he was willing to go Clarke's security that if elected he would carry out the promise in good faith, and that he was willing to have his bank issue a certificate of deposit in favor of Mr. King, to be held as security, that Clarke, if elected, would give Wood the appointment. I don't know that the certificate was issued except as they reported to me. After it was reported that King had the certificate of deposit, it was reported—I don't know by whom—that the Doniphan county delegation had sold out to Caldwell, and about the same time King came to my room at the hotel and inquired for Dan Adams. Adams was not present or about there at the time. King then handed me a sealed envelope, saying that it was a certificate of deposit for $3,000, which had been issued by Adams' Bank, requesting me to give it to Adams, and to say to him that his negotiation with Dr. Wood had failed. As soon as I saw Mr. Adams I handed the envelope to him saying to him what Mr. King had said to me.

Q. State what superscription was on the envelope—if any?

A. I do not remember.

Q. Is there anything more about that?

A. No, sir. There was a good deal of talk about it at that time.

Q. You say Mr. Clarke was not present at that conversation about the security.

A. I am satisfied, although I do not recollect any particular time when, yet that Clarke was told of the matter; that it was in some shape commnicated to Mr. Clarke. It is possible I may have told him myself.

Q. State what King said?

A. I don't know that I can do that, there is nothing more than I have stated.

Q What did Clarke say when you told him about the certificate? Or do you ever remember of Mr. Clarke's talking about that certificate?

A. My recollection is that it was reported to Mr. Clarke what was done. It might have been myself or Mr. Adams that reported it.

Q. And you have no recollection of hearing Clarke talk of that check?

A. I don't recollect any more than I have told. It was talked about generally at the time, and the general idea was, that the Doniphan county delegation had got more money than the value of this appointment. But by whom reported I do hot know.

Q. Generally believed was it?

A. I don't know whether it was generally believed or not with regard to the Doniphan county delegation having got more. (But the impression produced upon my mind was that it was true). I should not be likely to know of Mr. Caldwell's buying any votes, because there was no secret as to my being in favor of Mr. Clarke.

Q. Do you know of Dan Adams drawing any other checks or certificates of deposit during that Senatorial election except this one named?

A. I have no recollection.

Q. Did you ever hear him say?

A. Well, I have heard him talk so much that it would be difficult to say. I have no positive recollection of his saying that he drew any other.

Q. Do you know of any other certificate of deposit or check on Adams's Bank, having reference to the Senatorial election, than the one you have stated?

A. I do not, sir.

Q. Do you know of Clarke drawing checks during the campaign?

A. I do not, sir.

Q. Do you know where he kept his money during that time?

A. I do not. I presume that if he had any he kept it in Dan Adams' Bank.

Q. Do you know how much money Clarke used here from his own statement, or from what you saw?

A. I do not. I do not know of his using any money, except that he rented rooms.

Q. How many rooms?

A. I do not know that, nor never did know. I think I heard Clarke say himself that he had rented some rooms, but I do not remember the number. I occupied my own rooms and paid for them myself.

Q. Do you know what he paid to McMeekin per day or in gross?

A. I only know from a conversation I very recently heard. The conversation was between Mr. Clarke and Mr. Adams. My recollection is that the statement was that McMeekin had made out a bill of from twenty-five to twenty-six hundred dollars for rooms used during the campaign, and my recollection is that Mr. Adams stated (talking to Mr. Clarke about it) that the bill was at least one thousand dollars more than it should be, and, as I understood, that McMeekin had sued Clarke for the balance.

Q. Tell, Colonel, about the "soup house." I suppose you know something about that? Were you there?

A. Yes, sir, and helped to get it up. I only know that there was such a house there, where Clarke's friends met in caucus, and the rooms to talk in, and that refreshments were provided there at night. I, in connection with some other gentlemen, (I don't remember exactly who except that Dan Adams was there,) talked about the hotel being so crowded and the rooms so small that they could not have a caucus there privately, and proposed to cross the street and get a room in a new building, which contained several rooms, which could be had.

Q. How many rooms in all?

A. I do not remember how many. Three or five—may have been five. It was the whole floor. I do not remember who suggested it or made the arrangement. I know very well that I paid some of the expenses of it myself.

Q. Do you know what the whole expense of it was?

A. My recollection is that the whole expense was five, or six, or seven hundred dollars. I don't think it was a thousand.

Q. Who paid the balance after what you paid?

A. I do not know. I paid some two or three hundred dollars myself.

Q. When was the first time, as to the hour and day, that the Clarke men, as far as you know, made any overtures to Caldwell to support him?

A. Well, I never knew that there was any talk about supporting Caldwell until the night after the first ballot. I think I never heard of it until—don't know what time it was. I think it was in the caucus that night that it dissolved itself.

Q. Narrate the circumstances under which, after the caucus broke up, the arrangement was made with Caldwell?

A. I don't know that there was any arrangement with Caldwell. After the caucus broke up, I was with the Atchison county delegation in my own room until after daylight. I sent for them—those that were not there. The object of our delegation and of our friends was to consult what we would do ourselves, that is, what our county would do.

Q. Did the Atchison county delegation agree to support Caldwell?

A. The Atchison people agreed conditionally. The condition was that they would not pledge themselves yet to vote for Caldwell until they had had a conference with all the men who had voted for Clarke on the first ballot—the Clarke men as they were called—as to what they were all going to do.

Q. Did you send for Caldwell before you had an interview with the Clarke men?

A. Mr. Caldwell was sent for during the time.

Q. What was the object in sending for him?

A. The object was to talk to him, and to say that there had been a good deal of ill-feeling and rivalry between Leavworth and Atchison, and some of the delegation said they would not vote for Caldwell at all, or any Leavenworth man, until they could see and talk with him in reference to local interests. I think that questions, generally, were asked him about railroad matters.

Q. Did he satisfy you so far as to lead your men—Clarke men—to decide that they would vote for him?

A. It was generally satisfactory.

Q. Was anything said about re-imbursing Clarke for his expenses?

A. I don't think there was.

Q. Or about any expenses?

A. I never heard a word on the subject, and I don't

think I ever heard Clarke say anything on that subject. I may have heard him say something, but don't remember it now.

Q. Did you ever have any talk with Wood yourself about this?

A. Never.

Q. You say you never knew or heard anything about Clarke's accounts, check-book, etc.?

A. No, sir.

By Senator Stover.

Q. Are you acquainted with Len Smith?

A. I am, sir.

Q. Did you see him here at Topeka during the Senatorial canvass last winter?

A. I did—stopped at the same hotel.

Q. Were he and Caldwell operating together continually?

A. I took it for granted. I knew that he was electioneering for Caldwell.

Q. Did you have any conversation with him at Topeka last winter?

A. Frequent conversations.

Q. Did he ever state to you that he had certain amounts of money to use in this Senatorial canvass?

A. I cannot say that he ever stated it to me directly.

Q. Did he ever say anything to you about having one hundred and twenty-five thousand dollars to spend for Caldwell?

A. Not to me. I cannot say that Mr. Smith ever told me directly; but I heard Smith say while here, and, I think, in the presence of several gentlemen, that he was willing to spend one hundred thousand dollars rather than that Caldwell should be defeated.

Q. What else did he say upon this point?

A. I cannot remember any particular thing that he said. He was talking to me frequently.

Q. Did you say anything to him about being very indiscreet in talking about this money the way he did?

A. I think I said something to him. Once—in reference to it—I think I asked him if he were not afraid of being heard during the session of the Legislature to say that he would rather spend this amount than fail in his object. His reply was "No," or something of the sort.

Q. Did he intimate that he was not afraid of parties knowing that he had the money, because they would be apt to call for him if they knew?

A. I don't think he said it to me. I have heard such reports.

Q. Has any one ever told you that he has had any conversation with Mr. Smith about the money used?

A. Yes, some.

Q. Who were they?

A. Don't know of any particular man.

Q. Did you have more than one conversation with him about having money to use?

A. I do not remember but one.

Q. About how long was this before the vote came off?

A. I cannot tell.

Q. Who told you that he stated that if members knew he had money they would be apt to call?

A. I don't remember who told me.

Q. You were here during all the Senatorial canvass?

A. Yes, sir, I think so.

Q. From all the surroundings and your knowledge do you believe that there was money used to influence the votes of the members of the Legislature?

A. Well, sir, I cannot say I have any positive belief, one way or another.

Q. From the influences that you know were brought to bear on certain members, don't you believe it?

A. I supposed at the time that money was being used.

JAMES T. STEVENS,

Having been sworn, testified as follows:

Examined by the Chairman.

Q. Where do you reside?

A. Lawrence, Kansas.

Q. Were you here during the Senatorial election of 1871?

A. No, sir.

Q. Do you know I. S. Kalloch?

A. Yes, sir.

Q. Do you know Alexander Caldwell?

A. Yes, sir.

Q. Did you know of any business transaction between these two gentlemen last year?

A. Well, I did.

Q. State what that transaction was.

A. Some two or three weeks before the Senatorial election, Mr. Kalloch came to me and offered to sell me a note of $2,000, signed by himself, made payable to Len. Smith. Len's endorsement was on the back of it. I negotiated for the note, paid him all but four hundred dollars down, and sent him the balance the day before the Senatorial election. When the note came due, Smith and Caldwell were both in Washington. I waited until Smith came back. He came before Caldwell. I went over to Leavenworth to see him; asked him for the money; he stated that he did not have the note to pay; Caldwell was to pay it; he should not pay it. When Caldwell came home from Washington, I went over to see him about it; found him at the Mansion House; took him into a private room; told him what I wanted, namely: that I wanted money on the note that Kalloch had given to Len Smith, and Len Smith had signed. He replied that Kalloch had a little something to do yet before he would pay it. When he (Kalloch) did what was agreed upon, he would pay the note; I came home; sued the note; got a judgment; sent an execution over to Leavenworth. The last day that the sheriff had to make his return in, Mr. Crozier came over to Lawrence and paid the judgment. The transaction, gentlemen, you now have in a nut-shell.

Q. What did Caldwell say that Kalloch had to do "yet?"

A. He did not say.

Q. Did you see Crozier on the day he paid it?

A. I did, sir.

Q. Did he say for whom he made the payment.

A. No, sir, he did not.

Q. Did Caldwell say for what the note was given?

A. No, sir.

Q. Have you heard anything in regard to the use of money in the Senatorial election of last winter from any person?

A. Yes, sir.

Q. From whom did you hear it?

A. Mr. Kalloch.

Q. What did Kalloch tell you?

A. He told me that Caldwell had written him to come over to Leavenworth, and he went over. While there Caldwell told him that he wanted his influence to elect him as United States Senator, and to name a price that he would take. Kalloch then told me that he told Caldwell that he would not set any price, but that he would like to borrow some money of Caldwell, and thereupon asked him to loan him five thousand dolars; he then said he got three thousand in cash from Caldwell, and that if Caldwell was re-elected he was not to pay it back. If he were not elected, he was to pay it back. That is all that Mr. Kalloch told me.

Q About when was that conversation between you and Mr. Kalloch?

A. My best recollection is that it was not long after the Senatorial election—not more than a month.

Q Did you ever hear any one else say anything about this Senatorial election, and the use of money in connection with it, either by Mr. Caldwell or Mr. Clarke, or any other candidate?

A. Yes, sir, I have.

Q. Well, sir, who else have you heard speak in that way in relation to the election?

A. I cannot tell who it was that told me.

By Senator Whitney.

Q. On what date relatively to this Senatorial election did you buy this note of Kalloch?

A. Well, I should think it was just about a month before the Senatorial election.

Q. How long had the note been made when you bought it?

A. Nearly a month.

Q. When was it due?

A. Due at ninety days after date?

Q. Any other indorsement on it than Len Smith's.

A. No, sir.

D. M. ADAMS,

Having been sworn, testified as follows:

Examined by Chairman.

Q. Where do you reside.

A. In this city.

Q. What is your business?

A. Am engaged in the banking business.

Q. What business were you engaged in during the Senatorial contest last winter?

A. The same.

Q. Were you engaged in that contest in any way?

A. Well, sir, I took a small part in it.

A. In favor of whom?

A. I was supporting Mr. Clarke for the position of United States Senator.

Q. Did he have an account in your bank during that time?

A. He did.

Q. When did that account begin with reference to that election?

A. I think a day or two before the Legislature assembled. The day before I think.

Q. Which way did it begin, by draft or deposit?

A. By a deposit.

Q. How much did he deposit?

A. Twenty-five hundred dollars.

Q. Did he deposit any more during that canvass?

A. He did not.

Q. Did he draw that out?

A. He did; Mr. Clarke never drew any himself.

Q. Who did draw it out?

A. I did myself.

Q. On check?

A. Yes, sir.

Q. Were you authorized by him to draw it?

A. I was.

Q. Did you overdraw his account?

A. I did, sir.

Q. How much?

A. About sixteen hundred dollars. I have not examined the books, but I think it was about fifteen or sixteen hundred dollars.

Q. What was that money used for, by Mr. Clarke?

A. Well, sir, various purposes connected with the canvass.

Q. Are you able to state any item of expenditure of that money?

A. I am able to state the principal item of expense.

Q. What was it?

A. It was to Mr. McMeekin at the Tefft House.

Q. How much to him?

A. I think it is sixteen hundred and ninety dollars.

Q. What was that paid for?

A. His expenses at the house.

Q. For how long a time?

A. Were from the time he came there until the canvass closed.

Q. Was that sum paid for Clarke's personal expenses?

A. It was paid for Clarke's personal expenses, and for friends and invited guests.

Q. Did you know any of those invited guests?

A. Yes, many of them.

Q. How many were there?

A. I could not tell now.

Q. Did any other person deposit any money there about that time?

A. Oh yes, a great many; probably a hundred or two a day, but no one that I recollect of in connection with this canvass.

Q. Was not there ten thousand dollars deposited there by Anderson and Dennis?

A. Not that I recollect of.

Q. Was there any sum of money deposited there by one or both of those men, about that time?

A. Well, I presume there was, because they are regular depositors, and keep regular accounts there, but I don't think of anything special at that time.

Q. How many rooms had Clarke at the Tefft House?

A. Well, sir, I don't recollect.

Q. Who engaged those rooms?

A. Myself and Mr. James and Mr. Thomas of this county, were the committee that made the arrangements.

Q. Mr. Clarke assented to the arrangement that you made with McMeekin?

A. He did, sir.

Q. You state that there were sixteen hundred and twenty dollars paid to McMeekin. What became of the rest of the money that was deposited in and drawn out of that bank?

A. Well, sir, it was paid out for a great many different purposes.

Q. Are you able to state any purpose to which it was applied in any considerable sum?

A. There was quite an expense bill incurred before the Legislature met, on the part of two or three parties who traveled about the State to see members, which bill I paid after the Legislature assembled.

Q. Do you know how much that was?

A. I think about four hundred dollars.

Q. Any other item of expenditure?

A. Well, there was quite a large item of expense incurred in the renting of the second story of Rowley's building. There were some five or six rooms in that building rented and furnished as caucus rooms and refreshment rooms.

Q. How long was that maintained?

A. From the time the Legislature assembled until after the election of Senator.

Q Do you know what it cost to run that machine?

A. Well, sir, I cannot tell without examining pretty carefully into the bills, but my impression is that it cost somewhere from ten to twelve hundred dollars.

Q. Who paid that?

A. I paid it.

Q. The entire expense?

A. Yes, sir.

Q. For whom?

A. For Mr. Clark. It was an arrangement which the committee made originally without consulting Mr. Clarke, but he thought perhaps it was a good thing and assented to it.

Q. He then ratified the action of the committee, did he?

A. Yes, sir.

Q. What became of the balance of the money?

A. Well, I could tell if I could get to my books, and refresh my memory; but I am not certain that I could. I recollect at the time—a little while before the election—of an excursion to Kansas City, in which nearly all the members of the Legislature went, and I defrayed the expenses of quite a number of Mr. Clarke's friends who went down on that excursion. I don't remember how much it was. There were quite a number of Mr. Clarke's friends, who expressed a desire to go, and I furnished the means.

Q. Did Mr. Clarke have any other means here beside those deposited in your bank?

A. Not to my knowledge.

Q. Did you draw a certificate of deposit in favor of S. C. King during that Senatorial canvass?

A. I did.

Q. Against what bank was that drawn?

A. Against the Kansas Valley National Bank in this city.

Q. Was it an ordinary bank certificate of deposit?

A. It was.

Q. What was to be done with it?

A. Well, my understanding about it was that he had some negotiations with Senator Wood, in which he wanted to use it.

Q. Did you understand what those negotiations were?

A. I knew nothing only from Mr. King's representations.

Q. State what representations Mr. King made at that time.

A. My understanding of the matter, from Mr. King's representations, is this: that Senator Wood wanted the mail agency for Kansas, and that Mr. Clarke or his friends—don't know which—had given some assurance that he would have the position in the event of Mr. Clarke's election, and that Senator Wood was not satisfied with the assurance, and he wanted some security, and this certificate was wanted as security that this pledge would be carried out in the event of Clarke's election.

Q. In the event he was not elected what was to be done with the certificate?

A. It was to be returned to me.

Q. And then what—money to be paid?

A. No, sir, the certificate was to be returned to me.

Q. In the event that Mr. Clarke was elected, and Mr. Wood not appointed, then what was to be done with the certificate?

A. My understanding was that he was to draw the money on it.

Q. Against what deposit was that certificate drawn?

A. Against my own funds. I gave my own individual responsibility for that certificate.

Q. Then it was not drawn against any funds deposited by Mr. Clarke?

A. It was not, sir.

Q. Nor, in fact, against any funds that were on deposit?

A. Yes, sir, my own account, which is generally good for that amount.

Q. Was this check returned to you; and, if so, when?

A. It was returned; I cannot say when.

Q. Do you know of any other certificate being used in this way?

A. I do not.

Q. Do you know of any promises of office or appointments to office, made by any aspirants to office, to secure votes?

A. No, sir.

Q. Do you know whether Mr. Caldwell had any money with him personally.

A. I do not.

Q. Do you know Len Smith?

A. I do.

Q. Did he deposit any money in the Kansas Valley Bank at that time?

A. Well, I can't say whether he did or not; I don't know. I have not examined the books to see whether he did or did not. My impression is that he did not have any account there.

Q. Did he have any special deposit there?

A. I don't think he had.

Q. Have you any means of knowing whether he did have or not?

A. I have not here.

Q. Do you know whether he had any money when he came here or not?

A. I do not.

Q. Did you ever have any conversation with him in regard to money matters?

A. I don't think he ever did. He was on one side and I on the other, and I presume he was tolerably cautious in speaking of those matters to me.

Q. Do you know what arrangement was made between Mr. Clarke and Mr. Caldwell when Mr. Clarke withdrew from the contest?

A. I never knew of any arrangement. I have heard there was some arrangement between Clarke's friends and Caldwell, but have no personal knowledge of it.

Q. Do you know from whom you had the information?

A. Rumor; that is all.

Q. Do you know anything of it from Bob Stevens?

A. No, sir.

Q. From Mr. Clarke?

A. I never heard him say; Mr. Clarke told me he was advised to make some sort of an arrangement with Mr. Caldwell, but that he repudiated the whole thing, and never did have any arrangement.

Q. Did he say who advised him; which of his friends, as you call them?

A. I think he mentioned Mr. Bob Stevens.

Q. What business was Bob Stevens engaged in at that time?

A. I believe he was engaged in constructing railroads at that time—was General Manager of the M., K. & T. R. R.

Q. What was he doing here at that time?

A. He seemed to be taking part in the canvass?

Q. In whose favor?

A. Well, Mr. Clarke's, I should judge.

Q. Did he have any money on deposit at your bank at that time?

A. I think he had a small deposit.

Q. Do you know the amount?

A. About fifteen hundred dollars I think.

Q. When was that deposit made?

A. That was no deposit; that money had accumulated there for a long time, from the collection of interest on mortgages in Osage county, where he had a large amount of land several years ago, and the mortgages had been in our hands for collection; been accumulating during several months. He never deposited anything during the campaign.

Q. Do you know John McDonald, of St. Louis?

A. Yes, sir.

Q. Did he deposit any funds there?

A. He never did.

Q. What was he doing here at that time?

A. Well, I hardly know. I never met the man until I met him here; he didn't seem to be doing anything.

Q. Have you any knowledge of Mr. Len Smith, or Mr. Caldwell using any money during that canvass to secure votes for Mr. Caldwell, directly or indirectly.

A. Well, I don't know as I do.

Q. Do you know of Mr. Caldwell or Len T. Smith using any money during that canvass, directly or indirectly?

A. I cannot answer that question, for the reason that it would be a violation of the first principles of my business, and I cannot let you into the secrets of the banking institution that I preside over.

Q. Did any one borrow $10,000 at your bank about the time that that canvass was going on.

A. Not that I recollect of.

Q. Did Tom Anderson and Dennis borrow $10,000 there at that time?

A. They did not.

Q. Did they overdraw their accounts that amount?

A. Not that I recollect of.

Q. Did they (Caldwell or Len Smith) draw any checks in favor of any members of the Legislature at that time from your bank?

A. I object to answering that question for the same reason.

Q. Did Caldwell draw any checks on your bank in favor of members of the Legislature?

A. He never did.

Q. Did Len T. Smith?

A. Not to my knowledge.

Q. Are you able to state whether he did or did not?

A. I don't think he did.

Q. Did you have any conversation with Mr. Dennis or Mr. Anderson about the time of that canvass in relation to drawing checks upon your bank?

A. I don't recollect that I ever did.

Q. Did you have any conversation after the election with either of these gentlemen, in relation to any checks drawn by them, about that time, upon your bank?

A. I don't recollect that I did.

Q. Do you recollect whether any checks were drawn on your bank by either of them?

A. I presume there were, for the reasons that I previously stated that they had regular accounts there, which they keep yet, and have done for a number of years, but I do not recollect any particular checks that they drew at that time, or amounts.

Q. Do you recollect any checks drawn on your bank which they had signed, running to any of the members of the Legislature?

A. I don't recollect.

Q. Well, sir, from the business you were engaged in, or from any other source, did you learn that any amount of money had been paid to any member of the Legislature by Mr. Caldwell, or by any one in his interest, to secure votes for Mr. Caldwell at that election?

A. I have heard certain members mentioned and of sums paid to them for their votes for Mr. Caldwall.

Q. Who did you hear mention the names of these members?

A. Well, now I don't know that; I might specify a few, but my information is derived from rumor and general reports, rather than from anything definite which I could state.

Q. From the business you were engaged in at that time, and have been engaged in since, have you learned that any sum of money, or other valuable consideration, were paid to any members of the Legislature by Mr. Caldwell or by any one in his interest, to secure votes for Mr. Caldwell?

A. I do not know that I know of any sum that was paid to influence votes.

Q. From your business have you learned that any sum or sums of money were paid, or promised to be paid, by Mr. Caldwell, or by any person for him, to any member of the Legislature, or to any other person, for the purpose of influencing votes for Alex. Caldwell in the Senatorial election of last winter—1871?

A. I respectfully decline to answer that question.

Q. Was Colonel Abell here last winter?

A. I believe he was.

Q. In whose interest was he here?

A. I understand that he was here in the interests of Mr. Sidney Clarke.

Q. What was his general business at that time?

A. Well, I never met the gentleman until that time. I believe he was a railroad man, or attorney for some railroad.

Q. What kind of refreshments were kept in the headquarters over Rowley's store?

A. Well, sir, all those refreshments that are usually kept in a well regulated restaurant.

Q. Any liquors there?

A. I believe there was a private room where some parties took something of that kind.

Q. Do you know whether Mr. Caldwell executed his note to Tom Anderson or not?

A. I decline to answer that question.

Q. Is it a part of your business to collect notes on individuals and checks on other banking houses?

A. It is.

Q. Did Mr. Carney have any deposits at your bank during that time?

A. I don't think he did.

Q. Were you here at the election of 1867 at the time Mr. Pomeroy and Mr. Ross were elected?

A. I was here during a part of it only. I was absent in the East during the first portion of it.

Q. Have you any knowledge of the use of money or other valuable consideration for the purpose of influencing votes at that time?

A. I know nothing of that election.

Q. Did you pay a check for Charles Columbia about the time of the Senatorial election last winter?

A. I might have done so, but I could not tell without examining the books. I have no recollection of anything of the kind.

Q. Do you know E. C. Manning?

A. Yes, I know him.

Q. Did you ever have any conversation with him in regard to whom he was going to vote for last winter, and how much he wanted for his vote?

A. I did.

Q. You may state what that conversation was?

A. Well, gentlemen, that is a matter of history. It enters very largely into the campaign of last fall. Mr. Manning came to my room at the Tefft House. He said he was poor; it cost him a good deal to get elected, and he wanted a thousand dollars before he would vote for Clarke. He said, you have got the money, I know it, I need it and I am going to have it, or I will not vote for Clarke. I told him Mr. Clarke was a poor man, unable to pay any such sum; that he (Manning) had been sent here to vote for him, and that I would not pay him a dollar. He spoke harshly of Mr. Clarke for his meanness, and of his aversion for the same quality; left my room and I have never spoken to him since.

Q. Who was present?

A. Not any one. He had previously been to Mr. Clarke on the same errand, and admitted to me that he had been to Mr. Clarke.

By Senator Stover.

Q. Did any other members of the Legislature during the Senatorial election of 1871 intimate to you or say that they wanted, or required money for their vote, or that they would take money?

A. Yes, there was.

Q. Will you state who?

A. Mr. Busick came to my room and brought a young man with him, and introduced him to me. He was a stranger to me and I do not remember his name, and have never recollected his name since. He sat down and talked over the campaign generally, and informed me that he had not got his mind made up exactly as to how he was going to vote; thought pretty well of Mr. Clarke; thought pretty well of Governor Crawford; in fact, thought pretty well of all of them; and he (Busick) informed me that this young man was his friend, and any arrangement I made with him would be carried out in good faith, and he bowed himself out of the room immediately. This young fellow wanted $2,000 for Busick's vote.

Q. What other conversation was there?

A. I told him the same in effect that I told Manning That ended that interview.

Q. Any other case?

A. I don't think of any other.

By W. H. Clark.

Q. Did you ever hear T. L. Bond say that he had been offered any money for his vote?

A. I did.

Q. What did you hear him say and where was it?

A. I heard him state publicly in Mr. Clarke's room, in the presence of quite a number, that he had been offered $3,000 in cash to vote for Mr. Caldwell.

Q. Did he say by whom?

A. I don't recollect that he did. My recollection is that it was by a friend of Mr. Caldwell, and to vote for him. This statement was made in the presence of Sidney Clarke and others. I remember his manner well; he came in the door; made this statement and seemed to be quite excited.

Q. Did you hear any other persons make similar statements?

A. I did.

Q. Who?

A. Mr. Snead, of Saline county.

Q. What did he say?

A. I wont be certain about the sum: but he said he had been offered, I think, $2,500 or $3,000, if he would vote for Mr. Caldwell.

Q. Anybody else ever make similar statements?

A. Not to my personal knowledge.

Q. Was there a check or draft placed in your bank sometime near the time of the Senatorial election of 1871, drawn by Len T. Smith, and payable to Thomas Carney?

A. I decline to answer.

Q. Did Cyrus Leland ever make any statements to you about the sale of the Doniphan county delegation, or any members of that delegation?

A. He might have done so. I talked with all those Doniphan county men at the time, but I don't recollect any conversation with him more than any other of the delegation at that time.

Q. Did you ever hear from any person that any member of the Legislature of last winter received any money in consideration of their votes for Mr. Caldwell?

A. Yes, sir.

Q. From whom did you hear it?

A. Chester Thomas, sr.

Q. What did he say?

A. I understood him to say that Mr. Steele, of Sedgwick county, told him that Mr. Caldwell paid him five hundred dollars to vote for him.

By Senator Whitney.

Q. What did Tom Anderson ever tell you, if anything,

about buying members' votes in the Senatorial election of 1871?

A. I have had so many talks with Tom that I don't recollect anything just now.

Q. Did he ever tell you that he had bought anybody to vote for Mr. Caldwell?

A. I don't know as he ever stated it that way.

Q. Did he ever tell you that Caldwell was to pay him anything for services rendered in the election?

A. Well, I decline to answer that.

Q. Did a note made by Caldwell or Len Smith, in favor of Tom Anderson, or made by Tom Anderson, and endorsed by either of them, ever find its way to your bank during the Senatorial election of 1871, or afterwards?

A. I decline to answer that question.

Q. How much was Tom Anderson to get from Caldwell for his services to Caldwell in the Senatorial election?

A. I do not know from my personal knowledge.

Q. Did you ever hear Anderson say what he was to get?

A. Well, I decline to answer that question.

Q. Did Anderson or Dennis, or either, procure $10,000 from your bank, or from you personally, or about that sum upon a draft drawn on the treasurer of the Kansas Pacific Railroad during the Senatorial election of last winter?

A. I decline to answer that question?

Q. Now, I want to know a little more about this check of $3,000, or certificate of deposit, for that amount. Was that ever paid?

A. No, sir.

Q. How did you receive it back; in what manner?

A. My recollection is that it was handed back to me in an envelope by Colonel Abell.

Q. Was that before the Senatorial election?

Q. Yes, sir.

Q. Did that give you any authority to draw this check or certificate of deposit or any other certificate to aid in his election, except I mean for such expenses as you have narrated against this fund?

A. He never did; I never spoke to him on the subject of this certificate at all in my life.

Q. Did you tell him about it last winter after you gave it?

A. I do not recollect; to the best of my recollection I never spoke to him about it.

Q. Have you any paper in your bank now signed, or endorsed by Caldwell or Len Smith?

A. I decline to answer that question for the reason that it is a violation of the rules of our business to give such information were it true.

Q. Who acted as paymaster of the Caldwell fund, last winter, in your judgment or knowledge?

A. It was said that Len Smith and J. L. McDowell both acted in that capacity?

Q. Do you know what bank in Leavenworth Len Smith and Caldwell do their business with?

A. Caldwell does his business with Scott & Co., and Len Smith with Scott & Co. and the First National.

Q. Did Tom Anderson or any one else inform you what manner the Caldwell party transported their funds to Topeka last winter?

A. Not to my recollection.

Q. Did Tom Anderson or any one else of reliability ever intimate to you how much money Caldwell or Len Smith had here last winter?

A. I don't know that Tom Anderson ever said anything to me about it; but I have heard a great many statements from different parties.

Q. What was the amount?

A. I have always heard it estimated and believe that it was about $75,000.

Q. Did Peckham ever tell you how much he was to receive for his vote and influence?

A. He never did, only in a jocular way since the publication of these statements.

By the Chairman.

Q. Did Mr. Stevens draw against his deposit or account during the election of United States Senator?

A. Only a very small sum.

By Mr. Johnson.

Q. You have stated that you heard that Caldwell brought

to this town or used $75,000. Have you received your information from such a source or sources that you are satisfied that he used that amount?

A. Well, I might answer that briefly that I have.

Q. Will you name one of the channels of your information, naming first the one most reliable?

A. Well, I have refused to answer a good many questions this evening that might furnish some information on that subject.

JOHN M. STEELE,

Having been sworn, testified as follows:

By the Chairman.

Q. Where do you reside?

A. I reside in Wichita, Sedgwick county.

Q. Were you hear at Topeka during last winter at the time of the Senatorial election of United States Senator?

A. Yes, sir.

Q. In what capacity?

A. I was Representative of Sedgwick county.

Q. Do you know whether any money or other improper means were used during that canvass for any candidate?

A. No, sir.

Q. Do you know whether any candidate, or any friend of any candidate, offered to use money or any other valuable consideration in his interest?

A. No, sir.

Q. Do you know whether any of the candidates for United States Senator in that election, or any friends of that candidate, promised to pay any sum or sums of money to secure the votes of such candidate?

A. No, sir, I don't know of any such promises, or of anybody making them.

Q. Do you know of any promise to office in consideration of such votes?

A. Well, I don't know of any that I could say for certain.

Q. Do you know of any promises in reference to local land offices, or any thing of that kind in consideration of votes?

A. Well—yes.

Q. Finish your statement if you have anything more to say.

A. It was this way: our people in Sedgwick county wished to have the Land Office at Wichita, and I consulted with the different candidates on that subject; Mr. Crawford,my choice, said on the question of the removal of the Land Office, if he were elected, that if it was the interest of the district to locate it there, he was in favor of it. After I found Mr. Crawford had no show, I went to Caldwell, and he told me substantially the same thing.

Q. Did he promise to remove the Land Office to Wichita in the event of his election?

A. He did on condition that in his opinion it was to the best interest of the people of that district; those were the very words he used; I was willing to rest it on that, for I knew it had the advantage of location; it was the proper place.

Q. Did you see Mr. Clarke in regard to the matter?

A. Yes, sir.

Q. What did he say?

A Well, sir, he told me he would remove it to Wichita if he was elected; he told me so because he thought it was the proper place for it.

Q. Did you vote for him?

A. No, sir, I did not; I found he had promised it to two or three other places.

Q. Do you know a man by the name of Enoch Chase in this city.

A. I do not.

Q. He is father-in-law to Governor Crawford.

A. I dont know him.

By G. W. Clark.

Q. Did Mr. Caldwell place the Land Office at Wichita as he agreed to.

A. I got up some petitions, and members of the district

went to Washington, and had a hearing before the Kansas delegation, in Congress, and the commissioner of the General Land Office, and presented our claims, Augusta and Eldorado did the same; it was decided that Wichita was the proper place for the Land Office, and Mr. Caldwell was in favor of it.

Q. Was that the only condition that he thought it was the proper place for it?

A. It was; he was very careful what he said; I was in his room only once.

Q. He didn't make the offer provided that you voted for him?

A. No, sir, he didn't make any such remark.

By Mr. Johnson.

Q. Was that all the inducement you had to vote for Mr. Caldwell?

A. Well, it was thus: I suppose the main inducement was that when my name was called, he had some fifteen or twenty majority. Of course, I thought that if I persisted in voting against him, our people would not be likely to have his influence for the Land Office.

Q. Do you know Mr. Chester Thomas?

A. Yes, sir.

Q. Did you have any conversation with Chester Thomas in regard to the last Senatorial election?

A. Chester Thomas, if I remember him right, was a friend of Mr. Clarke, and wanted me to vote for Mr. Clarke, and tried to electioneer me for that purpose.

Q. Anything else.

A. No, sir, nothing more; he tried to persuade me to vote for Clarke as a proper man for our part of the country.

Q. Do you know of what politics Mr. Caldwell is?

A. Well, sir, he told me he was a Republican.

Q. Did you believe it?

A. Well, I have his word for it.

Q. Had you any other authority for it?

A. No, sir, I don't think I had.

Q. Did your belief in his being a Republican, influence your vote?

A. Well, if he had been a Democrat, I certainly should not have voted for him.

Q. Who named Mr. Caldwell before the joint session?

A. I forget; but I think it was Mr. Legate or Mr. Fenlon.

Q. In your conversation with Chester Thomas, didn't you intimate to him that some offers had been made by Mr. Caldwell to you, if you would vote for him.

A. No, sir.

Q. Was there anything said in that conversation between you and Mr. Thomas about five hundred dollars?

A. No, sir.

Q. You didn't tell Chester Thomas that you got five hundred dollars for your vote?

A. No, SIR-EE.

FRIDAY, February 9, 1872.

GEORGE NOBLE,

Having been duly sworn, testified as follows:

Examined by W. H. Clark.

Q. Where do you reside?

A. At Lawrence.

Q. What is your business?

A. Assistant Superintendent of the Kansas Pacific Railroad.

Q. What was your business during the Senatorial election of last winter?

A. The same business.

Q. Were you present here in Topeka during the Senatorial election last winter?

A. Part of the time—don't know that I was all the time.

Q. Do you know Alexander Caldwell?

A. Yes, sir.

Q. Do you know Len Smith?

A. Yes. sir,

Q. Did you see Len Smith here last winter?

A. Yes, sir.

Q. Do you know what he was doing here?

A. I do not know particularly what he was doing—don't know how to answer that.

Q. Did you hear him say anything about it?

A. No, I don't know that ever did?

Q. Do you know whether he was working in the interest of Mr. Caldwell?

A. I think he was.

Q. Did you at any time during the fall of 1870 borrow any money from Alex. Caldwell or Len Smith?

A. I borrowed some from Alex. Caldwell some time in November or December.

Q. How much?

A. Three thousand dollars.

Q. Did you give your note?

A. I did; five notes of six hundred dollars each and a mortgage on my property.

Q. Had you any conversation with Mr. Caldwell, about that time, about the payment of said notes?

A. I agreed to pay them when they were due, part of which I have done.

Q. Did Mr. Caldwell tell you at that time, that if you assisted him in securing his election to the United States Senate he would not collect those notes?

A. No, sir, he did not.

Q. Did he at any time?

A. No, sir.

Q. Was Mr. Caldwell at that time doing a banking business?

A. Not to my knowledge.

Q. Was he engaged in the business of loaning money?

A. I don't know that he was particularly.

Q. Was he a particular friend of yours?

A. Yes, sir, a personal friend of mine.

Q. Did he at any time give you to understand that he would not expect you to pay those notes in full?

A. No, sir, he never did. I have paid three of those notes; I have given him a check on the National bank, at Lawrence,—paid the notes with interest.

Q. Does Mr. Caldwell hold three notes yet?

A. Yes.

Q. Are they due now?

A. Yes, passed due.

Q. Has he ever asked you for the money since they have become due?

A. No, sir; he holds a mortgage for the full amount on my house.

Q. Do you know how much money the Kansas Pacific Railroad Company spent here in the Senatorial election last winter.

A. I don't.

Q. Do you know whether they spent any?

A. I don't know that they ever did spend any?

Q. Did you ever hear any of the officers of the road say how much?

A. No, sir; I never did.

Q. Did you ever hear any one connected with the road say that they spent any money in the Senatorial election?

A. No, I don't recollect that I ever did.

Q. Do you know, or have you ever heard, how much money Mr. Caldwell paid the Pacific Railway Company for their services in the Senatorial election?

A. No, sir.

Q. Did you ever have any conversation with Mr. Kalloch about these promissory notes that you gave to Mr. Caldwell?

A. I don't remember; I may have; I don't know that Mr. Caldwell was talked of at the time I got the money. I didn't get the money from him any cheaper than I should from any one else.

Q. Did you know of money being used in the Senatorial election of last winter for the purpose of aiding the election of any of the candidates for the United States Senate?

A. I don't.

Q. Have you ever heard of any being used from any reliable source?

A. No, sir.

THOMAS A. OSBORN,

Was sworn and testified thus:

Examined by the Chairman.

Q. Where do you live?

A. In Leavenworth.

Q. Were you at Topeka during the Senatorial contest in 1871.

A. I was.

Q. What was you doing here?

A. Trying to elect Mr. Caldwell to the United States Senate.

Q. Do you know whether Mr. Caldwell or any of his friends used any money in that canvass for him?

A. I do not.

Q. Did you have any conversation with Mr. Caldwell after the election?

A. I may have had; I don't remember distinctly.

Q. Do you know Len Smith?

A. I do.

Q. What was he doing here last winter?

A. Trying to elect Mr. Caldwell to the Senate, as I was doing.

Q. Do you know whether he had any money here to use for the purpose of securing votes for Mr. Caldwell?

A. I do not.

Q. Did you ever hear him say how much it cost to elect Caldwell?

A. I don't remember; I may have, but don't remember.

Q. Do you know Carney?

A. Very well, sir.

Q. Do you know what the agreement was between him and Caldwell, or Caldwell's friends, in relation to his being, or ceasing to be, a candidate for United States Senator?

A. I don't.

Q. Do you know whether there was any contract or agreement between them?

A. I do not; except as Governor Carney told me there was.

Q. When did he tell you so?

A. I think about five or six months ago.

Q. Any conversation with him since then?

A. Yes, sir; on last Monday night, at my house in Leavenworth.

Q. What was the subject of that conversation?

A. Various matters—private interests.

Q. Anything said about this contest last winter?

A. Yes, sir.

Q. Are you able to state what Mr. Carney said—the substance of it.

A. The substance of what Mr. Carney said was this: that he intended to appear before this committee and tell what he knew about the election taking place.

Q. Did he say what he knew?

A. Well, a great many things, he said; he said a good many things in reference to the contest last winter. He called my attention to a list of the members of the Legislature of last winter, asked my views in reference to different men in connection with it, and finally concluded by saying that he was coming up here to tell what he knew in reference to it.

Q. Did he say whether or not he knew of any money being used?

A. Governor Carney told me that he knew money had been used in the election.

Q. Did he say how much?

A. No; he did not.

Q. Did he say by whom it was used?

A. I don't think he did, sir.

Q. Did you ask him by whom it was used?

A. I did not.

Q. Are you not able to state that conversation as it occurred, between you and Mr. Carney, in relation to the use of money in that contest?

A. In reference to that conversation, I will say this: I am ready to say anything that I know to this committee in reference to that contest. Any conversations that Mr. Carney may have had then, or prior to that time, are matters that belong to him and me, and are matters of which this committee have nothing to do. On reconsidering the the question, I will answer that Governor Carney expressed in general terms his opinion, that money had been used in that canvass to elect Mr. Caldwell.

Q. Did he say how much money had been used?

A. He did not.

Q. Did he say by whom it had been used?

A. No; except in general terms, that Mr. Len T. Smith and Mr. Caldwell had used money.

Q. Did he name any member of the Legislature to whom money had been paid by them?

A. He did not.

Q. Did he mention any member of the Legislature to whom a check had been given?

A. He did not.

Q. Did he name any other person to whom money had been given to secure votes for Mr. Caldwell?

A. He did not.

Q. Did he state what information he had on the subject of the use of money at that time?

A. He said a great deal in reference to what he knew about it.

Q. Did he state what his means of knowledge were?

A. Well, sir, he said he was here and knew about the transactions?

Q. Did he state specifically in regard to the transaction, and if so, what specific statement did he make?

A. Governor Carney said to me: "I propose to go before that committee (meaning this committee) and tell what I know in reference to that election (meaning the election of last winter). Caldwell and Smith have treated me like a dog, and I intend to expose them. I know that they paid to members of the Legislature money for votes."

Q. What election was the subject of that conversation?

A. The Senatorial election of last winter—the election of Mr. Caldwell.

Q. Do you know where Mr. Carney is now?

A. I saw Mr. Carney on Wednesday and he told me to inform you he was ready to meet the committee at any time, if they would notify him, and it was his own request, and he will be disappointed if not called.

Q. Do you know whether Clarke used any money last winter or not?

A. I do not.

Q. Or any other person for Mr. Clarke, or any other candidate?

A. I do not, except from general rumor.

By J. Boynton.

Q. Do you know of any arrangement between Mr. Caldwell and Mr. Clarke to induce Mr. Clarke to withdraw?

A. I do not, sir, except by general rumor.

Examined by the Chairman.

Q. Do you know whether Mr. Caldwell promised any appointment to any persons to induce them to labor for his election?

A. I may have known of it at the time, but don't remember any now.

Q. Do you know of Mr. Clarke making any pledges of appointment to individuals, to secure his election?

A. None, except by rumor. I have heard that Clarke and Caldwell both promised a good many more offices than they could give.

By Mr. Wood.

Q. Did Governor Carney name any members of the Legislature who had received money for their votes?

A. My impression is that he did, but I could not give the name of any one, for I did not remember it.

Q. Would you know it if you saw a list of the names?

A. I don't know [The roll of the Legislature was here handed the witness, and after looking it over, he said]: yes, I think among the list was the name of Mr. Busick. I don't remember others, although there were quite a number of others.

Q. Can you state about how many names were mentioned?

A. It would be an estimate—I should say about twenty—perhaps less, or more.

By Mr. Johnson.

Q. What were your means for knowing last winter whether money was used by Caldwell, or Smith, or any of Caldwell's friends; was your relationship to that contest such that you were likely to know?

A. I was anxious to secure the election of Mr. Caldwell to the Senate, and was here for that purpose.

Q. Was the relationship such as would give you a general insight into their business?

A. Well, I thought I had some knowledge of the private workings of the canvass; I may have been mistaken.

Q. Then, sir, do you know of any instance, to the best of your knowledge, where money was used?

A. I don't, sir.

Q. Did you ever hear Len Smith say that he paid out any money in that canvass?

A. I have had a great many talks with Len Smith, and I don't know whether I heard it or not.

Q. To the best of your recollection?

A. I don't know that I did, and I don't know that I did not; my recollection is a matter of guess, and I am not prepared to say whether I did or did not.

By the Chairman.

Q. What was the relation between Mr. Caldwell and Mr. Smith at that time and previous to it?

A. They were very intimate, sir.

Q. Do you know where Mr. L. T. Smith is now?

A. Mr. Smith told me about the 25th of last month that he was going to New York, and would return in four weeks; that was in Leavenworth; that is all I know.

Q. Was that before this inquiry began?

A. My recollection is that it was before this investigation began.

Q. Don't you know as a matter of fact that Len Smith had a lot of money here last winter?

A. I don't know that he had a cent here. I loaned him some money to pay his little bills here; that was after the election.

Q. What is Len Smith's politics?

A. I take him to be a Democrat.

Q. What are Mr. Caldwell's politics?

A. I have always understood him to be a Republican—not an active Republican.

Q. Then I understand you, Mr. Osborn, to swear that you have no knowledge of any person using any improper influences or means to secure votes for Mr. Caldwell or any other candidate, last winter?

A. A good deal depends upon the meaning of the word "improper."

Q. State what means were used, then, to secure votes for Mr. Caldwell or any other candidate that you know of.

A. Well, sir, I cannot call to my recollection any particular vote that would enlighten you.

Q. Are you able to state whether promises of future rewards were used?

A: My general impression is that all the candidates promised everything they could think of, and a great deal more than they could fill, in money and offices, and everything else, and played off on them as often as they could. I want to say further: that in my judgment the last election was conducted as honestly as any other Senatorial election in Kansas, except the first Senatorial election when General Lane was elected, and then he had not money enough to carry him out of town.

By J. Boynton.

Q. Were you here in the campaign of 1867?

A. I was, sir.

Q. Do you know of any money being used then?

A. Only from the general talk. I knew further that there was some talk of checks and drafts being offered on the floor of the House of Representatives in joint convention for votes for Senator Ross, and the general talk was at that time that the Senatorial election for the two members had been carried by the use of money.

By the Chairman.

Q. You have stated that your judgment is that the last

Senatorial election was conducted as honestly as any other in the State, except one. Now I will ask you to state what your judgment is in reference to the means used to carry the last Senatorial election.

A. My judgment is that some money was used; but it is simply a matter of judgment.

By Mr. Johnson.

Q. As a matter of judgment, how much do you suppose that Mr. Caldwell was worth?

A. I can only tell you by common rumor—three or four hundred thousand dollars.

Q. You have no idea how much patronage he will have, if elected Senator.

A. That would depend on his good sense.

Q. Then you wish to convey the idea that Mr. Caldwell aimed to use three or four hundred thousand dollars in the election.

A. No, sir, I don't mean to say that.

By Senator Whitney.

Q. Do you know who paid the sums which were used in Caldwell's interest to elect him Senator.

A. I do not.

Q. Were you in Caldwell's room last winter during the canvass?

A. Yes, sir, quite frequently.

Q. Was not Len Smith there quite frequently?

A. He was there often; anxious to elect Mr. Caldwell, and working exclusively for that end.

Q. Did not Caldwell and Len Smith apparently have the most intimate and confidential relations?

A. I think they did, all through it.

Q. Was not Len Smith the principal manager of the movement to elect Caldwell here in Topeka?

A. Len Smith was one of Caldwell's principal friends, but I don't think he was the manager; he was regarded as among his chiefs.

Q. With authority to act for him?

A. I don't know what authority he had; perhaps he may have assumed a great deal.

Q. Were you about Governor Carney's rooms in 1867?

A. I was there all the while.

Q. Was there a room there that was used for the purpose of paying out the money?

A. Not that I know of, sir.

Q. How many rooms were there?

A. I don't remember, but I think four or five; several at any rate.

Q. Did Perry Fuller ever show you a check book that had been used in drawing checks for members of the Legislature?

A. No. sir.

Q. Did he ever tell you that he had bought members of the Legislature?

A. No, sir; I think I have an affidvait of a man in my desk at home made four years ago, in which he swears that money was offered him on the floor of the House as a member for his vote, to vote for Mr. Ross for the Senate.

Q. State his name.

A. His name is John D. Wells, and he lives in Marshall county?

Q. What county did he then represent?

A. Marshall county. I dont know whether I have that affidavit or not, but I think I have.

Q. Do you recollect who he swore offered him that money?

A. My impression is that it was the commissioners of Perry Fuller. I want it understood that this was money offered on the floor of the joint convention while the election was taking place.

GEORGE A. REYNOLDS,

Having been sworn, testified as follows:

Examined by the Chairman.

Q. Where do you live?

A. Lawrence, Kansas.

Q. Were you here during the Senatorial contest last winter?

A. A portion of the time.

Q. Whose favor or interest did you work in?

A. Well, I was not doing much work, but was favorable to Mr. Clarke's election for the United States Senate.

Q. Had he any money here to secure his election?

A. Not that I know of, sir.

Q. Had any one any money that you know of for him?

A. Not that I know of.

Q. Do you know R. S. Stevens?

A. Yes, sir.

Q. What business was he engaged in?

A. General Manager of the Missouri, Kansas and Texas Railroad.

Q. What was he doing here at that time?

A. He seemed to be in the interest of Mr. Clarke, and I think he was favorable to his election.

Q. How long was he here?

A. He was here during the election; until Mr. Caldwell was elected; when I come to think of it, I was here during the whole time.

Q. Do you know whether Mr. Stevens had any money here to be used in that canvass for Mr. Clarke?

A. No, sir; I don't know that he had a cent.

Q. Do you know whether money was used by Mr. Stevens to secure the election of Mr. Clarke?

A. None at all that I know of.

Q. Have you had access to the books of the Missouri, Kansas and Texas Railroad?

A. No, sir.

Q. Have you ever heard any conversation among the officers of that company in relation to the use of money in that election of United States Senator?

A. I had a conversation with, or rather the President of the company stated to me that Mr. Stevens paid some money here—bills that were in Topeka.

Q. How much?

A. My recollection is that it was about twenty-six hundred and fifty dollars.

Q. To what time did Mr. Parsons refer?

A. He referred to the time of the Senatorial election of last winter.

Q. What was the amount?

A. Twenty-six hundred and fifty dollars, I think; Mr. Parsons stated to me that amount of money was expended by Mr. Stevens in paying bills, such as the soup house affair—bills for gentlemen lobbying for Mr. Clarke.

Q. Anything more about that?

A. No, that is all.

Q. Do you know of any other use of money in the interest of Mr. Clarke, either from knowledge derived at the time the election was going on or from information received from persons who expended it afterwards, or from any other reliable source?

A. None whatever; I will state that it is only my recollection as to the amount of twenty-six hundred dollars and I have no further information about that; it all come up in incidental conversation.

Q. Do you know whether any money or other valuable thing whatsoever was used to secure votes for Mr. Caldwell?

A. No, sir; I do not.

Q. Do you know whether any money or other valuable consideration to secure votes for any of the other candidates?

A. No, sir; I do not.

Q. Do you know anything about the election of 1867?

A. No, sir; I have no recollection; I was in the Indian country at that time.

Q. Do you know anything about any contract between M. W. Reynolds, Mr. Pomeroy and Sidney Clarke, by which political influence was to be given and paid for?

A. Yes, sir.

Q State what that contract was? How much money was paid for it and what other securities were given?

A. I think it was the year 1866 that I was in Washington. Mr. Pomeroy and Mr. Clarke said to me at the Metropolitan Hotel that they desired to secure the influence of a paper published by my brother, the *Journal*, at Lawrence, and proposed, inasmuch as it was a considerable thing to maintain a paper in Kansas, to aid the paper by a money consideration. Thereupon each of them gave me for my brother five hundred dollars, which I forwarded to him, and gave me two promissory notes of a thousand dollars each, which I endorsed without recourse and sent to him the same day.

Q. What was the consideration for the payment of that money and the giving of those two notes?

A. It was that the paper should support the election of Mr. Pomeroy to the Senate and Sidney Clarke for Congress. That was the understanding.

Q. Was there any other consideration for the payment of that money and the giving of those two notes, save and except that the Lawrence *Journal*, edited and published by M. W. Reynolds, should support S. C. Pomeroy and Sidney Clarke for Senator and Representative in Congress at the then ensuing elections of those officers?

A. None whatever.

Q. Have those notes been paid?

A. No, sir, they have not, at least not in full. So far as I know they have not been.

Q. Do you know whether any promises were made by Mr. Clarke of appointment to office in consideration of votes in the event he should be elected this last winter?

A. No, sir.

Q. Or by Mr. Caldwell or any of the candidates?

A. No, sir, I do not.

By G. W. Clark.

Q. Mr. Reynolds, did you ever have any conversation with Senator Pomeroy concerning his election in 1867?

A. No, sir, I did not.

Q. Did he ever tell you how much it cost him to secure his seat?

A. No, sir.

Q. Did you ever see Perry Fuller's account books or check books.

A. I was somewhat familiar with the business of Perry Fuller & Co. I have seen charged on his books an amount of money to Mr. Pomeroy, and, I think, to Mr. Ross.

Q. Do you know the amount?

A. No, sir, and I don't know whether the money charged to them was used for election purposes.

By the Chairman.

Q. About what time were those items charged against these parties.

A. Well, it was in Washington, probably in 1867. or 1868, that I saw them, but I don't know the date at which they were charged to those gentlemen.

Q. Was the amount large or small that was charged?

A. I could not state the amount. I cannot answer the question.

Q. Was the amount a single item, or made up of a number of items?

A. I should think it was in items, two or three, or more.

Q. Did you ever have any conversation with Fuller in regard to the matter?

A. No, sir.

Q. Were you a member of the firm of Fuller & Co.

A. No, sir.

By W. H. Clark.

Q. Do you know W. H. Peckham, of Douglas county?

A. Yes, sir.

Q. Have you ever had any conversation with him about who he was going to support for Senator last winter?

A. I may have had, but don't recollect about him—oh, I presume I did a dozen of times, but I don't recollect what his answer was at either time.

Q. Do you recollect of his demanding money for his support of Clarke?

A. No, sir.

Q. Do you know Dr. McCartney, of Wilson county?

A. I do, sir.

Q. Have you heard of his vote?

A. I heard this about Dr. McCartney: "Mr. Moses Neal, of Humboldt, a friend of Dr. McCartney's, said to me, in Topeka, I think the night before the election, that he would like to vote for Clarke, (that is, Dr. McCartney would,) and was elected upon that issue in his county; would rather vote for Mr. Clarke for a thousand dollars than vote for Mr. Caldwell for fifteen hundred dollars; would like to know whether our side, as he called it, was going to put up any money; if not, he could get fifteen hundred dollars from Mr. Caldwell." I stated to him, "tell Dr. McCartney that we have no money to purchase votes for the election of a Senator." That was the whole of the conversation. Therefore he left, and the next day he (Dr. McCartney) did vote for Mr. Caldwell.

Q. Did Mr. Neal represent to you that he was the agent of Dr. McCartney?

A. No, not in the sense of an agent, but of a friend.

G. W. WOOD,

Being sworn, testified as follows:

Examined by Mr. W. H. Clark.

Q. Where do you reside, Mr. Wood?

A. Cheroke county, Kansas.

Q. What business were you in the last winter?

A. Well, sir, I was a part of the time in the Legislature, that is, a member of the Legislature.

Q. Were you here during the Senatorial election?

A. I was.

Q. Did you take any part in the campaign?

A. Well, I don't know hardly how to answer that. I, of course, cast my vote.

Q. Do you know Mr. Caldwell?

A. I know him by sight; was introduced to him, and was in his room several times.

Q. Did he or any of his friends ever ask you to vote for Mr. Caldwell for Senator?

A. Caldwell did not.

Q. Did any of his friends?

A. Well, there were men who pretended to be his friends that asked me to vote for him.

Q. Did any of them offer any inducements to you to persuade you to vote for him?

A. They did, sir.

Q. Who offered you inducements?

A. Well, sir, one of the men was a man by the name of Joel Thomas, who lives in Lawrence.

Q. What did he offer?

A. He offered me two thousand dollars in money if I would cast my vote for Alexander Caldwell.

Q. Did he show you the money?

A. He did not. He came up to my room and offered me the money, and I told him I was not for barter.

Q. Did he say he had been authorized by any one to make you that offer?

A. I don't think he did that time.

Q. Did he any time?

A. Yes. He came to me the next morning, the morning that the ballot was taken that elected Mr. Caldwell.

Q. What did he say?

A. He said that he had come. He approached me about like this: He said that they had bought enough votes to elect Caldwell; but he was authorized to offer me that morning a thousand dollars; that they had secured votes enough for from six to seven hundred dollars, but if I would cast my vote for Caldwell they would give me a thousand.

Q. Anything further?

A. No. I said, I am representing my constituents and I cannot afford to sell them out, and I don't believe Mr. Caldwell would do anything for them if he had the chance?

Q. Did he show you any money at that time?

A. I did not see any money at all; but he told me he was authorized to offer it.

Q. Any other offers made to you during the campaign?

A. Yes, sir. A man by the name of Kritz, or who gave his name as Kreitz, and said he was county treasurer of Jefferson county.

Q. When did he make you any offer?

A. On the day that the first ballot was being taken.

Q. Where?

A. Well, sir, he came into my room in the Ashbaugh House.

Q. What did he say?

A. He said he was authorized to pay me a thousand dollars if I would cast my vote for Alexander Caldwell.

Q. Did he say who authorized him?

A. I think he did. I told him I would not and could not accept the offer.

Q. Were there any other offers made to you?

A. No, sir.

Q. When did Joel Thomas make you this first offer?

A. The day that the first ballot was taken he made me the first offer?

Q. Before the ballot was taken?

A. I am not positive in regard to that.

Q. Did Kreitz say anything about how many votes they had bought?

A. He did not.

Q. Did you hear from any one how many votes Mr. Caldwell bought last winter?

A. I heard many assertions, but nothing positive.

Q. Did the friends of any of the other candidates make you any offer?

A. No, sir. They frequently approached me, but none made me any offer.

B. In what way did they approach you?

A. They tried to persuade me to vote for Sidney Clarke and some for Ross, and I told them it was inconsistent, and I could not do it. They told me that Clarke was our friend in regard to the Cherokee Neutral Lands; but I said I could never see it.

By Senator Whitney.

Q. How long have you known Joel Thomas?

A. I was acquainted with Joel Thomas—I first got acquainted with him four years ago this winter.

Q. What day did Joel get here from Lawrence?

A. I don't know, sir.

Q. Was the first time you saw him the day before the first ballot?

A. I am not positive.

Q. Did you see him on your way to the Legislature?

A. No, sir, I did not.

Q. When did you see him last anterior to his making the offer?

A. Oh, I think I saw him probably the day before in the Tefft House.

Q. Did you ever promise Joel at any time, either before or during the sitting of the Legislature, to vote for any particular person for the United States Senate?

A. I never did.

Q. Did you ever tell Joel that as a matter of friendship or favor to him, that you would vote for his candidate?

A. I never did.

Q. Did Thomas and Kreitz seem to be acting together in this matter or separately?

A. Separately apparently to me.

Q. Did either of them tell you what authority they had to make you this offer?

A. They did not, and I did not ask them.

Q. Was any other sum talked about at all except the sums you have named on the part of either of them?

A. There was not.

Q. Were you in Caldwell's rooms during the progress of the campaign?

A. I was.

Q. Whom did you see there—I mean in his private room?

A. I don't recollect. There were several gentlemen in. My impression is that Mr. Langdon and I went in together.

Q. Did you talk with Caldwell or Len Smith about the Senatorial election?

A. I did not, sir.

Q. Did Joel Thomas stay here until after the election was over?

A. I saw him in the House the day the final vote was taken.

Q. Did Joel tell you that he had approached any one else with an offer of money for his vote?

A. He did not.

Q. Did he speak of any one else?

A. He did not call any names.

Q. Did he speak of himself having secured any other votes?

A. He did not.

Q. Or this other man?

A. No, sir.

Q. Did you know of Thomas having private interviews with any other members?

A. I did not.

Q. Or that other man?

A. I did not.

Q. Did you ever talk with McCartney or Peckham about the Senatorial election while it was going on?

A. I never did with McCartney, but I did with Peckham.

Q. What did Peckham tell you about it?

A. I don't know that I could say. We talked frequently about how the election was being conducted, and who the probable candidate for the United States Senate was.

Q. Did he say he had any offer?

A. He did not. Mr. Peckham often asked me to support Caldwell if it was not inconsistent; but I said I could not do it.

Q. Did Peckham preside over Democratic caucuses on the subject before the election?

A. He did.

Q. Did he exert his influence at that time for Caldwell?

A. My impression is that he did not.

Q. Did he exert his influence for any one else?

A. Mr. Peckham and myself exerted our influence that the Democrats should stand together as a body, and vote in a body, first, last and all the time.

Q. That was Peckham's policy as well as your own?

A. It was.

Q. When was it that he made up his mind that he would go for Caldwell?

A. When he saw that the Democrats could not be controlled to support one man, then he thought it was policy to support Caldwell before any other candidate.

Q. Has Peckham ever told you since the election anything about Caldwell and his promise to him?

A. No, sir.

By G. W. Clark.

Q. Were you acquainted with Mr. Phinney?

A. I was acquainted with Mr. Phinney.

Q. Do you know of his receiving any money for his vote?

A. I do not; nor of any other member receiving it.

FEBRUARY 12th, 1872.

T. S. FLOYD,

Having been sworn, testified as follows:

Examined by the Chairman.

Q. Where do you reside?

A. County of Sedgwick and State of Kansas.

A. Do you know one J. M. Steele?

A. I do.

Q. Do you know what his financial circumstances were when he came to the Legislature last winter; if so, state?

A. They were considered very low.

Q. Had you the means of knowing what money he had then?

A. Not to a certainty.

Q. Did you have any conversation with him then in regard to what money he had?

A. Only so far as a bargain there was between us. He said he had not the means to fulfill the engagement, and if I would withdraw the trade he would like to have it done.

Q. How much money did it take on his part to fulfill his engagement?

A. One hundred dollars.

Q. Do you know what his financial condition was when he returned from the Legislature?

A. Not for a certainty; only as I saw it manifested in his business and every day affairs of life.

Q. What did you see that indicated the use of money, and in what amount?

A. He increased his business about fifteen hundred or two thousand dollars.

Q. Do you know where he got the extra funds which he put in his business?

A. I do not.

Q. Do you know in whose favor for United States Senator J. M. Steele was elected?

A. Yes, sir; he was elected and was pledged to all his prominent supporters for Governor S. J. Crawford.

ENOCH CHASE,

Having been sworn, testified thus:

Examined by the Chairman.

Q. Where do you reside?

A. Topeka, Kansas.

Q. Were you acquainted with one J. M. Steele, a Representative from Sedgwick county, in the Legislature last winter?

A. I was.

Q. Had you any business transactions with him last winter, and if so, state what it was, and all about it?

A. Well, I had a note against J. M. Steele, of Wichita, of $200; I called on him for payment, and he paid me with interest.

Q. Do you know how much money he had at the time he made this payment to you?

A. I do not; he seemed to have plenty of money. He paid me two one hundred dollar bills, and eight dollars beside. He made this payment to me two or three days after the Senatorial election.

CHESTER THOMAS,

Having been sworn, testified as follows:

Examined by Chairman.

Q. Did you have any conversation with J. M. Steele, last winter, about the Senatorial election? if so, state all of that conversation and the circumstances.

A. I did; he authorized me to go to the friends of Caldwell; he told me to tell them they could get a vote for $800, and told me not to tell them whose vote it was. I went to James L. McDowell and Len T. Smith and talked to them. Len Smith told me, in his business-like way, that they could get all the votes they wanted now for $500. Then McDowell and I went off by ourselves and talked about the same transaction, and from McDowell's conversation I ascertained that Mr. Steele had been "fixed"—that they had "got him." This is the languare that was used. I understood from the circumstances that Steele had five hundred dollars. I then went back to Mr. Steele, and told him he was already sold out, and he had his money, and I could tell him how much he got, and told him he had $500 in his pocket. His first remark was: "I told you not to mention my name under any circumstances." He said they (meaning, as I understood, Caldwell's friends) were buying their way through anyway, and it made no odds how much money he got. This conversation with McDowell was right after the first ballot, and they complained that he (Steele) had not voted as he agreed, but thought he would vote right in the end.

Q. When you told Steele that he had $500 in his pocket, did he deny or explain it in anyway?

A. I don't think he denied or admitted it directly.

Q. When and where had you these conversations with Mr. Steele?

A. After the first ballot, and before the last ballot, in the Tefft House.

H. D. BAKER,

Having been sworn, testified as follows:

By J. Boynton.

Q. Where do you reside.

A. Saline county, Kansas.

Q. Was you in this city last winter during the Senatorial contest?

A. I was.

Q. Do you know of any money or other corrupt influence being used to obtain votes?

A. No, sir; I do not know of any.

Q. Did you hear anything about money being used or offered?

A. Yes, sir; I heard there was money offered and used.

Q. Did you see Bob Stevens here last winter?

A. Yes, sir.

A. Did you hear him say anything on that subject?

A. Yes, sir; I heard him say something on that subject, but I did not hear him offer any money.

Q. Did you hear anybody offer any money?

A. Well, sir, I think I did.

Q. Who was it, and to whom was it offered?

A. I could not say it was money either; Mr. Hopkins, a gentleman who was in the lobby here, and myself were talking about the vote of the member from my county, and he (Hopkins) said he could make it to the gentleman's interest if he would support Caldwell.

Q. State all of the conversation between you and Hopkins in relation to the vote of the member from your county?

A. In the conversation, Mr. Hopkins asked me if I knew the member from my county intimately; I told him I did. He then asked me if I knew who he was going to support for United States Senator; I told him I thought he was going to support Clarke. He then said Caldwell had come here for the purpose of being elected United States Senator, and that a man had just as well make something out of it as not; that a man was a fool for bucking against him, and that if Snead would support Caldwell he could make something by doing it, and asked me to have a conversation with Snead and let him know what Snead said.

Q. Do you know Mr. Busick, a Representative from Lincoln county?

A. Yes, sir.

Q. Did you ever have a conversation with him on the subject?

A. Yes, sir; I roomed with Mr. Busick a part of the time, and heard him talk frequently about the money that was being used in the election.

Q. Did you ever hear him say anything about a bribe having been offered him?

A. Yes, sir; he told me that some one of Mr. Clarke's friends—I think it was Bob Stevens—offered him two thousand dollars for his vote for Clarke.

SPECIAL REPORT.

Mr. Snoddy, Chairman of the Joint Committee of the Legislature to investigate charges of bribery and corruption in Senatorial elections of 1867 and 1871, submitted the following partial report relating to the refusal of Daniel M. Adams to answer certain questions, together with the following resolution, which, on motion of Mr. Moore, was adopted:

Mr. President: The Special Committee appointed under House Concurrent Resolution No. 15, have to report that in the progress of their examination they called Mr. D. M. Adams and asked him the following questions which he declined to answer, to-wit:

Questions asked Daniel M. Adams by the Joint Committee of Investigation which the said Daniel M. Adams refused to answer:

Question. Do you know of Mr. Caldwell or Len T. Smith using any money during that canvass, directly or indirectly?

Answer. I cannot answer that, for the reason that it would be a violation of the first principles of my business.

and I cannot let you into the secrets of the banking institution that I preside over.

Q. Did they draw any checks in favor of any of the members of the Legislature at that time upon your bank?

A. I object to answering that question for the same reason.

Q. From your business, have you learned that any sum or sums of money were paid or promised to be paid by Mr. Caldwell, or by any persons for him, to any member of the Legislature, or to any other person for the purpose of influencing votes for Alex. Caldwell in the Senatorial election of last winter—1871?

A. I respectively decline to answer that question?

Q. Do you know whether Mr. Caldwell executed his note to Tom Anderson or not?

A. I decline to answer that question.

Q. Did he ever tell you that Caldwell was to pay him anything for services rendered in the election?

A. Well, I decline to answer that.

Q. Did a note made by Caldwell or Len Smith, in favor of Tom Anderson, or made by Tom Anderson, and endorsed by either of them, ever find its way to your bank during the Senatorial election of 1871, or afterwards?

A. I decline to answer that question.

Q. Did you ever hear Anderson say what he was to get?

A. Well, I decline to answer that question.

Q. Did Anderson or Dennis, or either, procure $10,000 from your bank, or from you personally, or about that sum, upon a draft drawn on the treasurer of the Kansas Pacific Railroad during the Senatorial election of last winter?

A. I decline to answer that question?

Your Committee ask the adoption of the following resolution:

Resolved, That D. M. Adams, a witness who has refused to answer certain questions set forth in the Special Report of the Special Committee, be required to answer the said questions kindred to and connected with them.

JAS. D. SNODDY,
Chairman Special Committee.

On motion, the above resolution was adopted, and Mr. D. M. Adams was instructed to answer the questions propounded by the Investigating Committee.

I hereby certify that the above is a true and correct copy of the original report now incorporated in the Senate Journals.

In testimony whereof I have hereunto set my hand and seal, this 26th day of February, A. D. 1872.

GEO. C. CROWTHER, [SEAL.]
Secretary State Senate.

D. M. ADAMS RE-CALLED.

Q. Do you know of Mr. Caldwell or Len T. Smith using any money during that canvass, directly or indirectly?

A. I paid considerable sums of money to another party, upon the check or draft of Len T. Smith, during that canvass.

Q. To whom did you pay that sum, and what was the amount?

A. I paid it to T. J. Anderson; the amount was $7,000.

Q. Do you recollect the day that check was cashed?

A. January 23d, 1871.

Q. Did you have any conversation with Mr. Anderson about that check, and the purpose for which it was drawn?

A. I did not; he said he wanted the currency on it.

Q. Did he get the currency?

A. He did.

Q. Was that before or after the election of Mr. Caldwell?

A. It was before.

Q. Did you cash any other draft, drawn by Len Smith, than this at that time?

A. Not that I recollect of.

Q. In whose favor was that draft, drawn by Len Smith?

A. To the order of Thomas Carney, and by him endorsed; that is, drawn in favor of Thomas Carney.

Q. Did they draw any checks in favor of any members of the Legislature, on your bank?

A. Well, I must say in reply to that, that at the time I refused to answer that question I supposed they had drawn some checks, but on examination I find they had not.

Q. From your business, have you learned that any sum or sums of money were paid, or promised to be paid, by Mr. Caldwell, or any person for him, to any member of the Legislature, or any other persons, for the purpose of influencing votes for Alex. Caldwell in the Senatorial election of last winter?

A. Well, I have learned that Mr. Caldwell did agree to pay a certain sum of money to Major Anderson for his service in endeavoring to secure his election.

Q. Did you learn when that agreement was made?

A. Sometime before the meeting of the Legislature.

Q. Have you learned whether or not Mr. Caldwell paid, or promised to pay to any one else any sum of money for his influence at that time?

A. I have heard that he agreed to pay Governor Carney a certain sum of money, but that is hearsay and common report; I have always supposed it was correct.

Q. Have you ever learned from you business relation that Mr. Caldwell, or any person for him paid, or promised to pay any sum of money to any members of the Legislature in consideration of their vote for him?

A. I have heard that (this is hearsay again) the Doniphan county delegation was paid $7,000 to vote for Mr. Caldwell; $1,000 a piece for the entire delegation.

Q. From whom did you get that information?

A. Well, sir; it is a matter of common report. I have heard it probably hundreds of times, and I don't know that I ever heard of it differently; I have always heard it alike.

Q. Do you know whether Mr. Caldwell executed his note to Tom Anderson or not?

A. I do not.

Q. Did he ever tell you that Caldwell was to pay him for services rendered in that election?

A. He did.

Q. Did a note made by Caldwell or Len Smith, in favor of Tom Anderson or made by Tom Anderson and endorsed by either of them ever find its way into your bank during the Senatorial election of 1871, or after that?

A. There was such a note that found its way into our bank.

Q. For what amount?

A. Thirty-five hundred dollars

Q. Who made the note?

A. It was made by T. J. Anderson.

Q. Payable to whom?

A. Alexander Caldwell.

Q. Endorsed by whom?

A. Alexander Caldwell.

Q. What date was on the note?

A. Well, sir; I have not seen the note for some little time, and I cannot recollect the date, but it was shortly after the Senatorial election.

Q. When was it to be due?

A. Eighteen months after date.

Q. Did you ever hear Anderson say what he was to get?

A. I have.

Q· What did he say he was to get?

A. Five thousand dollars.

Q. State whether any part was ever paid, and if so how much?

A. The amount of this note—to my understanding—was part payment.

Q. Was anything said by Tom Anderson in regard to the other fifteen hundred dollars?

A. Well, that it was to be paid to him.

Q. Did Anderson and Dennis, or either of them procure ten thousand dollars at your bank, or from you personally or about that sum upon a draft drawn upon the Treasurer of the Kansas Pacific Rrailroad during the Senatorial election of last winter?

A. I believe there was such a draft.

Q. By whom was it drawn?

A. I think it was drawn by . nderson, Superintendent Kansas Pacific Railroad.

Q. In favor of whom?

A. I think in favor of the bank; I don't recollect certain, that is, Kansas Valley National Bank.

Q. Who presented it?

A. T. J. Anderson.

Q. Was it cashed?

A. It was.

Q. Do you know for what purpose that money was drawn out at that time?

A. I do not.

Q. Do you know at what date it was drawn?

A. I think I could tell by referring to a Journal of the Legislature; it must of been drawn on 23d of January.

Q. What was the amount of that check or draft?

A. Ten thousand dollars.

Q. Was there any other check or draft drawn about that time similar to this one you have spoken of?

A. Not to my recollection.

Q. Do you know how much money Mr. Clarke and his friends had been here in the city of Topeka or elsewhere within reach to be used in that canvass?

A. I never supposed that there was any money to be used by Mr. Clarke but what was deposited with me. I never knew of any, and never had any reason to believe there was any but what I have mentioned, and that I think I stated to be about forty-two or forty-three hundred dollars.

Q. Is that all the money that he had here, or that he was able to control to secure his election, or advance the prospects of his election?

A. It was to the best of my knowledge and belief.

Q. You may state who was Mr. Caldwell's financial agents here during that canvass?

A. It was generally understood that Len T. Smith and James D. McDowell acted in that capacity.

Q. Have you had any conversation with James L. McDowell since that time in regard to that election?

A. I never have.

Q. Do you know where they deposited these funds in this city at that time?

A. I think in their pockets.

Q. On what bank was this seven thousand dollar draft drawn in favor of Mr. Carney?

A. Scott & Co., Leavenworth.

By Senator Whitney.

Q. For what purpose did Tom Anderson tell you this seven thousand dollars which he obtained on the Carney draft was to be used?

A. He did not state.

Q. Do you know what that money was for?

A. I was always satisfied what it was for.

Q. Please state.

A. It was for use in the Senatorial election.

Q. Did Sidney Clarke authorize you to draw certificates of deposit in behalf of members of the Legislature in exchange for their votes for him for Senator?

A. He never did.

Q. Was this Carney draft paid promptly by Scott & Co?

A. It was.

Q. Where is this thirty-five hundred dollar note in behalf of Anderson at this time? What became of it?

A. It is in the National Bank, not due yet.

Q. Where was this Tom Anderson note payable?

A. It was made payable at the Kansas Valley National Bank of Topeka.

By Mr. Johnson.

Q. When you speak of Major Anderson getting that money, you mean Tom Anderson?

A. I mean Thomas J. Anderson.

THOMAS MURPHY,

Having been sworn, testified as follows:

Examined by the Chairman.

Q. Where do you reside?

A. Atchison, Kansas.

Q. Were you in Topeka during the Senatorial election of 1871?

A. Yes, sir.

Q. In what capacity were you here?

A. I was a member of the Legislature from (I forget the number of the district) Atchison City.

Q. State whether or not you know of the use of any money in that election, last winter, to influence or control the votes of the members of the Legislature?

A. Not of my own personal knowledge?

Q. Have you ever had any conversation with Mr. Caldwell in reference to the use of money in connection with that election.

A. No, sir.

Q. With Sidney Clarke?

A. Yes, sir.

Q. Did he state who had used or offered to use money?

A. No, sir.

Q. State what the conversation was between you and Mr. Clarke in reference to the use of money?

A. I desired Mr. Clarke's election. I told him that it was my opinion, from the rumors afloat, that money was being used to secure the Senator's election, and asked him if he had any money to use for the same purpose. He stated he had not.

Q. Is that all the conversation you had with him in relation to the money matter?

A. That was all, sir.

Q. Do you know Mr. Butts, usually called "Billy Butts?"

A. Yes, I know Mr. Butts.

Q. Did you ever have any conversation or transaction with him last winter in relation to the Senatorial election?

A. Yes, sir.

Q. State what it was?

A. Well, sir, I was anxious to secure Mr. Clarke's election, and I had a conversation with Mr. Butts to try to get him to vote for Mr. Clarke, on the grounds that he was favorable to our interests in Congress relative to our Atchison, Topeka & Santa Fe Railroad, and that Mr. Butts, living where he did, was equally interested with us in the matter. Mr. Butts said, as near as I can recollect, that he was favorable to Mr. Clarke, but added in a jocular manner that he wanted some consideration for his supporting him. I asked him if I could make that known to Mr. Clarke, and have an interview with him. He stated that I might do so. I so informed Mr. Clarke. Mr. Clarke replied that he would like to see Mr. Butts; but if money was the consideration he required he had none to pay him. I told Mr. Butts what Mr. Clarke's reply was and that is the last I knew about it.

Q. Do you know whether any promise of any appointment to office being made by any of the candidates for Senatorial election to members of the Legislatnre?

A. Only by common hearsay. I will state, in connection with that Butts matter, that when he spoke of a consideration there was nothing mentioned between him and me, that is, no particular consideration mentioned as to what it should be.

Q. Did you have any other conversation with any other member of the Legislature in relation to the use of money, or of any other consideration?

A. No, sir.

Q. Were you here during the election of 1867?

A. I was here, but not as a member.

Q. Did you know of any money, or check, or anything of that kind, being used in that election?

A. I do not.

Q. Or promises of office, or other influences of that kind, to secure votes?

A. No, I do not.

T. J. DOLAN,

Having been sworn, testified as follows:

Examined by the Chairman.

Q. Where do you reside?

A. Atchison city, Kansas.

Q. What were you doing at Topeka last winter during the Senatorial election?

A. Well, I was here like a good many others, I presume, seeing a United States Senator elected.

Q. Did you see one elected?

A. Yes, sir.

Q. What part did you take in it?

A. I did not take any special part that I know of, further than that I came as a friend of Mr. Clarke's.

Q. Did you remain a friend of Mr. Clarke's throughout the contest?

A. Yes, sir.

Q. Do you know anything about what was called the "soup house?"

A. I presume I know something about what you term the "soup house."

Q. Well, the rooms over a drug store across the street from the Kansas Valley National Bank?

A. Yes, sir.

Q. Who was running and operating that machine?

A. I don't know who paid the expenses. I was there a portion of the time.

Q. There in charge of it?

A. Not in direct charge.

Q. Were you superintending it?

A. A portion of the time.

Q. What had they there?

A. Well, they had eatables and cigars.

Q. Anything else?

A. They held caucusses there.

Q. In whose interest was that establishment kept up?

A. I think it was kept in the interest of Mr. Clarke.

Q. Were you in Caldwell's room between four and five o'clock on the evening before the election took place on the next day?

A. No, sir, I was not.

Q. Were you ever in Caldwell's room during that contest?

A. I was once.

Q. When was that?

A. I want to correct. I was in the room joining the parlor there; but whether that was his room or not I do not know. I was in that room once.

Q. When was that?

A. I think that was the night before the election, between eleven and twelve o'clock.

Q. Where did you go from there?

A. I went from there back to the room over the drug store.

Q. Where did you come from when you came to Caldwell's room?

A. I came from that room.

Q. What was the purpose of your visit to Mr. Caldwell's room?

A. The purpose was: I had no definite purpose in view further than to state to Mr. Caldwell that there would not be any arrangement made by Mr. Clarke's friends, by him agreeing to do certain things for the Atchison folks, that I thought they would support him.

Q. By whose direction did you take that message?

A. Not by anybody's request.

Q. Went of your own notion?

A. Yes.

Q. What were those certain things you told him you thought would induce the Atchison delegation to support him?

A. They were in regard to some of our local matter in the Legislature·

Q. What were they?

A. One was in regard to the Central Branch Railroad. The other was to prevent any future legislation in regard to the Atchison and Topeka Railroad. In other words, my object was to have him agree not to change the present bill authorizing them to build the road from Atchison to Topeka and then south.

Q. Well, sir, did he make any promise in regard to these things?

A. Yes. He promised his aid, for the Central Branch Railroad would be of as great interest to Leavenworth as to Atchison, and therefore it was to his interest to aid in its extension; and that as far as regards the Atchison & Topeka Railroad he did not propose to change the present bill, or to vote for a change.

Q. Was there anything else upon which you desired to see him?

A. No, sir.

Q. Did you communicate the result of your visit to any one?

A. I think I did.

Q. To whom?

A. I do not remember now whom. It was to some of the Atchison folks.

Q. You went there for no other purpose?

A. That was all, sir.

Q. Who were present at that interview between you and Mr. Caldwell?

A. There were several other gentlemen in the room, but I do not remember who they were.

Q. Did you have a private interview, or was it in the presence of those other gentlemen?

A. I considered it private. Those gentlemen were in the room, but not close enough to hear.

Q. Was that the first time you had seen Mr. Caldwell during that canvass?

A. I had seen him at the Tefft House and in the saloon, bar-room or office below.

Q. Had you talked with him before during the canvass?

A. No, sir.

Q. Were you acquainted before?

A. Yes, sir.

Q. Did you know a man by the name of O. E. Scip?

A. Yes, sir.

Q. Did you have any conversation with him before you came down here last winter in relation to the Senatorial election?

A. I guess I talked with him.

Q. Had you any arrangement with him by which that election was to be a matter of speculation between you and him and other gentlemen?

A. No, sir, I had not.

Q. Do you know Mr. Wood, of Doniphan county?

A. Yes, sir.

Q. Do you know anything about his conduct last winter in relation to this Senatorial election?

A. Of my own personal knowledge I do not. I heard of it from others.

Q. Do you know anything of certificates of deposit being drawn in his favor?

A. I did not see it. I saw the envelope.

Q. Do you know who drew it?

A. Not of my own personal knowledge.

Q. Do you know what became of it?

A. Well, I don't think I saw it returned, but I knew when it was returned.

Q. Where were you then?

A. At Topeka.

Q. At what place?

A. I don't remember exactly.

Q. Who was present?

A. Col. Abell.

Q. Any one else?

A. I don't know. Mr. King returned it to Col. Abell, or left it for him to give it to Mr. Adams.

Q. Do you know whether any money was used, or other valuable consideration, by any of the candidates last winter for United States Senator to secure votes?

A. I do not know of my own personal knowledge.

Q. Did you see money paid to any one to secure influence in the election of any particular candidate?

A. No, sir, I did not.

Q. Do you know from having heard the parties say who paid the money?

A. No, sir.

Q. Do you know in any other way that any money was paid?

A. Well, I do not know positively of any money being paid to anybody.

Q. Do you know whether there was any promised to be paid or not?

A. No, sir, I do not.

Q. State, if you know, whether any money was paid, or promised to be paid, by any person to secure votes for any of the candidates during that canvass?

A. I do not.

Q. Have you been informed by any person who knows, that money was paid to any one to secure votes or influence in order to secure votes?

A. Well, I just remember that there was a current report; it was a common report, which was all I heard.

By Senator Whitney.

Q. Do you know Senator Wood?

A. Yes, sir,

Q. Had you any talk with him last winter about the Senatorial election?

A. Yes, sir. Our conversation was of a general character.

Q. Any conversation with him about a $3,000 certificate of deposit?

A. No, sir.

Q. Had you any talk with him about getting the mail agency in consideration of his voting for Clarke?

A. I think not.

Q. Do you know of his holding a certificate of deposit for that or any other sum awhile?

A. I think Mr. King held it.

Q. You don't know of his transferring it to Wood?

A. I don't know that he did.

TUESDAY, February 17, 1872.

OWEN E. SEIP,

Having been sworn, testified thus:

Examined by W. H. Clark.

Q. Where do you reside?

A. Atchison city.

Q. Were you present in Topeka during the Senatorial campaign last winter?

Q. Was there anything said in any conversation with those parties about using money or any other improper influence to secure votes for any named candidate?

A. No, sir.

Q. Did you ever have any conversation with Tom Dolan about the Senatorial election?

A. Yes, sir.

Q. Did he make any statements about money or any improper influence being used to secure votes for any candidate?

A. I and Mr. Dolan had some talk of coming over here and assisting Mr. Clarke if we could, but not as to any money matters. We expected, to be sure, that if we assisted Mr. Clarke so as to secure his election we should have some favors from him, such as appointments.

Q. Did you come?

A. No, sir.

Q. Did you have any conversation with Dolan during the Senatorial election about how that campaign was conducted?

A. Yes, I think I had.

Q. Was there anything said about money being used or offered by any party?

A. He told me that there was no money used that he knew of.

Q. Did Mr Dolan come over?

A. Yes, Mr. Dolan was here.

Q. Had you and Mr. Dolan and Mr. Murphy any agreement about how you would conduct the Senatorial campaign, before Mr. Murphy's election to the Legislature?

A. No, sir; I don't know as we had any agreement, though we had frequently talked the matter over. Murphy frequently asked me to assist him to get into the Legislature, and being a personal friend, I was willing to do so.

Q. Was there any understanding between you and Murphy, and Dolan, that Mr. Murphy was to vote for any person other than Mr. Clarke, provided a consideration was paid?

A. There was an understanding to this effect, that Mr. Murphy should not vote for any other candidate except Mr. Clarke, until he had consulted with me and Mr. Dolan, but there was no money consideration.

Q. How came you to make such an agreement as that?

A. Because it just came up that he wanted Mr. Clarke elected, and if Mr. Clarke had no chance, that Mr. Murphy should consult with us as to the candidate who should next be voted for, and the reason for it was that we expected to make some arrangement if he did vote for another man to have some appointment.

Q. Did Mr. Murphy vote for any other person than Mr. Clarke?

A. I don't know.

Q. Do you know whether he voted for Caldwell on the last ballot?

A. I don't, sir.

Q. Were you ever consulted about his voting for any other person?

A. No, sir; I did not come here as I agreed; I went to Pennsylvania, and the Legislature was almost over when I returned.

Q. Do you know whether Murphy consulted with Mr. Dolan?

A. I do not, sir.

By the Chairman.

Q. Have you ever had any conversation with Mr. Dolan and Mr. Murphy about that agreement since the election of Mr. Caldwell?

A. I did.

Q. What did Mr. Dolan or Murphy say?

A. They told me this: that they came down here and did all they could for Mr. Clarke, until Mr. Caldwell had votes enough, and they could not make any arrangement.

Q. Did not Murphy say that he voted for Caldwell?

A. I don't recollect; he might have told me so; it is likely that he did tell me so.

JOHN G. LINDSAY,

Was sworn and testified thus:

By the Chairman.

Q. Where do you live?

A. Anderson county, Kansas.

Q. Were you here last winter?

A. I was.

Q. In what capacity?

A. I was a member of the State Legislature.

Q. Were you here during the Senatorial campaign?

A. I was.

Q. Were you acquainted with the different candidates for United States Senate.

A. Was personally acquainted with most of them.

Q. Did you know Len Smith?

A. I knew him.

Q. Did you see him here last winter?

A. I did.

Q. What was he doing here?

A. I do not know as he had any special business here.

Q. Did you have any conversation with him during the time you were here?

A. Very frequently, sir.

Q. Did you talk with him or he with you, anything about Senatorial candidates?

A. He did.

Q. Did he talk in favor of any one of the candidates more than another?

A. Yes, sir.

Q. In whose favor?

A. The Hon. Alexander Caldwell.

Q. Did he not appear in the manner of his conversation to be engaged in aiding in the election of Alex. Caldwell?

A. He earnestly advocated the election of the Hon. Alex. Caldwell.

Q. Did not that appear to be his business here last winter?

A. Well, he talked more about the Senatorial election than any other one subject.

Q. Did he state to you, at any time, that he or any of the friends of Mr. Caldwell, had money here to use for the purpose of securing the election of Mr. Caldwell?

A. He did not.

Q. Did he ever talk to you about ever using any in that campaign?

A. He did not.

Q. Did any of the candidates make any offers of money, to prevail upon you to vote for them?

A. Emphatically, NO!

Q. Did any of the friends, of any of the candidates, offer to buy your vote with money or anything else?

A. No, sir; they did not have money enough to buy my vote.

Q. Did you have a draft drawn on Leavenworth by the Hon. Alex. Caldwell, and payable to your order, due in a month, in January, 1871?

A. No, sir.

Q. Did you transfer to W. A. Johnson, of Anderson county, a draft of twelve hundred dollars, drawn by Len Smith, of Leavenworth, January, 1871?

A. No, sir; I never heard of any such draft.

Q. Did you not transfer to W. A. Johnson, during January of last year, a draft for a certain amount, drawn by some person?

A. No, sir.

Q. Did you ever state to any person that you had

received twelve hundred dollars for your vote for Mr. Caldwell?

A. No, sir; and the man that makes such an assertion is a liar, if there is such a man, and had better not come in pistol-shot of me.

Q. Did you hear of any member of the Legislature getting money for his vote last winter?

A. I heard a great deal of outside talk about members of the Legislature selling their votes, but I never heard any specific charges made against any particular member of the Legislature for selling his vote.

Q. Did you receive any promise of any consideration whatever for your vote on the first ballot for United States Senator, last winter?

A. I did not; I voted for Mr. Snoddy, who was then my first choice for United States Senator.

Q. Did Thomas Carney hold your note last winter for twelve hundred dollars, signed by you, and signed or endorsed by a man named Usher?

A. No, sir.

Q. Did Alex. Caldwell hold such a note?

A. No, sir.

Q. Did any party in Leavenworth hold such a note?

A. No.

Q. Did you not make your note in Leavenworth, some time last fall (that is a year), the fall of 1870, for a considerable sum of money, payable at sixty days from date?

A. I did not.

Q. Did you give any note in Leavenworth, during October or November, for any amount, in 1870?

A. With Colonel Houston, I endorsed a note made by Isaac Hiner, in favor of some bank in Leavenworth, for about seven hundred dollars.

Q. Was that the only note which had your name on, in Leavenworth, in the fall of 1870?

A. It was not; I had a mortgage note there as collateral security for three hundred dollars that I borrowed from Scott's bank, which I have since paid.

By Mr. Johnson.

Q. Do you know if there was any betting going on last winter in the election of Mr. Caldwell?

A. Well, I heard men offer to bet money that he would be elected, but I did not know of any bet being made.

By J. Boynton.

Q. Did you hear any member of the Legislature say they had been offered money for their votes in the Senatorial campaign of 1871?

A. I did; I heard several members of the Legislature say they could get money for their votes.

Q. Well, for whom did they say they could get money for their votes?

A. I heard members of the Legislature say they could get money for voting for Clarke and for Caldwell.

Q. Have you ever heard any one say that he was offered any definite amount?

A. No, sir.

Q. Do you know anything about the Senatorial election of 1867?

A. I was in Topeka during the entire month of January, or nearly the entire month of that year, and saw what was going on.

Q. Do you know of any money or rather corrupt influences being used during that campaign, to secure votes for any candidate?

A. Not of my own personal knowledge?

Q. Did you hear anything about it, and if so, what?

A. I heard a great deal about money being used. I heard Perry Fuller expended forty thousand dollars to secure the defeat of Mr. Carney. I heard men say who voted for Mr. Carney that they were offered money to vote against him.

Q. From what candidate or his friends did those offers come?

A. I heard that such offers came from Mr. Pomeroy and Perry Fuller.

Q. Who was Perry Fuller working for?

A. Well, I first thought he was in favor of any person who would defeat Mr. Carney. At the last he favored Mr. Ross.

Q. Is that all you know about that election?

A. It is about all that I know personal, except that I have always thought that Mr. Carney was beaten with money. But I do not know as it was so of my own personal knowledge.

ELIJAH SELLS,

Having been sworn, testified as follows:

Examined by the Chairman.

Q. Do you know James D. Legate?

A. I do, sir.

Q. Did you see him any time last winter during the Senatorial election?

A. Yes, sir; he was a member of the Legislature.

Q. Had you any conversation with him, or he with you, in regard to the use of money in that canvass?

A. We had several conversations, running through the whole canvass. I cannot report any conversation; but he made this general impression: money was being freely used.

Q. Did he say about how much money Caldwell had to use?

A. He may, but I do not remember.

Q. Who was he working for?

A. Well, I can hardly tell you. He sometimes seemed to be for Caldwell, and sometimes against him, as his conversations ran. I can state about the conversation, and you can draw your inferences as I did. He said he was instrumental in bringing out Mr. Caldwell, and his object was to bring a man out from Leavenworth that would defeat Governor Carney without much hope of securing Caldwell's election. But that if he (Caldwell,) made himself so strong that he was likely to succeed, he would have to stick to him. That was the impression made upon my mind by the conversation.

Q. Did he say anything about the means that Caldwell had to use in gathering strength for himself.

A. I cannot state in positive words, but the impression he produced on my mind was that money was at the capitol.

Q. Do you know whether any money was used by any of the candidates?

A I do not.

Q. Or any offer of money?

A. I do not.

H. P. WELSH,

Having been re-called, testified as follows:

Examined by Chairman.

Q. Did you hear any conversation between any person lately, in relation to proceedings before this Committee, and this investigation, if so, who, when, what, and where was it, and all the circumstances connected with it?

A. I heard a conversation last Thursday night at the Tefft House, in the room adjoining No. 113, where I slept; I did not see any one; I do not know who was in the room, only I judge from their voices and their talk. This is a small room, and there is a door opening from that into a large room; that door was locked, but did not close very tight; I could see the light through the door; the persons in there were a man, I believe, called Colonel Abell, Sidney Clarke, and a man whom I heard Sidney Clarke introduce to Mr. Whitney as Mr. Dolan; as to the conversation, it was about this investigation; I was asleep at first, and was awakened by the talk and turned over, to listen as any one naturally would to what was said; I could not hear all that was said because the conversation was broken off by some one coming up stairs, which was frequent. At other times the conversation was so low I could not hear it. And to give a statement of what each one said, would be impossible from those circumstances. There was another gentleman there—Dan Adams—from what he stated he had just been up before this Committee.

Q. Can you state what he said?

A. Well, he went on in this conversation in relation to —I cannot tell exactly—but he appeared to be telling how he had got Snoddy down before the Committee, and raised the laugh on him, and so on; but what he said, I cannot recollect.

Q. Are you able to state any more of the conversation by him?

A. I cannot; he said a great deal sometimes talking loud, and sometimes low.

Q. What time did Whitney come there?

A. Well, sir; he came in sometime after Mr. Adams came in, what time in the night I do not know; he was the last one to go into the room.

Q. What did he state; if any thing?

A. Well, sir; when Mr. Whitney talked, he talked low; I could not hear what he said.

Q. Do you remember any reply that was made?

A. Something which created a laugh always; but what he said, I could not tell.

Q. Do you know what the subject was at the time?

A. Those other men after he got through were talking about the investigation.

Q. Do you know anything they said in the conversation in which they were engaged?

A. No; I could not.

Q. How long were they in there after Mr. Whitney came in?

A. I should think about one-half hour.

Q. Whose room was that they were in?

A. I understood it to be Colonel Abell's room.

Q. Are you able to state any of the conversation that Adams had there?

A. Well, they were talking about some young man's testimony; I do not think Mr. Whitney was there then; and I would not be positive, but my impression was that it was Bond's testimony.

Q. Was the conversation conducted in an ordinary tone of voice or a lower tone?

A. Generally a lower tone. Adams, I recollect distinctly, stated before Mr. Whitney came in, to this effect: "You know when they had an excursion down to Kansas City, our boys came to me and said they were pretty hard up, and I stated I let them have twenty-five or fifty dollars," not mentioning who they were.

Q. Did he say anything about the use of any greater sum than you heard?

A. No.

JOHN R. MULVANE,

Having been sworn, testified as follows:

By the Chairman.

Q. Where were you last winter during the Senatorial election, and what business were you then engaged in?

A. Cashier of the Topeka bank, residing here in Topeka.

Q. Were there any drafts or checks cashed at that bank during that Senatorial canvass, which were drawn upon any of the banks in Leavenworth?

A. Yes.

Q. How many, and what were the amounts of each—by whom were they drawn, and upon what bank or banks?

A. January 23d, 1871, J. W. Morris, Vice President of the First National Bank; of Leavenworth. We cashed a check of his on their bank for $5,000, on the evening of that day.

Q. What time in the evening?

A. I suppose, as near as my memory will serve, between nine and ten in the evening.

Q. Were you in the habit of keeping the bank open and doing banking business at that hour?

A. No, sir, the bank was not open; Mr. Smith, the President of the bank, and Mr. Morris came to my house about nine o'clock. Mr. Smith asked me to go down to the bank with him. I went down to the bank, being the only man that could get at currency. Mr. Morris produced a check of $5,000 on their bank at Leavenworth, and I gave him $5,000 in currency for it.

Q. Did Mr. Morris or Mr. Smith tell you for what purpose the money was drawn out at that time of the night?

A. They did not.

Q. State whether any other drafts or checks were drawn at that time, and the circumstances.

A. I think it was the 24th or 25th that Robert Crozier drew on the same bank for $1,200. That is the only two checks. All others that passed through our bank were such as had nothing to do with this business of yours.

Q. What time of the day were these $1,200 drawn by Crozier?

A. During banking hours.

Q. What relation does Mr. Crozier sustain to the First National at Leavenworth?

A. He is the Cashier.

Q. Was it a check drawn by him as Cashier, or his individual check?

A. His individual check.

Q. To whose order were these checks drawn?

A. To the order of Jacob Smith.

Q. Who did you pay the last check to?

A. I cannot remember; it came in over the counter regularly. It must have been paid to Mr. Crozier himself.

Q. Did Jacob Smith's endorsement appear on both these checks?

A. Yes, sir.

Q. And no other?

A. No other.

JACOB SMITH,

Having been sworn, testified thus:

By the Chairman.

Q. Where do you live?

A. Topeka.

Q. What business were you engaged in during the Senatorial canvass last winter?

A. Farming, merchandizing and banking?

Q. Do you know whether or not one Mr. Morris drew a check or draft on the First National Bank, Leavenworth, and which was cashed at Topeka Bank?

A. I do.

Q. Do you know about what date that was drawn?

A. I cannot exactly state that.

Q. Was there more than one check of that kind drawn?

A. Not by Dr. Morris.

Q. Do you know what Dr. Morris wanted to use the money for?

A. I do not.

Q. What time was that check cashed at your bank?

A. I judge about nine o'clock at night.

Q. Who was it drawn in favor of?

A. I think it was myself.

Q. Did not Mr. Morris say anything to you about the purpose?

A. Not to my knowledge.

Q. Did he make no explanation why he did not apply to have the check cashed during banking hours?

A. Not to me.

Q. Did he make any explanations to any one else that were communicated to you?

A. Not to my knowledge.

Q. What was Morris doing here at that time?

A. Well, he was here looking on, watching politicians, I presume.

Q. Was he engaged in the Senatorial canvass during that time?

A. He was around the lobby here at the Tefft House.

Q. Who was he in favor of for United States Senator?

A. I don't know positively, but I should judge Caldwell.

Q. Was it not unusual to open your bank at that hour of the night?

A. It was, but we have done it before. I think we have done it for the railroad once or twice, although it certainly was unusual to open it at that hour.

Q. Was there any other check cashed at your bank drawn on the First National, Leavenworth?

A. I think there was one of $1,200.

Q. Who drew that?

A. I think it was Judge Crozier.

Q. Do you know what that one was drawn for?

A. I do not.

Q. What was Crozier doing here at that time?

A. He was looking to politicians I presume.

Q. Was he interested in the election of United States Senator?

A. I think he was electioneering for Caldwell.

Q. Did any of Clarke's, or Walker's, or Crawford's friends, draw any money out of your bank at that time?

A. They did not to my knowledge.

Q. Did you go with Morris that evening?

A. I think I did.

Q. Do you recollect where you met him first?

A. I do not, but think it was up at the Tefft House.

Q. Do you recollect the conversation between you and Dr. Morris that evening before you went to the bank about that money?

A. I do not.

Q. Do you recollect or not whether he made any explanation why he applied for the money at that hour?

A. I think not to me.

Q. Did he assign any reason why he could not wait for banking hours in the morning?

A. I don't think he made any statement to me about it He might or might not.

Q. You are President of the Topeka Bank, of which Mulvane is Cashier, are you?

A. Yes, sir.

Q. And were at that time?

A. Yes, sir.

By Senator Whitney.

Q. Do you remember what part of the Tefft House you met Mr. Morris in?

A. I think it was in the office.

Q. Did any else ask you to raise money on that check of Morris's.

A. Not to my knowledge.

Q. Had you ever any talk with Len Smith about cash ing checks or raising money?

A. He asked me one day, and I told him he had better get some one else?

Q. How much did he ask you to cash for him?

A. I don't remember the amount now.

Q. Did he have the checks drawn?

A. No, sir; I think not.

Q. Was it a large amount that he wanted you to cash for him?

A. I do not remember; some two or three thousand dollars; possibly more.

Q. Did he say what he wanted it for?

A. No, sir; I think not.

Q. Did Len Smith ever say anything about buying votes here?

A. No; I think not.

Q. Or about wanting to buy votes?

A. Not to me, I think.

Q. Why did you tell Smith he had better get some one else to cash those checks for him?

A. I thought the honest yeomanry might pick him up before the close of the Legislature.

Q. Do you know how much money the Caldwell party brought to this town and dispersed here?

A. I do not.

Q. Do you know anything about the election of 1867? anything definite about corruption, or anything of that sort, in that election?

A. Well, I don't think I do. I know there was—that is, I heard there was—money used.

By the Chairman.

Q. At the time Len Smith spoke to you about cashing checks for him, did he state for whom those checks were to be drawn?

A. No; I think not, sir. He wanted to raise some currency and gave his checks, and asked me to cash them, and I refused on the ground that I thought it was not prudent for him to throw out his checks.

Q. Why?

A. Well, as I stated before, he might be picked up.

Q. By whom?

A. The honest yeomanry.

Q. For what?

A. For giving checks.

Q. There is no harm in giving checks is there?

A. No.

Q. Is it not a fact that you refused to cash those checks for Smith for the reason that if you were to do so those checks would furnish, as you thought, evidence of the use of money by Smith in that election?

A. Well, that is what I thought of.

Q. And that was the ground of your refusal?

A. Yes; I did not want to be mixed up in it.

Q. Had you any knowledge, then, that Mr. Smith wanted that money for that purpose?

A. No; I merely surmised it.

Q. Did he say or intimate the purpose for which he desired the currency upon those checks?

A. Not to me.

Q. Well, from what did you surmise the purpose for which he wanted the money?

A. Well, as it is customary for men to do those things, as I learn by rumor only, I surmised it in that case.

By Senator Whitney.

Q. Was that just before Morris came to get this money?

A. Yes.

Q. Immediately before?

A. No; the beginning of the session, I believe.

Q. What did you say to him?

A. I told him to be careful, to look out.

Q. Did not Len tell you what he wanted the money for? Did he tell you how much he would probably want to draw?

A. No; I think he did not. I think he wanted at that time two or three thousand dollars.

WEDNESDAY EVENING, February 14, 1872.

G. E. BATES,

Having been sworn, testified thus:

Examined by the Chairman.

Q. Where do you reside?

A. Junction City, Davis county, Kansas.

Q. Do you know a man of the name by A. W. Byers?

A. I don't know him personally.

Q. Did you have any conversation with him last winter in regard to the Senatorial election?

A. Not to my recollection.

Q. Did you directly or indirectly have anything to do with him in connection with the election?

A. No, sir.

Q. Have you any knowledge of any money being used in that election to secure votes for any candidate?

A. I have not.

Q. Do you know of any money or other valuable thing being offered by any of the candidates for votes?

A. No, sir, not to my own knowledge.

Q. Have you such knowledge by information from persons to whom the offer was made or by whom it was made?

A. I think I have in one instance.

Q. State what it was.

A. J. H. Snead, Representative from Saline county last winter, told me in the streets at Topeka that he had been offered money for his vote.

Q. Did he say by whom the offer had been made?

A. Not to my recollection. He stated, however, who the party wanted him to vote for.

Q. Who was he to vote for in the event of his receiving money?

A. Alexander Caldwell.

Q. Did he say how much money?

A. He told me at the time, but I cannot be positive how much.

Q. Are you able to state your recollection now?

A. My recollection would be that it was $3,000, but I cannot state it positively.

Q. Do you know of any other instance where money or other valuable consideration was used or offered to be used in that canvass?

A. No, sir, I do not think I do.

By Senator Whitney.

Q. Do you know anything of the Senatorial election of 1867?

A. I was here at the time.

Q. Do you know of your own knowledge of any money or promise of money being used in that election to influence votes?

A. There was one member of the Legislature, Richard D. Mobley, of Ottawa county, Kansas, who told me he was offered money by one of the Fletchers to vote for Carney.

Q. Did he say how much?

A. My recollection is that it was $2,500, but I am not certain.

Q. Any other instance?

A. Not that I know of my own knowledge.

Q. Were you frequently in Clarke's room last winter?

A. Yes, sir, pretty near every day during the canvass.

Q. Did you ever see any checks drawn or check-book lying around in his private room?

A. Never did.

Q. Did you ever know anything about a certificate of deposit being drawn?

A. No, sir. I have no knowledge of his financial matters whatever.

Q. When did Mobley say relatively to the election that the offer was made?

A. Just as they were going into the hall before the joint convention.

W. H. PECKHAM,

Being sworn, testified as follows:

Examined by Mr. W. H. Clark.

Q. Where do you reside?

A. Douglas county.

Q. Where are you doing business now?

A. Topeka.

Q. What business are you engaged in?

A. Jewelry and drugs.

Q. How long have you been engaged in that business?

A. Since the 16th of last April.

Q. From whom did you purchase your drug store?

A, Dr. Greeno.

Q. Were you a member of the Legislature last winter?

A. I was.

Q. Were you present during the Senatorial campaign?

A. I was.

Q. Are you acequainted with Len Smith?

A. I am.

Q. Had you any conversation with him during the Senatorial campaign about who he wanted you to support for United States Senator?

A. Yes.

Q. Did you have any conversation with Mr. Caldwell about the Senatorial election?

A. No.

Q. Did Mr Caldwell or any one for him make any offer of money or any valuable consideration to you in consideration of your vote for Mr. Caldwell for Senator?

A. No, sir.

Q. Did any one offer you anything?

A. No.

Q. Did you ever call on Mr. Caldwell or Mr. Smith for money after the election?

A. No.

Q. Did you call to see Mr. Caldwell at any time after the election?

A. Yes, I did.

Q. Did you ever call on him in Leavenworth?

A. Yes.

Q. Was there any conversation then about the Senatorial election?

A. Yes.

Q. Anything about any money?

A. No.

Q. Did you ever tell any person that you were going to get $2,000 for your vote for Caldwell?

A. I never told anything as a fact.

Q. Did you ever tell any person at any time that you were going over to Leavenworth to get some money from Caldwell?

A. No, I did not.

Q. Or Len Smith?

A. No.

Q. Do you know of any money being used during the Senatorial election for votes?

A. I do not; I never saw any used.

Q. How much did you see around?

A. Oh, I don't know; I saw some.

Q. Whom did you see have any?

A. Oh, many; but perhaps no more than business men may be supposed to have.

Q. Did Len Smith ever tell you he had money here to secure the election of Mr. Caldwell?

A. He did not.

Q. Do you know of any one having any money here to use in the election to secure votes?

A. No.

Q. Were you present in Dr. Greeno's store frequently during the Senatorial campaign?

A. I was.

Q. Did you talk any in there about the campaign?

A. I believe I did.

Q. In your conversations do you usually say what you mean?

A. In a business capacity—yes.

Q. Did Mr. Clarke ever make you any offer to purchase your farm if you would vote for him?

A. No, sir; he never did.

R. D. MOBLEY,

Having been sworn, testified as follows:

Examined by Chairman.

Q. Were you present here in Topeka at the Senatorial election in 1867, when Mr. Pomeroy and Mr. Ross were elected?

A. I was, sir.

Q. Do you know of any money or other valuable thing that was used or offered to be used by any person to influence the votes of members of the Legislature in favor of either of those gentlemen or any other gentlemen who were candidates for election at that time; if so, state.

A. I do not know of any money being used. John Fletcher asked me one day what my price would be; I told him about four or five times as much as it was reported Finn was offered, which was $600. After we had gone into the joint session, he said if I would cast my vote for Thomas Carney, I should have his (Thomas Carney's) check for that amount. I refused to receive it and voted for Mr. Ross.

Q. Do you know of any other offer to use money to influence votes in that session?

A. I do not of my own personal knowledge.

Q. Were you here at the Senatorial election last winter?

A. I was.

Q. Do you know of any such transactions last winter?

A. Not of my own personal knowledge.

ISAAC SHARP.

Having been sworn, testified as follows:

By G. W. Clark.

Q. Where do you reside?

A. In the city of Council Grove.

Q. Did you ever have any conversation with Mr. Hammond in regard to the Senatorial election of 1871?

A. Yes, sir; I have.

Q. State what the conversation was.

A. Since this investigation has been agitating the public mind, I have had two or three different conversations with him; all of which arose incidentally, principally in his own house; in which he stated that he did not propose to come before this committee if he could possibly avoid it. He said they would have to be sharp to catch him, for he knew "too d—d much to tell." He stated that during the Senatorial canvass referred to, he himself, in connection with two other citizens of our town, G. M. Simcock and Charles Columbia, cooked Mr. Phinney's goose, our Representative in the Legislature at that time, and succeeded in securing his vote for Mr. Caldwell, or neutralizing its effect as against him; and he did not care a d—n which way he put it; that Mr. Phinney had come to him since and desired that he would give a certificate stating he knew nothing about it, but he refused to do that, and stated he would not put himself on the record as knowing anything about it.

Q. Did you ever hear Mr. Hammond say how much money Mr. Phinney got for his vote?

A. Yes, sir. I do not now recollect that I heard him say that he saw or knew anything about it, but in a general way; but I heard him speak of his (Phinney's) $1,000.

Q. Did you ever hear Mr. Hammond say that he ever received any money for securing Mr. Phinney's vote?

A. He used the phrase that all he "ever got was to keep the bread riot from rising in Topeka." He said he took his principally in the liquor commodity.

Q. Were you in Topeka in 1871, at the Senatorial election?

A. I was.

Q. Do you know of any money being used to influence votes?

A. No, sir; I have no personal knowledge.

By Senator Stover.

Q. Did you ever hear Mr. Hammond make any statement about manipulating Mr. Snead's vote?

A. Yes, sir.

Q. Please state about what he said.

A. Well, he said he had Mr. Snead in tow for some two or three days to get his vote for Mr. Caldwell, and he had to keep him pretty drunk; and in keeping him drunk he was pretty drunk himself.

Q. Did he say he had succeeded?

A. He had a negotiation completed; all the terms agreed, and the price he was to receive, the money having to be received through Mr. Hammond. But at the time he came to get his man, Snead was too drunk and could not be found; and he lost his commission or proportion of ducats. I think that was the language used.

Q. Do you know of any money or other valuable consideration to secure the votes of any members or the influence of any party?

A. Mr. Len T. Smith proposed to me that I might just as well make a little money out of this transaction as any other person; that my position with the Democratic party in the State was better than that of any other man and in that way of making money; and he could make it to my interest of perhaps a couple of thousand dollars if I were to use my influence with the Democratic members to induce them to vote for Mr. Caldwell.

Q. Did Mr. Smith state to you at that time that he was the agent of Mr. Caldwell, or give you to understand that he was working with authority from Mr. Caldwell?

A. Not in any direct language. I saw him and Mr. Caldwell often together, and Mr. Caldwell himself told me that any benefit I could be to him, Mr. Smith would not forget me for it.

Q. Was Smith present at that conversation with Caldwell?

A. Yes, sir. It was after the conversation I had with Mr. Smith before. I recollect Len Smith laughing and saying, "I guess we shall not make anything out of that thing."

S. D. MACDONALD,

Having been sworn, testified as follows:

Examined by the Chairman.

Q. Where do you reside?

A. Topeka, Kansas.

Q. Do you know anything about the use of money in the Senatorial election of 1867?

A. Yes, sir.

Q. State what you know about it?

A. Well, I was in Mr. Downs' room in the Capital House during the latter part of the session of 1867, and while I was there talking with Mr. Downs, Mr. Finn, a member of the Legislature, came in for money, and Mr. Downs told him he might take $500 or nothing; and he paced the floor sometime and seemed indisposed to take it, but finally consented, and Mr. Downs gave him what he said was $500, and I think he told him he must give a receipt in full. I understood that to be for his services in the Senatorial election, but more than that I know nothing.

Q. Is that the only instance in which you know of the use, or the offer of the use of money in that campaign?

A. Yes, sir.

Q. Do you know anything of the Senatorial campaign last winter in that respect?

A. No, sir.

Q. Do you know for whom Mr. Finn was to use his influence for that consideration?

A. I do not know certain, but my impression was that it was for Ross.

Q. Was it for his vote, or influence, or what?

A. I understood it to be for his vote, from the fact that he was upbraided by Mr. Downs, who told him he was an infamous character, and that he wanted as little to do with him as possible.

J. C. VINCENT.

Having been sworn, testified as follows:

Examined by Senator Whitney.

Q. Were you here last winter during the Senatorial election?

A. I was, as a member of the Senate.

Q. Do you know of any member of the Legislature having been approached with any corrupt offer for his vote?

A. I do not.

Q. Did any member of the Legislature tell you during the Senatorial election, or since, that he had been approached in that way?

A. There was.

Q. State who it was.

A. Mr. Peckham told me that he had an opportunity of making $2,000.

Q. Please state the time and place, and all that was said on that subject.

A. We have had half a dozen different conversations about it since the election.

Q. When was the first of those conversations?

A. It was soon after the election; how many days I cannot tell exactly.

Q. Who did he say made the offer?

A. He never told me.

Q. What was he to do in consideration of the $2,000?

A. This conversation was a general conversation, and he took it for granted that I knew what he was to do, and I do not think he specified.

Q. Was he to cast his vote for any particular person for United States Senator as a part of this consideration for the money?

A. As I answered a few moments ago, I am satisfied that he knew that I understood that he was to use his influence in the Democratic caucus.

Q. On whose behalf?

A. Caldwell's.

Q. To secure votes for Mr. Caldwell?

A. To help him in his election, as a matter of course. That is the inference I drew, but he did not say so.

Q. You refer to a caucus of Democratic members of the Legislature?

A. I do.

Q. Did he say that he got the $2,000?

A. He said that he did not.

Q. For what reason?

A. He did not give any reason, for he knew that I knew—took it for granted that I knew why he failed.

Q. Did you know?

A. I knew that the caucus burst up a little in advance.

Q. In advance of what?

A. Before the time arrived in which they could be used.

Q. Did he speak to you as if he had agreed to use his influence in the Democratic caucus on behalf of Caldwell for the sum of $2,000?

A. He never said so.

Q. Was that the inference that he led you to draw?

A. It was.

Q. And did you further infer from his conversation that he failed to receive the $2,000 because he had failed to manage the caucus as he had agreed, or as he supposed he could do?

A. That was certainly the inference that I drew.

Q Did he ever say to you that he still had a claim on Caldwell for the $2,000?

A. He never did.

Q. Did he ever tell you who made him this offer?

A. He never did.

Q. Did he not buy this drug store of Greeno upon the supposition that some of Caldwell's friends were going to pay the $2,000 for his influence last winter?

A. I do not believe that he did.

Q. Do you know of his going to Leavenworth to see Caldwell since the election, either by actual knowledge or from anything he told you?

A. I do not know that he went expressly to see Caldwell.

Q. Did he go to see Caldwell among other objects?

A. I know that he went to Leavenworth, but not that he went to see Caldwell.

Q. Did he see him at any time he went there?

A. I do not know.

Q. Or Len Smith?

A. I cannot answer positively that he saw Len Smith.

Q. Did he not go to Leavenworth to get money from some source?

A. I do not know that he did.

Q. Did any person, either for himself or as agent for another, offer to purchase Peckham's farm as a consideration or inducement that his vote should be cast for Sidney Clarke for Senator?

A. Mr. Peckham did tell me so.

Q. State what he said about that.

A. He said that he had been asked before this committee if Sidney Clarke had offered to purchase his farm in consideration of his vote. This conversation was this evening. He said to me that Clarke did not, but another party did.

Q. Did he state who the other party was.

A. No, sir, I never heard about this transaction before.

J. T. LAUTER,

Having been sworn, testified as follows:

Examined by the Chairman.

Q. Were you here during last winter at the Senatorial election?

A. About four or five days.

Q. Do you know whether any money or other valuable thing was used in that canvass for the purpose of controlling votes?

A. I do not.

Q. Did you see any money transaction in connection with it?

A. No, sir; only by rumor.

Q. Do you know E. C. Manning?

A. I have seen him.

Q. Did you see him at any time about the time of the election last winter?

A. I saw him here; I believe he was a member.

Q. Did you ever see him have any money about that time?

A. Well, I might have seen him handle money about that time, but do not remember anything definite.

Q. Did you ever talk to any of the members of the Legislature about having had offers of money or other valuable thing in exchange for thei r votes?

A. No, I never did. I do not think any member of the Legislature ever told me that he had an offer.

By Mr. Wood.

Q. Did you ever hear any one say that he had been approached with money or other valuable consideration for his influence in the Senatorial election of 1871?

A. Yes.

Q. State who and what the consideration was.

A. I heard Mr. Carson say that he was furnished money o pay members to vote for Caldwell.

Q. Did he say who furnished the money?

A. I don't think he ever told me who—I only inferred it.

Q. What was your inference?

A. I inferred that it was Anderso n.

Q. Did any one else than Carson ever tell you?

A. No, sir; he was the only one.

Q. Who and what is he?

A. I do not know what his business is.

Q. Where does he live?

A. Garnett.

By Senator Stover.

Q. Did Carson say how much he had in his possession to influence votes?

A. He said he paid one member $1,000.

Q. Did he state the member's name.

A. No.

Q. Did he speak of any other case?

A. Yes, he said there were others, but did not say who they were, or how many, or how much money.

Q. Did Carson state for whom he paid the money?

A. He stated that he had paid it for a vote for Caldwell.

Q. Did he state who authorized him to pay the money?

A. He did not any further than I have stated.

ROBERT CROZIER,

Having been sworn, testified thus:

Examined by the Chairman.

Q. State your place of residence and your business.

A. I reside in Leavenworth; my present business is that of Cashier of the First National Bank of Leavenworth.

Q. Were you at Topeka during the Senatorial contest last winter?

A. I was.

Q. How long were you here?

A. I was here from about the third day of the session until the day following the election.

Q. What were you doing here?

A. I was exerting myself to the extent of my ability to help elect Mr. Caldwell to the Senate.

Q. Do you know whether any money or any other valuable thing was used in that election to secure or obtain votes in that Legislature for Caldwell?

A. I do not.

Q. Did you know whether any money or other valuable

thing was used in that contest to secure votes for any candidate for United States Senator?

A. I do not.

Q. What amount of checks were drawn on the First National of Leavenworth, by persons that were here in the interest of Mr. Caldwell, during that time or that they were cashed during that contest, or afterwards, at the First National?

A. I cannot tell how many checks might have been drawn by persons here in Mr. Caldwell's interest or the First National Bank, as there were several persons here who kept accounts in the First National, and I did not observe whether they drew any checks here or not; I can state as to one check in particular, and that is all I can: that check was drawn by myself. My impression is that Dr. Morris drew a check on the First National Bank for some amount, but what amount I cannot tell now.

Q. How much money did Len Smith draw out of that bank at the time he first came up here, and at any other time during that contest?

A. I cannot tell without reference to the books of the bank.

Q. Have you no general knowledge about the amount?

A. No, I cannot say that I have; Mr. Smith's accounts fluctuated very much, sometimes he has very much, and sometimes not much; and I cannot tell you how his accounts changed at that time.

Q. Did Mr. Caldwell keep his account at the First National at that time?

A. Mr. Caldwell has kept an account there for the last four years.

Q. Do you know how much money he drew there at that time?

A. That particular account has not been disturbed for the last two years, I think; it is a trust fund, although standing in the individual name of Mr. Caldwell; he keeps his regular account on Scott & Co. The check I drew—referred to above—did not result in changing Mr. Smith's account at all; it was drawn the day of the Senatorial election; after the election, and the next day Mr. Smith handed me the amount of the check at Leavenworth.

Q. Did you get that check cashed in this city?

A. Yes, sir.

Q. What did you do with the cash?

A. I gave it to Mr. Smith.

Q. You drew the check then as an accommodation for him?

A. Yes, sir; for Mr. L. T. Smith. Mr. Smith came to me after the banks in this city had closed; said he wanted $1,200 to pay some bills, and asked me if I could get him that much currency. I told him I thought I could; started to go to the Topeka Bank; met Mr. Jacob Smith on the side-walk; asked him if he would cash my check on the First National Bank for $1,200; he said he would, and did so. I handed the funds to Mr. Len Smith.

Q. Where was that check cashed?

A. Mr. Smith stepped into his bank; I stepped into his hardware store. That is my recollection.

Q. You have no means of stating what amount of money Mr. Smith drew out of the First National about the time he came here to go into that contest?

A. Not with me here.

Q. Have you ever examined the account with reference to that?

A. I never have.

Q. Do you know what Morris did with the cash for the check which he drew on the First National?

A. I do not know that he got cash for the check he drew on the First National.

Q. State if a check for $5,000, signed by J. W. Morris, drawn on the First National Bank of Leavenworth in favor of Jacob Smith, endorsed by Jacob Smith, did not come into your bank at Leavenworth, from the Topeka Bank, a very short time after that Senatorial election?

A. I don't think I ever saw such a check. It might have gone down while I was here.

Q. Do you know from the record at your bank that such a note as I have described was collected from the First National Bank by the Topeka Bank about that time?

A. I never saw such a check, nor never saw any entries concerning such a check in any of the books of the First National Bank.

Q. Did you have a conversation with Mr. Morris concerning it?

A. I had a conversation with Dr. Morris about some currency, but what it was, or what the amount of the currency was, I cannot now tell.

By Senator Whitney.

Q. Does Len Smith keep any other bank account at Leavenworth than with your bank?

A. Yes, sir; he keeps an account with Scott & Co.

Q. Do you recollect how large a balance Smith had at your bank about the first days of the meeting of the Legislature, last winter.

A. I do not.

Q. Did Smith make any arrangement with you at any time about the meeting of the Legislature, about honoring his drafts which might be drawn on him; if so, what arrangement?

A. None whatever. I do not think Mr. Smith's account was there at that time.

Q. Did Smith keep a bank account in any of the eastern banks at that time?

A. Not to my knowledge.

Q. Did Senator Pomeroy have a bank account with you at Leavenworth?

A. No, sir; never has had.

Q. Were you here at Topeka during the Senatorial election of 1867?

A. I was a portion of the time.

Q. Do you know of any money, or other corrupt means being used to influence that election, from any reliable source or sources?

A. No; I know nothing at all; nor did I at that time, except by public rumor.

Q. Did you ever hear any members of the Legislature say anything about any offers that they had received, or any approaches in a corrupt way, on the subject of their votes for Senator?

A. I do not think I did.

Q. Did you ever have any talk with Governor Carney about the Senatorial election of last winter?

A. Yes; considerable talk.

Q. Did he state to you the reasons why he withdrew?

A. Yes; he gave me a reason, which was that he did not want to jeopardize the election of a Senator from Leavenworth.

Q. Did he state anything to you about being reimbursed for his expenses?

A. Never a single word.

Q. Did you have any talk with him within two or three weeks, relative to the Senatorial election of last winter?

A. No, sir; I don't think I have spoken to him for a month.

By Mr. Johnson.

Q. Did you have frequent conversations with Len Smith last winter, during the pendancy of the Senatorial election?

A. I talked with him more or less every day.

Q. What appeared to be his business at that time?

A. He seemed to be exerting himself to accomplish the election of Mr. Caldwell.

Q. In this conversation with Len Smith, did he ever intimate to you or tell you that money was being used for the election of Mr. Caldwell?

A. He never did then or since.

Q. Did you ever receive information from any reliable source, that money was being used?

A. I never heard any one say that money had been used as of his own knowledge. I heard Mr. Smith talk about his hotel bill; and though I do not remember exactly what the amount was, yet I think he said either that "his" bill, or "the" bill was in the neighborhood of $2,000.

By Senator Whitney.

Q. Did the agency of Len Smith and his friends in behalf of Caldwell seem to be fully approved and understood by Mr. Caldwell?

A. Why, Mr. Caldwell and Mr. Smith were in frequent conversation; they conversed a great many times. Yes, it did seem so.

Q. Did the relations between John McDowell and Mr. Caldwell seem to be intimate during the Senatorial election?

A. They did.

Q. Was Jas. L. McDowell here actively engaged in securing the election of Mr. Caldwell?

A. I think he was.

W. C. WEBB,

Having been sworn, testified as follows:

Examined by the Chairman.

Q. Were you a member of the Legislature last winter?

A. I was.

Q. From what district?

A. The fifty-third, Fort Scott city district.

Q. State whether you know of any money or other valuable thing being offered, or purposed to be given, to any member of the Legislature by any of the candidates for the United States Senate, or any persons acting in their interest, to influence votes?

A. I do.

Q. State where, when, by whom, and the circumstances attending that offer or proposed gift.

A. In the city of Fort Scott, in the month of December, 1870, at my office in that city. Mr. C. S. Wheaton, the then Sheriff of Bourbon county, called on me and commenced the interview by inquiring whether I was in any way committed to any candidate for the United States Senate, to which I answered distinctly, I was not. He then desired to know if I had any choice among the men talked of for that office. I told him I had, I was in favor of a Fort Scott man, either Judge Lowe or George A. Crawford. He asked me if I could support Sidney Clarke. I stated no, I could not. He wanted to know why, and I assigned various reasons, the purport of which was, that I was not satisfied with his political action. And in addition to that, my constituency had elected me, well knowing that I was hostile to Sidney Clarke. To which he said that Clarke's friends had also supported me as Representative. I said I knew that, that was true; but they knew very well too that I was not in favor of Sidney

Clarke. He then took a pencil and sheet of paper that was lying on the table before him, and on that made a dollar mark, a figure two and three ciphers after it. He showed it to me, and I looked at it and asked him what it was, what does it mean? Which question I asked because there was no points. I then asked this question, is it two thousand or twenty? He said two thousand dollars. To that my reply was in these words: Sidney Clarke could not buy me for ten times two thousand dollars. He answered, I don't propose to buy you. I said, O! no, you do not, but Mr. Clarke would be very glad to have my services at almost any price; but I could not support Mr. Clarke at all, Mr. Wheaton. He then said, that of course if I could not vote consistently for him it was all right; but two thousand or twenty five hundred dollars was a good deal better than nothing. The paper upon which the two thousand dollars was written I have in my possession still.

Q. State if you have ever before stated these facts to any person, if so, to whom and when and where?

A. I did state all these facts at the Tefft House in the room of George A. Crawford before the Senatorial election, and stated them to George A. Crawford, Judge Lowe, Dr. J. S. Redfield, S. A. Manlove and C. A. Morris, all of Fort Scott, and to all at the same time. I mentioned the circumstance of the offer that had been made me, and that it had been made in Mr. Clarke's interest; but I did not name the person who made the offer.

Q. State if Mr. Wheaton was here during the Senatorial election.

A. He was. I understood him to be here in the interest of Mr. Clarke from his general speech, demeanor and associates.

Q. State, if you know, to whose election for United States Senator Mr. Wheaton was favorable at the time of the interview at Fort Scott.

A. He was then a warm personal and political friend of Sidney Clarke, and favorable to his election for United States Senator.

A. Do you know of any money or valuable thing used, or attempted to be used, by any one else, to influence votes in that election?

A. I do not.

Q. Were you here at the election of 1867?

A. I was not.

By Senator Whitney.

Q. Did Wheaton say that he had authority from Clarke to make this proposal?

A. He did not, nor even that Clarke knew of it.

Q. Did you hear any member or members of the Legislature of last winter say that they had been approached with any current offer for their votes?

A. I can not say that I did.

By the Chairman.

Q. Was Mr. Wheaton a wealthy man or otherwise at the time he made that offer?

A. I should say not wealthy; but he was worth several thousand dollars

THURSDAY, February 15, 1872.

E. B. PURCELL,

Having been sworn, testified thus:

Examined by the Chairman.

Q. Were you here at Topeka during the Senatorial canvass or any part of it last winter?

A. Yes, sir. The greater part of it.

Q. Had you any conversations with Alexander Caldwell during that time?

A. I was with him more or less.

Q. Did you have any conversations with him with regard to procuring votes for him?

A. Not in any particular way. We talked over the matter.

Q. In any of your conversations with Mr. Caldwell was there anything said about the use of money?

A. No, sir.

Q. Do you know whether there was any money used to procure votes for him?

A. No, sir.

Q. For any one?

A. No, sir.

Q. Did you have any conversation with any one in which the subject of money was mentioned as a means to procure votes for any of the candidates in that election?

A. No, sir.

Q. What was Len Smith doing here last winter?

A. I suppose he was here as many others during the Senatorial campaign. What he was doing I do not know.

Q. Do you not know that he was here in the interests of of Alexander Caldwell?

A. I never heard him say he was, nor Mr. Caldwell either.

Q. Do you not know that he was here in the interests of Alexander Caldwell?

A. I would simply suppose he was. I never heard him say so or anything of that kind.

Q. Was Jim McDowell, of Leavenworth, here.

A. Well, McDowell was here.

Q. What was he doing?

A. He was about the Tefft House. And I suppose he was here because it was the Senatorial campaign. I never heard him say.

By Mr. Johnson.

Q. Did you have any conversation during that campaign with Len T. Smith?

A. I spoke to him several times, past the time of day, and had more or less talk at different times.

Q. Did you and he have any conversation in regard to the Senatorial election?

A. I presume the greater part of the talk would bare on that subject.

Q. Did you have any conversation about the Senatorial election?

A. I would judge it was on that subject.

Q. Do you mean to say that you are not positive it was.

A. It was.

Q. Now, sir, from that conversation with Len Smith, in whose interest do you suppose he was working?

A. Every thing would indicate that he was in favor of Mr. Caldwell.

Q. Did Len Smith, to your knowledge, have any business here except pertaining to that particular campaign or election of United States Senator?

A. I do not know that he had.

Q. From your conversation what was Mr. Smith's business here?

A. I cannot tell what was his business here.

Q. What, then, did he appear to be engaged in.

A. He was here because it was a Senatorial contest, and was taking interest in Mr. Caldwell's favor.

Q. What relation are you and Alexander Caldwell?

A. We are cousins.

J. HAMMOND,

Having been sworn, testified as follows:

Examined by Senator Stover.

Q. Were you here at the Senatorial election last winter?

A. I was.

Q. Do you know of any money being used during that campaign to secure the vote or influence of any member of the Legislature?

A. Not to my certain knowledge.

Q. Have you information that there was?

A. Nothing positive.

Q. Have you what you consider reliable information?

A. No, I cannot say that I have?

Q. Please state what information you have?

A. Well, I cannot say that I have any information.

Q. Are you acquainted with Mr. Snead?

A. I am.

Q. Did you have any conversation with him during the campaign?

A. Yes, sir, I did.

Q. Do you know whether any money or other improper influence were brought to bear on Mr. Snead to secure his vote for Mr. Caldwell?

A. At one time there was some money offered (at least that was my understanding,) by George Smith of Leavenworth. The money was offered to secure Snead's vote.

Q. How much.

A. There was no certain amount specified.

Q. Did you make any proposition?

A. I did.

Q. What conclusion did he come to?

A. He came to the conclusion that he would vote for Caldwell.

A. Well, I cannot say whether he said he would accept the proposition or not. The statement was made by me.

Q. To whom?

A. To him—Snead.

Q. Of how much?

A. Two thousand dollars.

Q. To vote for whom?

A. For Caldwell.

Q. What did he say?

A. He said he was elected in the county he came from on the Clarke issue, and that he could not well support Caldwell. But at the same time he was a poor man and that it would assist him some, though I cannot recollect the words he said.

Q. Did Mr. Geo Smith, of Levenworth, authorize you to make this tender to him?

A. I can not say positively that he authorized me to do so; he said that there was a certain person whom I might draw upon.

Q. Who?

A. Mr. G. M. Simcock.

Q. Did you draw?

A. I did not, sir.

Q. Do you know of any other attempts that were made to secure votes or influence of members of the Legislature?

A. I only know two, Snead and Phinney.

Q. What do you know about Phinney's case?

A. A conversation was had after I had talked with this man Snead. Mr. George Smith, of Leavenworth, came to me and asked me if I knew how Phinney's vote could be secured; stated at the same time that Phinney was a Clarke man, and that they did not know how to reach him; he asked me if I had any influence over him or could control his vote; I said to him: I cannot myself, but could lay plans that would secure his vote; he then asked the question if it would do to approach him with money, my reply was that he had better not; he then said, he had rather give him or make him a present of one thousand dollars than buy him for five hundred; he then asked me the question, what would be the business that I would suggest to work upon him to secure his vote; my remark was to telegraph to Charlie Columbia or write him to come down and then to G. M. Simcock to approach him, for him to go to the Fifth Avenue Hotel, and take dinner and after Simcock and Columbia had had a talk I would come in and agree with him on their proposition for Phinney, we were then to go to Caldwell at the Tefft House, where Mr. Caldwell agreed that if he would use his influence in bringing the Kaw Lands into market. Mr. Simcock and I went to Mr. Caldwell's room, and Caldwell agreed to use his influence to bring these lands into market; then Mr. Phinney promised each of us, Simcock and me, that he would vote for Caldwell.

Q. Do you know what arrangement was made between Mr. Phinney, Mr. Simcock and Mr. Columbia?

A. No, sir.

Q. They never told you?

A. No, sir; I never asked them.

By the Chairman.

Q. What was George Smith doing here.

A. I cannot tell what he was doing but suppose he was working in the interest of Caldwell's election.

By Senator Whitney.

Q. Were you here in Topeka during the Senatorial election of 1867?

A. Yes, sir.

Q. Do yo know of any money or other corrupt means being used at that time to influence votes for Senator?

A. No, sir; I do not.

JAMES PHINNEY,

Having been sworn, testified as follows:

By Senator Stover.

Q. Were you a member of the Legislature last winter?

A. Yes, sir.

Q. Were you here during the Senatorial campaign?

A. Yes.

Q. Do you know of any money, or other valuable consideration, being offered to members of the Legislature to secure their votes?

A. No; only myself.

Q. Please state to the Committee the circumstances.

A. Mr. Sidney Clarke came to me when I was eating supper one evening, and asked me why I did not go to his room. I said to him that he had men enough there to do his business without me; and then he inquired the number of my room, and the number of Senator Stover's room at the same time; said he would come to my room and see me. Then I did not see Mr. Clarke until—I don't recollect what day it was—a day or two before the Senatorial election. He passed through the hall, in the Tefft House, just as I was going out of the door. He asked me if that was my room; I told him it was. Then he wanted me to step back into the room, and wanted to talk with me a few minutes; said he was in a hurry, and I said I was also; that I had but a few minutes to talk. He wanted to know then what I was going to do about voting for Senator; I told him I had made up my mind to support Governor Crawford for Senator. That seemed to surprise him. He stated that would not do at all; I must vote for him. I told him that I did not think so: that I should vote for Crawford; had made up my mind to do that. He then wanted to know what was the matter, and said he had calculated on my vote, and wanted to know why I was not going to vote for him. I told him I would not vote for him or any other man who thought there were certain parties who, as they represented, could control my vote. He said there was nobody representing that they could control my vote. I told him that then I had been very much mistaken in thinking so, but I still thought so. He wanted to know then what was the matter, and said he had calculated upon my vote, as before. I told him that there were a great many of my friends "out there" who supported him, and I told him that I myself was one of them; that I had supported him five or six years, thinking we were going to get our homes there. I told him that he had never done anything for our county; that he had never bestowed any political patronage upon us or anything of the kind. He said: "Now, Mr. Phinney, I want to satisfy you. I want you to vote for me, and anything I can do for you, I will." He told me then that he would give me a position in the Land Office if I wanted it; stated that was one of the best offices in the state; that it paid $3,000 a year. He said the position had been offered to Maxon once, and he would not accept it. I asked him then if he would give me the old man Aikin's place. He said: "No; but I will do this, Mr. Phinney: I will give you a position in the Augusta, or the Humboldt, or the Junction City Land Office, and (says he) your expenses shall all be paid." He said: "I durst not do it myself, but I will speak to Dan Adams to do it." That is what I said as near as I can recollect. He then asked me: "Is that satisfactory to you?" I said, "That is satisfactory." I did not tell him I would vote for him. That is about the conversation as near as I can recollect. I never saw Mr. Clarke again until after the Senatorial election.

Q. Was the understanding when you were elected a year ago last fall, that you were to vote for Mr. Clarke?

A. I did not understand it so, and I have affidavits with me here of the two parties that I was pledged to the contrary before I was elected. The parties are Isaac Baxter, of Car's Creek, Morris county; and Mr. Heabrink, of Council Grove. One of these pledges I made before I was nominated for Representative, and the other after I was nominated and before I was elected.

Q. Did Mr. Clarke make a direct statement to you that if you would vote for him he would secure this position in the Land Office for you, and pay your election expenses?

A. Yes, sir.

By Senator Whitney.

Q. Were you in Topeka during the Senatorial election of 1867?

A. I was in Kansas, but not in Topeka, and I know nothing about that election.

By Mr. Johnson.

Q. Whom did you support for United States Senator?

A. I supported Mr. Crawford. Mr. Crawford on the first ballot, and Mr. Caldwell on the second.

Q. Did Mr. Caldwell make you any promises?

A. No, sir.

Q. Did you have a talk with Mr. Sincock in the Fifth Avenue Hotel, in connection with another gentleman?

A. Yes, Sir.

Q, Did you and Mr. Sincock, and Mr. Columbia have a conversation at the Fifth Avenue by yourselves?

A. I do not recollect that he had.

Q. Did you and Mr. Columbia, Mr. Sincock, and Mr. Hammond go from the Fifth Avenue to the Tefft House, that day?

A. Well, I cannot be positive; we went several times, but I would not be positive as to that day. My impression is that we did.

Q. In that interview with Mr. Caldwell did he make you any promises?

A. Mr. Caldwell never made me any promise any more than that if he were elected, he would do the best he could for our part of the country.

Q. Was there any particular thing specified?

A. If he were elected he would bring those Indian lands into market.

JOHN P. USHER,

Having been sworn, testified as follows:

Examined by the Chairman.

Q. Did you hear any conversation at any time between Mr. Perry, President of the Kansas Pacific and Mr. Alexander Caldwell in relation to the payment of any money by the company as a part of the expense of the election of Mr. Caldwell for United States Senator?

A. I did not. I do not think I have seen them together since the election.

Q. Did you have any conversation with Mr. Perry, President of the road, in which he stated that Mr. Caldwell claimed that the road should pay an amount of money to go to pay his election expenses?

A. Yes, I did.

Q. When and where was that conversation?

A. According to my recollection it was the last time I saw Mr. Perry. I met him up the road in a car when he was coming down from Denver the other day.

Q. What did Mr. Perry tell you?

A. He said (as well as I can remember,) that after Caldwell's election, he went up to Leavenworth to see him, and congratulate him on his election, and to his surprise Caldwell told him that he wanted him to pay $30,000, which he, (Mr. Perry,) declined to pay. Mr. Perry said he was very much surprised at the demand, and so expressed himself to Caldwell, intimating that as he had been successful, and had been elected United States Senator, that was honor enough, without making a demand of that sort of him, and he should not respond to it at all.

Q. Did Mr. Perry in that conversation say anything about seeing Colonel Dennis and Mr. Anderson in regard to any promises which Mr. Caldwell claimed to have been made by these gentlemen for the Kansas Pacific Railroad?

A. Yes, he did.

Q. State what.

A. He said, as I understood him, that Caldwell claimed that he was justified in making that demand in consequence of some promise that he had had here from Mr. Perry's friends.

Q. Are you able to state any other part of that conversation which you have not already stated, Judge?

A. He said that he did not believe it, and they would come up here and see whether it was so or not; he wanted to know. Accordingly they did come. Len Smith and Caldwell came, as I understand.

Q. Do you know what the result of the inquiry was?

A. He said that these gentlemen did not admit what Caldwell said, but did not stand as square as he would have liked them; that he was not satisfied but that there might have been something said, but at any rate he would not pay anything.

Q. Did Mr. Perry, in any part of this conversation, state to you the ground or the purpose upon which or for which Caldwell made this demand?

A. I don't know as he did. I do not know as he said why, or whether he was out so much, or what he said about it. At any rate he was importunate for the money, and came once or twice about it.

Q. Did Mr. Perry state what Caldwell claimed the promise was that he said was made by Dennis and Anderson?

A. I do not think Mr. Perry explained that.

MOSES NEAL.

Having been sworn, testified as follows:

Examined by Mr. Whitney.

Q. Do you know Dr. McCartney?

A. I do.

Q. Were you here last winter during the Senatorial election?

A. I was.

Q. Did Dr. McCartney have any conversation with you in regard to the Senatorial election?

A. Yes.

Q. State what it was.

A. Dr. McCartney told me that he was at a loss whom to vote for, and said he felt inclined to support Mr. Clarke, but he remarked, that "the other side" was offering pretty good figures. I asked him what he could get. He said that he had been offered $2,500.

Q. Who did he mean by the "other side?"

A. I understood from what he said that it was—well, we were talking about Clarke and Caldwell, and my understanding was that it was Caldwell, although he did not say.

Q. You were talking about no one else than Clarke and Caldwell?

A. No, sir.

Q. Did he say what he intended to do about it?

A. He did not, but again remarked that he would prefer to vote for Clarke.

Q. Was there anything more of that conversation?

A. He said that he would rather vote for Clarke by $1,000. I told him that I did not believe that Clarke would give it.

Q. What did he reply to that?

A. I could not say.

Q. Was this conversation before any vote had been had at all?

A. It was.

Q. Any other talk with him on the same subject afterwards?

A. I think I told him, either at that time or afterwards, that if I were in his place I would vote for Clarke on the first ballot any way. He said that he "felt to do it," as he thought that his constituents would prefer that he should.

Q. Did you have any other conversation with him on the same subject?

A. Nothing, I think, but, perhaps, just about the same. Nor anything after the election.

Q. Did he tell you who offered him this $2,500?

A. He did not. His remark was "the other side."

Q. Do you know whether he got any money?

A. I do not.

Q. Did you ever here any one say that he did get any money?

A. I did not.

Q. Do you know of any money or other corrupt offer being made to influence votes?

A. Only by hearsay.

F. A. ATHERLEY,

Having been re-called, testified as follows:

Examined by Chairman.

Q. State whether or not you know of Mr. Butler, a Representative from Coffey county in the Legislature in the session of 1871, receiving any valuable consideration for his vote for United States Senator at that time?

A. Of my own knowledge I do not.

Q. Did you ever make any inquiry or investigation in any of the Lawrence banks of this State, and find there that checks had been cashed—drawn—in favor of Mr. Butler about the time of that Senatorial election?

A. I have not

Q. Have you any knowledge whatever of his receiving any money or any checks in consideration of his vote?

A. None at all.

FRIDAY EVENING, February 16, 1872.

I. S. KALLOCH,

Having been sworn, testified thus:

Examined by the Chairman.

Q. Were you here at Topeka during the Senatorial election of last winter?

A. I was.

Q. Do you know Alexander Caldwell?

A. I do.

Q. Do you know whether he used any money in that canvass or not?

A. I do not know.

Q. Do you know whether any one used money for him?

A. I do not.

Q. Do you know Len Smith?

A. I do.

Q. Was he here?

A. He was.

Q. What was he doing?

A. I do not know.

Q. Was he doing anything here?

A. I do not know what he was doing particularly.

Q. Did you have any conversation with him at the time he was here during the winter?

A. I had no more, I think, than passing the time of day with him.

Q. Did you have any conversation with Caldwell?

A. Yes.

Q. In relation to what?

A. Well, I conversed with him often in relation to the campaign and its prospects.

Q. In any of those conversations was there anything said about the use of money or other valuable consideration for the purpose of influencing votes?

A. Nothing at all with reference to the use of money.

Q. In reference to anything else that was valuable?

A. I do not recollect of anything.

Q. Do you know whether Sidney Clarke had any money to use in that campaign?

A. Sidney Clarke said to me at one time that he had "perfected arrangements" by which he could take care of that portion of the Legislature that might be for sale.

Q. When was that conversation?

A. That was in Lawrence a few days before the Senatorial contest.

Q. Did he at that time or any other time tell you what those arrangements were?

A. No, sir.

Q. Did you at that time or any other time ascertain from him or from any other source what those arrangements were?

A. No, I cannot say that I did. I have no positive knowledge.

Q Do you know of any other of the candidates using money or proposing to use money or other valuable consideration to secure votes than the two that I have mentioned?

A. I do not.

Q. Did you ever have any talk with John McDowell with regard to the Senatorial election?

A. I do not recollect of any. I might have had, but do not recollect.

Q. Have you had any conversation with members of the Legislature since the election of Caldwell in which they stated that money was paid or offered to be paid to them to secure their votes?

A. No, sir.

Q. Have you no knowledge at all Mr. Kalloch about the use of money in that contest by Mr. Caldwell or his friends for or in the interests of Mr. Caldwell?

A. Not the slightest particle that I recollect of or know.

By W. H. Clark.

Q. Do you know whether Gov. Carney before the election loaned any money to any parties who were then candidates for the Legislature?

A. I do not.

Q. Do you know of his giving any money?

A. I do not.

Q. Or any checks, drafts, or any evidences of indebtedness?

A. I don't know.

Q. Do you know of any agreement between Mr. Caldwell and Mr. Carney made during the Senatorial campaign of last winter?

A. I know nothing of it personally.

Q. Do you know of Mr. Caldwell paying any money to any newspapers in the State to secure their support for him for Senator?

A. I do not.

By Mr. Johnson.

Q. Mr. Kalloch, in whose interest were you working during the Senatorial election last winter?

A. Mr. Caldwell's.

Q. Did you have a conversation with Len Smith in regard to the Senatorial election last winter during the pendency of the election?

A. I must have had some conversations with Len Smith, but don't recollect anything particular about it.

Q. Did Len Smith ever tell you anything about the means that were being used to secure the election of Mr. Caldwell?

A. No, sir.

Q. Did you talk with him frequently on that subject?

A. No, sir.

Q. Did you ever have a talk with Tom Anderson with regard to the Senatorial election?

A. I presume I did during its pendency, but recollect the particulars of no conversation.

Q. Do you know of Mr. Caldwell, Mr. Len Smith, or Mr. Tom Anderson ever making any promise of money or other valuable consideration to any member or members of the Legislature for their support of Mr. Caldwell?

A. I do not.

Q. Was your connection or intimacy with those parties such that you would be likely to have known if any such transactions had transpired?

A. I should not have known of any such transaction.

Q. Why?

A. Well, I would not.

Q. Do you know of any arrangement whereby certain persons were not to know of those transactions?

A. No; I do not.

By J. Boynton.

Q. Mr. Kalloch, what influences were used to secure the election of Mr. Caldwell?

A. Well, I used all the influence I could to get men to support him, because I thought he was the best man we could get under the circumstances, by talking with them. What influences other men used I am not posted in.

Q. Was Mr. Caldwell a politician?

A. Something of a politician, I think.

Q. What were his politics?

A. He presided at a Republican meeting that I addressed in Leavenworth some two or three years before his election.

Q. Were you here at the Senatorial election of 1867?

A. I believe I was.

Q. Do you know of any money, or other corrupt influence being used in that election by any of the candidates.

A. No; I cannot say that I do.

Q. What did you ever hear about it?

A. I heard Perry Fuller say that he came here to put somebody there for the Senate—came here prepared to do it: if that is an answer to the question. I do not know that anybody paid or received any money at that time of my own knowledge.

Q. Did Perry Fuller say what means he had for putting any man there?

A. Yes, he did. He said he had money enough to "put a man through."

Q. Did Fuller say he was going to use the money for that purpose.

A. He did.

Q. Do you know in whose interest he was working.

A. Yes; I suppose I do.

Q. For whom.

A. For Mr. Ross. At the time of the conversation he had with me, he was not working for any one, but afterward he supported Mr. Ross.

By the Chairman.

Q. Did the friends of Mr. Ross, who were members of the Legislature, support any other candidate for the Senate at that election?

A. I think they did.

Q. Whom?

A. Mr. Pomeroy.

Q. Was the election of Mr. Pomeroy and Mr. Ross, at that time, the result of a combination of the supporters of Mr. Ross and the supporters of Mr. Pomeroy?

A. Well, I think not.

Q. How long did Fuller get here before the election?

A. I do not recollect exactly, but think it was only a few days.

Q. How long were you here during last winter, at the time of the election of Mr. Caldwell?

A. I was here most of the time from the assembling of the Legislature to the time of the election.

Q. Were you here upon any other business than to aid in the election of Mr. Caldwell?

A. I was not.

Q. Did he pay your expenses while here?

A. He did pay them.

Q. Did he promise or pay you any other recompense?

A. No, sir.

Q. Did you ever have any arrangement with Mr. Caldwell by which, in the event if he was elected to the United States Senate, you were to receive any valuable consideration for what services you might render in securing that election?

A. No; I never did.

Q. Do you know of any one who had such or similar arrangements with him for the purpose?

A. I do not.

By Senator Whitney.

Q. When Perry Fuller told you, in 1867, that he had money enough to "put a man through," please define what you mean, or what you understood him to mean, by that expression?

A. Why, I understood him to mean what he said; that is, elect a man Senator.

Q. Did he at any time decide upon his nominee?

A. I think not.

Q. Do you know what time relative to the election he decided to take up Ross?

A. Well, it was very soon after his arrival; I think at the day of his arrival at Topeka.

Q. Do you know how much money he used in that election?

A. I do not; I do not know that he used any money.

By Mr. Johnson.

Q. How much were your expenses here last winter, Mr. Kalloch?

A. I do not know. By board and many extras, I would say in reference to a former answer I have given, that I always presumed that Mr. Caldwell paid my expenses—I never paid them myself.

Q. Do you know what your expenses were while you were here?

A. I do not know the price of board at the time, but it would be no more than the board during the time I was here.

MONDAY, February 19, 1872.

WILLIAM SPRIGGS,

Being sworn, testified as follows:

Examined by the Chairman.

Q. Where do you live?

A. Near Garnett, Kansas.

Q. Were you here last winter during the Senatorial election, and if so, do you know of the use of any money in that election to influence the votes of members on the vote for United States Senator?

A. I was here; I do not know of my own knowledge.

Q. Did any one tell you of the use of money in that election? If so, state what was told you—state all about it?

A. Well, Frank Drenning said that he placed two thousand dollars in the hands of the Treasurer of Nemaha county to be delivered to the two members of the House from Nemaha county if they voted for Mr. Caldwell for Senator; that if Mr. Caldwell had not been so slow, he would have got them for $1,000—five hundred each. After the election was over, Mr. T. J. Anderson wanted me to take an order to Garnett on Mr. Carson. He said a member from Linn county (Crocker, I think,) had received of him one thousand dollars to vote for Mr. Caldwell. He said that Jas. D. Snoddy had brought such pressure upon Crocker that he had backed down and got alarmed, and delivered the $1,000 to Carson, to be delivered to him (Anderson,) and Carson had failed to do it. I refused to take the order. George Smith, of Leavenworth, Kansas, told me that he had paid out little over twenty thousand dollars to different members of the Legislature for their votes for Mr. Caldwell. That it was his own money; that he paid it at the request of Mr. Caldwell, and that Mr. Caldwell was to refund it to him.

Q. Did Drenning say where he got the money, or who authorized him to pay or deposit the money?

A. He said Caldwell could have saved one-half of this sum if he had not been so slow.

Q. Did Anderson say he had paid part of the money to Crocker, or that he had paid it to him through Carson?

A. I can't be positive about that, but the impression is that he had paid it to Crocker himself.

Q. State, if you know, what Len T. Smith was doing here last winter during the Senatorial canvass?

A. He was engineering Mr. Caldwell's election. I think Len T. Smith and Caldwell roomed together. I supposed Len T. Smith to be Caldwell's heaviest banker.

Q. Were you here during the Senatorial election of 1867?

A. Yes.

Q. Do you know of any money or other corrupt influences being used to secure votes of the members of the Legislature for candidates for the United States Senate?

A. Not of my own knowledge.

Q. What have you heard in regard to such influences being then used?

A. The only thing direct was from Perry Fuller. He told me the evening after the election of United States Senator, that Pomeroy and Ross' election had cost him forty-two thousand dollars. He told me he considered he had made fifty-eight thousand dollars; that he had set apart one hundred thousand, and had got through with forty-two thousand dollars. He said he had left Kansas and established himself in New York city in business, and his object was to control the entire Indian trade of the West; that if Tom Carney was elected with such a house as he had at the door of the Indians, he would at least divide that trade with him. He said that trade was worth a half million dollars annually.

Q. Did he speak of any particular case?

A. No.

Q: Was Perry Fuller working for Pomeroy as well as for Ross in that canvass?

A. He was apparently as earnestly.

Q. For whom were you working last winter in the canvass?

A. I just came here with a view of working for Governor Crawford; If Carney was a candidate, I intended to work for him. I thought Governor Crawford had no chance, and I went to work for Caldwell about a week before the election.

Q. Did Anderson tell you whose money the $1,000 that he wanted you to get of Carson, was?

A. No, he did not; I think I learned from him at that time, or at some other time that the Kansas Pacific Railway Company was assisting Caldwell.

WILSON SHANNON, JR.,

Having been sworn, testified as follows:

By the Chairman.

Q. Where do you reside?

A. At Lawrence.

Q. Were you here during the Senatorial election of 1871, and if so, you may state what you know about money or improper influences being used in that canvass and election to secure votes?

A. I was here during all that Senatorial contest. A few days before the Senatorial election took place, Mr. W. H. Peckham, then a member of the Legislature, came to me in this city; he told me that if Clarke did not come down within the next twenty four hours he was going over to Caldwell. He wanted me to so notify Clarke or his friends; I was going for the train and I went to Lawrence; when I returned the next week Mr. Peckham was a strong Caldwell man; sometime after that, shortly after the Legislature adjourned, I met him in Lawrence, and he then told me he was sorry he voted for Caldwell, and if he had known what he knew then, he would have voted for some one else. He made several trips to Leavenworth ,and he stepped off and told me what I have stated.

By Senator Stover.

Q. Did Mr. Peckham give you to understand that he wanted money from Clarke before he would vote for him?

A. Yes, he did.

Q. Did you understand that Sidney Clarke had money to use in that contest, and if so, how did you get that information or understanding?

A. Sidney Clarke came to my law-office, in Lawrence, a few days before the Legislature met, and he told me he had secured a certain number of rooms in the Tefft House for the benefit of his friends. He told me he had from forty to fifty thousand dollars to secure his election, and that he could get all the money that was necessary from his friends east; I understood at that time it was from Washington. He told me that he was satisfied that the Senatorial election was a question of dollars and cents, and the man that had the most money was going to win, and told me he was going to start what I call a "bread riot" the "soup house" on the corner. I had told Peckham what Clarke had told me. Mr. Peckham told me he had spent several hundred dollars to secure his election and he wanted to make himself whole, if not a litte more so; and after the thing had run along here for ten days, and said if Mr. Clarke did not come down with some of that money he had, he should go over to Caldwell. Clarke often talked and gave me his plans, and gave me to understand that he had money enough to buy his way through and was going to do it, or try to.

Q. Did Sidney Clarke give you to understand that Senator Pomeroy was to furnish him money if he needed it?

A. Yes, that is what I understood from his conversations. He said he could raise so much money in Kansas and, if he needed more; I understood from him that was to call on Pomeroy and he would furnish it.

Q. Do you know of any cases where money was paid to members of the Legislature to vote for Caldwell or Clarke or any other person?

A. Not of my own knowledge.

Q. Have you reliable information that money was used to secure votes.

A. I am morally satisfied that there was, and along in the forepart of January, 1872, I came up to Topeka to file briefs, and met T. J. Anderson at the Kansas Pacific depot, and he came up to me and congratulated me on the stand and opened up on the Caldwell bribery; told me he knew all about the members who had sold out and the amount paid to each one; and that he had a list in writing of the names who had sold out, and that he would give it to me for publication in our paper if Caldwell and Len T. Smith did not come down during that week. Told me he was going down to Leavenworth to see them about the matter that week, and if they did not settle up he would give me the list for publication in our paper. He said, Wils, it puts me in a bad shape. I promised a good many things and they have gone back on me, and it leaves me in a bad shape, and he could not stand it, and he would give me the list for publication. He said he was going to get even with those fellows. I went home, and in a week or so we came out in an article on the "Caldwell Bribery," as we called it, and mentioned Anderson's house. I then met him afterwards at Cline's restaurant, and he said, you fellows have played hell, putting my house in the papers; Len Smith sent me word that it was all fixed up, and he had nothing more to say about it. This was the evening of the complimentary oyster supper at Cline's during this session. Since that time Tom Anderson and I have had no conversation about this. He would not talk about it.

Q. Do you know where W. H. Carson is, and had you any conversation with him about testifying before this Committee?

A. I don't know where he is only from information, and that is that he is in Missouri. I had quite a long conversation with him about testifying before the Committee.

Q. State all that conversation?

A. Mr. Carson came into my law office in Lawrence last week. He told me he had been subpœned before this Committee, and wanted to know what the punishment would be if he did not answer questions if he was brought before the Committee I told him if he refused to answer questions the Committee would report him to the Legislature, and the Legislature would order him to be brought before the body for contempt. He said he would go to jail rather than he would answer any questions, and that he notified his wife that if she heard of his being in jail she need not be alarmed. I told him the punishment the Legislature could inflict for not answering was to confine him during its session. He said he was coming up here and was going to lay around a day or two, and asked if Caldwell was paying anything to witnesses for not testifying. I told him I did not know. He said he thought he would go to Missouri, after I told him what the penalty would be.

Q. Did any one else tell that members had sold out, and if so, who so told you? State all about it.

A. Tom Anderson had a list, and Prentis told me Tom Anderson had a list of those who sold out, and finally Sidney Clarke come to our law office with Mr. Cree on Monday evening, the 15th of January, 1872. Mr. Clarke proposed to furnish the list of the members of the Legislature who sold out in the Senatorial election of 1871, and taking the statutes of 1871, in which is a list of the names of the members of the Legislature of that year, he marked or checked off the names of those he said sold out to Caldwell, which are as follows: G. W. Hogeboom, Sol Miller, J. Wood, A. Barber, A. W. Bayer, Abram Bennett, W. C. Butts, C. B. Butler, R. E. Cable, E. H. Cawker, Felix T. Gandy, J. B. Kennedy, John G. Lindsay, J. M. Luce, E. C. Manning, A. A. Moore, T. H. Moore, James Phinney, E. Warner, H. P. Welsh, S. G. Whittaker, J. L. Williams, Wm. Williams, and John Willitts. This is the list that was furnished to us together with a list of witnesses by whom he said it could be proven that those members had sol out to Caldwell.

Q. Did Mr. Clarke give you any statement of any particular case.

Q. Yes; he gave us the statements as pubulished in the *Democratic Standard*, of January 18, 1872, except as to D. B. Johnson and W. H. Peckham. The statements in that article are published notes of the verbal statements made by Clarke, taken at the time he made them.

Q. Did you have any conversation with Len T. Smith about the election of Caldwell? If so, state what it was.

A. Len told me he was going to elect Caldwell, and said they had all the money and everythnig else they wanted and were going to elect him.

Q. Do you know a man by the name of Hopkins an insurance agent from Leavenworth? If so, what was he doing here last winter?

A. I do know him; judging from what I saw of him he was here to secure the election of Alexander Caldwell; I saw him working for Caldwell; and if Len Smith wanted to talk to a member of the Legislature confidentially he could see him in his room, and let Hopkins talk to him. He was one of the most active workers for Caldwell, and during the night before the final vote I saw him talking to members in the House, and go into their rooms, and pass back and forth to and from Caldwell's room out into the hall, and into the members' rooms; that night he was more active than any man in the Tefft House, and for a week before he was one among the most active men for Caldwell.

TUESDAY, February 20, 1872.

J. B. DAVIS,

Having been sworn, testified thus:

By the Chairman.

Q. Where do you reside?

A. Augusta, Butler county, Kansas.

Q. Were you here last winter during the Senatorial canvass, and, if so, do you know of money, or other improper influences, being used by any one to secure votes for United States Senator?

A. Of my own knowledge, I do not.

Q. Did you ever have any conversation with any one who professed to know, and who stated that money was so used? If so, state with whom and what the conversation was.

A. I had a conversation with some one, I do not remember with whom, and we were discussing how much it cost Caldwell to get elected, and we differed as to the amount. I claimed that it cost him nearly or quite one hundred thousand dollars, and the other party claimed that it cost him somewhere in the neighborhood of fifty thousand dollars, and we agreed to leave it to T. J. Anderson to say which was nearest right. I afterwards met T. J. Anderson on the street and asked him to tell me which was the nearest right as to the amount, at the time stating the conversation between me and this other party, and Mr. Anderson said in substance that my estimate was the nearest correct, and that it cost Mr. Caldwell in the neighborhood of ninety thousand dollars.

Q. Did you hear or have a conversation with any other person on this subject? If so, state what that conversation was?

A. I heard a conversation in Kansas City between Mr. R. T. Vandoren, Mr. Sidney Clarke and John Hutchins, about the time this session of the Legislature convened, in which it was stated by some of the parties that Dr. Morris, an officer in some Leavenworth bank, let Caldwell have about thirty-five thousand dollars, and that they had some trouble about currency, and came to Kansas City to get it. It was also stated that Dr. Morris would be a good witness as he could tell something about Caldwell's bank account at that time. During the Senatorial contest last winter I had a conversation with Mr. Sidney Clarke concerning the so called "merchantable members" in which Mr. Clarke told me that some of his friends had secured the Doniphan county delegation to vote for him for Senator and the money was paid to them; that they afterwards returned the money to his friends and accepted a higher bid from Caldwell or his friends. I understood from Clarke or some one else that the Doniphan delegation had determined to go in a body. Mr. Clarke told me that he thought that either twelve or fourteen thousand dollars, (he was not certain which,) had been paid to secure the Doniphan delegation for Mr. Caldwell.

EDWARD RUSSELL,

Having been sworn, testified as follows:

Examined by the Chairman.

Q. Did you ever have any conversation with S. C. Pomeroy in relation to the Senatorial election of 1867? If so, state that conversation?

A. I had conversations with Senator Pomeroy in relation to that election; I could not narrate all of them. Senator Pomeroy made this remark to me when we were together in his room at the Capital House in Topeka: that he had spent a fortune in defeating Thomas Carney for the United States Senate, at the same time he pointed to his check book then lying on the table. I remember no other remark that I am positive of.

Q. When was this conversation?

A. It was either just before or just after the vote in the Joint Convention by which E. G. Ross was elected.

Q. Was it before or after Pomeroy was elected?

A. That I cannot say. My impression is that it was before—in the night—about midnight; but I wont be positive of that.

Q. Was Carney at that time a candidate against Pomeroy?

A. He was.

Q. Was it known the night before the vote in Joint Convention at that election who would probably be elected on the next day in the Joint Convention?

A. It was an absolute certainty that Pomeroy would be elected or it was so regarded.

Q. Do you know anything about Perry Fuller's connection with the Senatorial election of 1867? If so, state all you know in that regard, and what you saw him do?

A. I know that he was in very frequent conference with Senator Pomeroy. My impression is that they occupied rooms together or adjacent to each other, and in going into Pomeroy's room both day and night at almost all hours I found Perry Fuller there and in consultation with Senator Pomeroy. On one or two occasions I saw him take what, from its general appearance, seemed to be a check-book, and delivering it to some one in my presence and the presence of Senator Pomeroy.

Q. When, with reference to the election of Senator Pomeroy and Ross, were these consultations and this check drawn?

A. Before the election of either of them.

E. C. MANNING,

Having been sworn, testified as follows:

Examined by the Chairman.

Q. Where do you live?

A. I live in Winfield, Cowley county, Kansas.

Q. Were you here last winter during the Senatorial contest. If so, in what capacity, and what, if anything, do you know of money or other improper influence being used, or offered to be used, by any candidate or his friends for him, to secure votes for United States Senator?

A. I was here last winter as Representative of Cowley

county. A certain gentleman offered me eighteen hundred dollars or thereabouts to vote for Mr. Caldwell for United States Senator. He offered to lift a note in bank that was overdue that he knew I could not lift. I don't recollect what the exact amount of the note and the interest on it was, but it was in the neighborhood of eighteen hundred dollars.

Q. Who was the gentleman who made you that offer?

A. I decline to answer that question.

[Whereupon the Committee, by vote, required Mr. Manning to answer. Whereupon Mr. Manning still refused to answer.]

Q. What further did he say to you in regard to that offer?

A. He told me to call on Tom Anderson, and he would give me the note if I accepted the proposition. I replied that I would be a bankrupt before I would accept such a proposition, and he replied that I was a fool, and then asked me what I would take and vote as he proposed.

Q. When, with reference to the election, was this offer?

A. It was the evening before the first vote for Senator.

Q. Where was that note at the time of this conversation?

A. It was at the Topeka Bank, I suppose. It was payable to the Topeka Savings Bank.

Q. Did you have any conversation with Sidney Clarke last winter in regard to the Senatorial election? If so, state what it was?

A. He told me about a week before the first vote that he expected a man here on Wednesday with plenty of money to be used in securing his election. He said he would have one hundred and fifty thousand dollars to back him, (Clarke). That party's name was Bob Stevens. Two or three days after that he authorized me to say to any member of the Legislature who would vote for him, that if they would vote for him for United State Senator, and he was elected, that each member so doing should be paid whatever price they asked. I did not make any such proposition to any member. He asked me once or twice if I knew of any members whose votes could be secured for him with money. About this time or a short time previous I had asked Mr. Clarke to loan me one thousand dollars, with which to make a part payment upon the note I had in the bank which I have mentioned, I stating to him distinctly that I had made an arrangement with Mr. G. W. Veale, of this place, to endorse my note that I should give him (Clarke) for the one thousand dollars, which loan was to have been for one or two years time, with interest at ten per cent. I stated to Clarke my circumstances, and that I asked this of him as a friend; that my desire was to get this note out of bank, where it was drawing one and one-half per cent. per month; that Mr. G. W. Veale was my endorser upon my eighteen hundred dollar note, and had proposed that if I could borrow the one thousand dollars he would endorse for me, and would take the note out of bank for me, and would take some property which I proposed to throw over to him for the balance due upon the note. Clarke told me he thought he would let me have the money, and for me to see Dan Adams; that he thought I could get the money of him. I called on Adams, and he said he could not let me have the money. I told Veale of my failure and asked him if he knew anywhere else where the money could be had. I did not ask this loan in consideration of any service it could render him in the Senatorial election.

Q. Did you ever demand of Sidney Clarke at any time any money or other valuable thing in consideration of your voting for him for United States Senator last winter?

A. I did not.

Q. Did you ever narrate this statement in regard to this thousand dollars before to-night?

A. Yes, I have. Perhaps not in the same words. I told it to friends of mine in Cowley county.

Q. Did Clarke tell you that Bob Stevens was going to back him up with money?

A. He told me that a man would be here on Wednesday with one hundred and fifty thousand dollars and that that man was Bob Stevens.

WEDNESDAY, February 21, 1872.

D. R. ANTHONY RE-CALLED.

Examined by the Chairman.

Q. Did you ever have any conversation with Senator Pomeroy in relation to the election of 1867, in which there was anything said about the use of money on his part, in that election? If so, state all of that conversation.

A. I cannot state all of that conversation, for I do not remember it.

Q. State what part you do remember.

A. As far as the part of the conversation that relates to money, he said it cost him a good deal of money. That is about the substance of what was said about the use of money. The most he specified was his hotel bill, which he spoke of as large through paying for so many there.

Q. Did you ever have any conversation with Perry Fuller in relation to that election, and the use of money therein by him for any one else? If so, state what that conversation was.

A. I did. I had a conversation with him in Dan Adam's Bank, and at other places. While in the bank he showed me a check book in which were the stumps of twenty odd checks, (I did not count them,) amounting he said to about eleven thousand dollars which he had paid to secure Ross' election and he told me what bank it was on; my idea was that it was on some banking firm in New York; but my memory is indistinct on that; he told me the names of the members of the Legislature at the time, and in whose favor those checks were drawn.

Q. Have you any other knowledge of the use of money in that Senatorial contest? If so, state.

A. The balance is only hearsay.

FRIDAY, Feburary 23, 1871.

W. G. RAYMOND,

Having been sworn, testified as follows:

Examined by the Chairman.

Q. Were you here last winter during the Senatorial contest?

A. Yes, sir·

Q. Do you know Len Smith, and did you see him last winter?

A. I do, and saw him here.

Q. Did you ever have any conversation with him in relation to that Senatorial contest? If so, state when, and what it was, and all the circumstances which transpired in connection with it.

A. He had a conversation with me at the Tefft House in the hall between the rooms of Caldwell, Walker and Crawford. I was near by him, and started to go to the room of Mr. Walker; he threw his right arm over me and led me up toward the wall. He says don't leave yet; we are dead broke just now, but as quick as Tom Anderson returns from the bank or depot, (I don't recollect which he said,) we will have plenty of greenbacks to carry the matter through. My recollection is that the money he spoke of getting, he said, was railroad funds. I know he spoke of some particular fund, and think it was railroad funds. I left immediately, and went into Caldwell's reception room to see if I could see anything. In a few moments Major left Caldwell's reception room and went out, going down stairs. I remained in the room for sometime; Major Anderson returned; Mr Caldwell was in the reception room, and he locked arms with Anderson, and went into his private room. They were in the room from five to ten minutes, and Anderson came out; I looked to see if I could see any greenbacks on or about the Major when he came in, and saw that his coat on the left breast had the appearence of having something in the inside breast pocket of considerable size; and when he came out that appearence was gone, and his coat was alike on both sides. I remained in the reception room for perhaps an hour or two. I think that Mr. Caldwell remained for that time in the private room during which time; over a half dozen of members of the House went into the private room and come out in a short time, and I think some other citizens went in who were not members.

Q. Did more than one member go in Mr. Caldwell's private room that day while you were there, at a time.

A. I don't think there was but one at time.

Q. Can you fix the date of the transaction you have been relating?

A. As near as I can do it, it was the morning of the day before Mr. Caldwell's election, or it may have been the morning before that. It was one or the other of these days.

Q. Do you know why Len Smith spoke to you in the manner he did?

A. I don't know unless he was mistaken in the person he was talking to. I believe he mistook me for some one else I am led to this belief by his subsequent conduct toward me.

Q. Where do you reside?

A. At Auburn, Shawnee county, Kansas.

FRIDAY, February 23, 1872.

W. S. BANKS,

Having been sworn, testified as follows:

Examined by Chairman.

Q. Where do you reside?

A. In Leavenworth.

Q. Were you in Topeka during the Senatorial canvass of 1871?

A. No; none of the time.

Q. Did you ever have any conversation with Alexander Caldwell in regard to that canvass?

A. Yes; several of them.

Q. In any of those conversations, was there anything said by him about the use of money, in any way, to secure his election to the United States Senate?

A. Whatever was said in regard to the means used to secure his election was strictly in confidence.

Q. Please state what was said by him in regard to the means used to secure his election?

A. I decline to answer that question.

Moved by Mr. Johnson that the witnesses be compelled to answer the question. Motion put and carried unanimously. And the witness answered as follows:

A. In regard to that, the question is so broad that if I were to state all he said about all the means used to secure his election, it would take one all afternoon.

Q. Did he ever say anything to you about using or even having used money to secure his election to the United States Senate?

A. Yes.

Q. What did he say about using or having used money to secure his election to the United States Senate?

A. He said the campaign had cost him a great deal more than anybody had any idea of; told me he had to pay Thos. Carney's campaign expenses. He said the amount he paid Carney was not much more ten per cent. of the whole amount the campaign had cost him.

Q. Did he say what the whole amount was?

A. No; but he said if he could show me his check book I would be surprised at the amount it had cost him.

Q. Did he make any statement from which you could approximate the whole amount that the campaign cost him?

A. Nothing further than to say that it cost him about twice as much as the entire salary of the office would come to for the entire term of six years.

Q. What is the amount of the salary of the office for the term of six years, if you know?

A. I don't know, but understand it to be thirty thousand dollars, not including mileage.

Q. Did he say to whom this amount was paid, or in what manner this amount of money or any part of it was expended in the campaign?

A. He did not particularize any further than the one item I have mentioned, which he said was paid to Carney.

Q. When was this conversation?

A. In March of 1871—it may have been in February—it was shortly after his election.

Q. Did you ever have more than this one conversation with him about having used money to secure his election?

A. I had several conversations with him about having used money to secure his election?

Q. Did you ever have more than this one conversation with him about having used money to secure his election?

A. I had several conversations with him; I don't know that all which I have related was stated at one conversation. He his spoken to me repeatedly in general terms about the expense of the campaign.

Q. Were these conversations substantially the same or were they contradictory?

A. All of them were substantially the same.

Q. Did you know about the time of those conversations anything about Caldwell's financial affairs?

A. No, I did not know anything about them—only he said the campaign had left him very hard up.

Q. Did you ever hear him say anything about the cost of buying a Legislature of this State in a Senatorial canvass?

A. I cannot remember exactly what remark I have heard him make tending in that direction.

Q. Can you state the substance of those remarks?

A. Yes; that it was a costly business.

Q. Were those remarks made in connection with the conversation that you have related?

A. Yes.

Q. Did you ever have any talk with Len T. Smith about the canvass for and election of Caldwell to the United States Senate? If so, state what he said?

A. The only material point I remember is his conversation a few days after Caldwell's election. He said Mr. Caldwell felt very poor since his election because he said it cost like hell to buy a Legislature. I think he was drinking some at the time he made this remark.

Q. Do you know, or did Caldwell ever tell you what connection Len. T. Smith had with Caldwell's election?

A. I have heard Mr. Caldwell say that Len T. Smith managed things for him in that canvass and election. I judge from his (Len T. Smith's) conduct that he was interested in Caldwell's election.

By Mr. Johnson.

Q. In these conversations, did he say or intimate that any other parties had been or were to pay any part of the expenses of his election?

A. No.

Q. During any of these conversations did he say anything about the Kansas Pacific Railway Company assisting him or furnishing him any money to pay the expenses of his election?

A. No.

Q. Did he ever say anything about any person spending any money for him in securing his election?

A. He said that Len T. Smith, Lucian Scott and others had been liberal in spending money in connection with the campaign, but that he had always had to furnish the money

By Senator Stover.

Q. Do you know, or have you been informed, reliably, whether Mr. Caldwell or any of his agents or friends paid any money to buy parties since this investigation began on account of Caldwell's election?

A. All the information I have is through Colonel Anthony. He told me that Tom Anderson said he would not leave the State until he got his money from Caldwell or his agents; that he would not take any promises or notes, but must have the currency in hand. Anthony told me the next day after this conversation that Anderson told him he had got his money, and was going to leave. He said that Anderson said he had got the money from Lucian Scott. The amount which Anderson said he had received was five thousand dollars.

Q. When were these conversations?

A. About the 15th of February, 1872.

Q. Did you have conversations with Caldwell before the meeting of the Legislature of 1871, about the use of money to secure his election to the United States Senate?

A. He remarked to me once or twice before the canvass that it was going to cost him all his loose money. I was careful not to know anything about that; Len Smith seemed to be running that part of it.

Q. Have you heard or do you know of Caldwell or his friends using money or other influences to get witnesses to leave the State since this investigation began.

A. I have heard frequent rumors; it is the common talk in the city of Leavenworth, that Carney, T. J. Anderson and Len Smith have been induced to leave the State or remain away from the State on account of this investigation.

Q. Did you ever have any conversation with Thos. Moonlight about money being paid to members of the Legislature to induce them to vote for Caldwell? If so, state what he said.

A. Moonlight said he was witness to a transaction where money was paid by an agent of Caldwell's to one, or it may have been two members of the Legislature, to secure his or their votes for Caldwell for United States Senator.

Q. Did Mr. Caldwell ever pay, or offer to pay, you any money for your services in his behalf, in his election to the United States Senate?

A. He offered to pay me twenty-five hundred dollars last November. I did not accept his offer.

Q. Did he offer you money at other times on this account?

A. No.

CIVIL ACTION.

M. W. Reynolds vs. S. C. Pomeroy and Sidney Clarke.

Be it remembered that heretofore, to-wit, on the twenty-second day of February, A. D. 1870, and at the February Term, A. D. 1870, of the District Court, sitting in and for Douglas county, State of Kansas, among others, the following proceedings, to-wit, were had:

Milton W. Reynolds, plaintiff *vs.* Samuel C. Pomeroy and Sidney Clarke, defendants. Civil action.

This day came the said plaintiff, by Riggs, Nevison & Foote, his attorneys, and the said defendants, by their attorneys, A. H. Horton, Akin & Barker, and in open court the said parties waived a trial by jury in this action, and submitted the same to the court upon the issue joined between the parties, and the court, after hearing the evidence and arguments of counsel, do find as facts in this case as follows: That on the twelth (12) day of March, A. D. 1866, the defendants made the promissory notes as stated in the petition, and delivered the same to G. A. Reynolds, the agent of M. W. Reynolds; that the consideration for the notes was the promise on the part of M. W. Reynolds, through his agent, George A. Reynolds, to use his newspaper, the Lawrence *State Journal*, to influence the re-election of Sidney Clarke to Congress and the re-election of Samuel C. Pomeroy to the United States Senate; that M. W. Reynolds did, in pursuance of his agreements, endeavor to influence and secure the re-election of Sidney Clarke to Congress, up to the time of the nomination of Clarke by a convention of the delegates of a party of the people of Kansas in September, 1866, and did endeavor to influence and secure the re-election of Samuel C. Pomeroy to the United States Senate up to the time of the election of Pomeroy by the Legislature of the State of Kansas in January, A. D. 1867; and the court do therefore further find, as a conclusion of law in this case, that the contract attempted to be entered into was against public policy and void. It is, therefore, considered and adjudged by the court here that said plaintiff ought not to have his said action against the said defendants, or either of them; and it is, therefore, further ordered and adjudged by the court that the said defendants recover of said plaintiff the costs herein expended—taxed $. To all of which findings and judgment of this court the said plaintiff, by his counsel, duly excepted and gave notice of a motion for a new trial of said action.

STATE OF KANSAS, }
Douglas county, } I, B. D. Palmer, Clerk of the District Court, sitting within and for said county and State, hereby certify that the above and foregoing is a true and correct copy of the order and proceedings of the court in the above case as the same now appear of record in my office.

Witness my hand and the seal of said court this 21st day of February, A. D. 1872.

S. S. B. D. PALMER,
Clerk.

Depositions of sundry witnesses taken before me, Nicholas Callan, a Notary Public, in and for the county of Washington, in the District of Columbia, on the 31st day of January, 1870, between the hours of 8 o'clock, A. M., and six o'clock, P. M., at the office of said Nicholas Callan, No. 448, 15th street, in said county and district, pursuant to the annexed notice, to be read in evidence on behalf of the defendants in the cause pending in the Douglas county District Court, in Douglas county, State of Kansas, in which Milton W. Reynolds is plaintiff, and Samuel C. Pomeroy and Sidney Clarke are defendants in said cause.

Samuel C. Pomeroy, of lawful age, being by me first duly examined, cautioned and solemnly sworn, deposeth and saith: That his home is in Atchison county, in the State of Kansas, and that he has resided in said State since 1854; that he is now at Washington, D. C., in attendance upon the session of the Senate of the United States, and must of necessity remain at Washington, D. C., during all the present session of Congress, which will extend beyond March 1, 1870, and cannot be present at the February term, 1870, of the District Court of Douglas county, Kansas, on account of his public duties as such United States Senator from Kansas, and, further, that he knows the plaintiff, and signed the notes mentioned in the petition of the plaintiff in the above entitled suit; that there was no consideration paid to himself or to Mr. Clarke, either by George A. Reynolds or Milton W. Reynolds, at the time of signing said notes by him and Mr. Clarke; and at the date of the said notes neither himself nor Mr. Sidney Clarke was owing or indebted to either Geo. A. Reynolds or Milton W. Reynolds for any money whatever; that the notes were signed and delivered without consideration being paid to either himself or Mr. Clarke, or to any one for us; that Geo. A. Reynolds, the payer of the notes, acted for the plaintiff, M. W. Reynolds, and was his agent in this transaction; that while the plaintiff well knew under what circumstances the said defendant signed and delivered the said notes to Geo. A. Reynolds for the benefit of the plaintiff at the time said notes were signed and delivered, and was familiar with all the facts concerning the purposes for which said notes were given and delivered, both at the date of the note and even before he received them from his brother, Geo. A. Reynolds; that the plaintiff obtained said notes with full notice of all the facts connected with their delivery to Geo. A. Reynolds. And he further states that at the date of the notes, the said Milton W. Reynolds was connected with the *State Journal*, so called, a newspaper published at Lawrence, Kansas, and was editor of said paper, and continued to be editor and publisher of that paper until about February, 1869, when it was merged into what is known as the Lawrence *Republican Journal;* and the deponent further states that he was at the time, is now, and was for a long time before the date of said notes a member of the Republican party, a life long advocate of the principles of freedom to all, and of the equality of all men before the law; and that being thus interested in the success of the principles of the Republican party, and of the success of the members of that party in Kansas especially, he did, at the instance of the plaintiff, at the date of signing said notes, together with his co-affiant, Sidney Clarke, express a willingness to aid and assist said plaintiff in the publication of the said *Journal* at Lawrence, Kansas, provided the said plaintiff would continue to publish such paper as a Republican paper, and would in such paper support, sustain and advocate the principles and faith of the Republican party then existing in Kansas and other States of the Union, and would in his paper in future, after the date of said note, support and urge the election of the nominess of the Republican State Convention of Kansas for the year 1866 and thereafter, and the nominees of the Douglas county Republican Convention of the same year; that in consideration of the execution and delivery of the said notes to the said plaintiff by the defendants, the said Milton W. Reynolds then agreed, and the said Geo. A. Reynolds, for and his in behalf, agreed that the said *State Journal* should be published by him as a true Republican paper, devoted to the success of the Republican party in Kansas, and the advocate of the nominees of the party in Kansas in 1866 and thereafter; and especially promised, in consideration of obtaining said notes so sued on, that he, the plaintiff, would directly and indirectly, through his writings in the said *State Journal*, published at Lawrence, Kansas, endeavor to procure the election of all the nominees of said State Convention in Kansas, at the November election of that year, for and to the offices for which they were so nominated, and would also support and endeavor to procure the election of the Republican Senators at the hands of the Legislature of Kansas of 1867. And deponent further states that upon said agreement and promises on the part of the plaintiff said notes were executed and delivered to Geo. A. Reynolds, for Milton W. Reynolds, his brother; and, further, that in 1866, after the date of said notes, and before they became due, the Republicans of the State met in convention and nominated a full set of candidates for state officers in Kansas, and among the persons so nominated was S. J. Crawford for Governor and the Hon. Sidney Clarke as candidate for Representative to Congress from the State of Kansas, and the said S. J. Crawford and the said Sidney Clarke, with the other persons so nominated at said convention, were the regular nominees of the Republican party of the State for that year, to be supported by the Republican electors at the fall election; and this deponent further states, that the said plaintiff, soon after the date of said notes, in violation of his covenants, and promises, and agreements, and long before either of said notes became due, refused and neglected to publish his said paper, the *State Journal*, as an exclusively Republican paper, and failed and refused to fulfils his said promises and agreements; and did, before said notes became due, support and sustain Democratic principles in his said *State Journal*; and did refuse and fail to support and advocate, by his writings in said paper, the election of the said S. J. Crawford to be Governor of the State of Kansas and the said Sidney Clarke to be Representative in Congress from said State at the fall election in 1866; and did fail to support and advocate the election of other of the regular Republican State Convention candidates of 1866; and did fail to support and endeavor to elect the county Republican candidates from Douglas county for the same year; and did, in violation of said promise and agreements, directly and indirectly sustain and advocate, through the columns of the said *State Journal*, the election of

James L. McDowell for Governor of Kansas at the fall election of 1866; and did advocate and support the election of Charles Blair to be Representative in Congress from Kansas at the fall election of 1866; and the said McDowell and the said Blair were then the Democratic nominees and candidates for positions against the said S. L. Crawford and the said Sidney Clarke; and during the said political canvass of 1866 the said plaintiff supported the claims and urged the election, through the columns of said *Journal*, of the said Democratic candidates, and also other Democratic nominees of the Democratic Convention of Kansas for 1866, and also several Democratic nominees in Douglas county for the same year. And the deponent further states that during the said canvass of 1866 in Kansas, after the date of said notes, and before the same became due, the said *State Journal*, published and edited at Lawrence, Kansas, by the said plaintiff, was injurious and detrimental to the Republican party and cause in Kansas, and used its columns to the injury and detriment of the nominees of the Republican party in Kansas for 1866; and the course of said paper was injurious to the said Sidney Clarke and to all the advocates of Republican measures and principles in the State. And deponent further states, that at the time, and after the said notes became due, they were never presented to him for payment by said plaintiff, and it was distinctly understood between the parties, that the support of the Democratic party by the plaintiff discharged both Sidney Clarke and this deponent from any obligation to aid the paper of which the plaintiff was the proprietor. And the deponent further states that neither of said notes were ever protested, and that from the time they were given until just before the commencement of this suit, he had no intimation that anything would be claimed from the obligation. And the deponent further states, that in January, 1867, after, or about the time of his re-election to the Senate of the United States, he had a conversation with the plaintiff, who declared that he was in sentiment as much a Republican as the deponent himself, and that his support of the Democratic or Johnson party and its candidate during the preceding canvass was only because of his desire to sustain his brother, Geo. A. Reynolds, in his office as agent of the Seminole Indians, and that he judged it better on that account to sustain the Johnson party; but that hereafter he intended to support the Republican party, at least he should support the Senators from the State—meaning the deponent and Hon. E. G. Ross; but he made no claim for payment of any money; he exhibited no notes, and did not speak of any. Deponent does remember paying the plaintiff the sum of two hundred and fifty dollars; but that sum was paid at the time of this deponent's visit to Lawrence and Topeka about the beginning of the year 1867, and had no relation to these notes, and at this time no notes were presented or spoken of; but that sum was paid him upon his representation of his expenses at Topeka and Lawrence, and that of his friends in the canvass for Senators, about the first day of that year, (1867).

S. C. POMEROY.

Also of Sidney Clarke, of lawful age, who, being first duly examined, cautioned and solemnly sworn, deposes and says: That he resides in the city of Lawrence, and State of Kansas, and is acquainted with all the parties to this suit; that he is at present a member of Congress from the State of Kansas, and in attendance upon the second session of the Forty first Congress, which will continue beyond the 4th of March next, which renders it impossible for him to be present at the February term of the District Court of Douglas county; and he further states, that in the case of the above mentioned suit he signed the two notes of one thousand dollars each with Senator Pomeroy; that he frequently conferred with Geo. A. Reynolds and Milton W. Reynolds in reference to the position of the *State Journal* towards the Republican party; that Geo. A. Reynolds informed him, and he also understood from Milton W. Reynolds, that he was one of the chief owners of the *State Journal*; that the said Geo. A. Reynolds informed deponent that he exercised a controlling influence over the columns of the paper, and had furnished the greater part of the capital for the purchase; that both of these men complained that they found it very hard to sustain their paper from the subscriptions and advertisements, and claimed that they ought to receive some support from the Republican party; that after consultation with Senator Pomeroy an arrangement was finally made, and agreed to by Geo. A. Reynolds and Milton W. Reynolds, that they would support in the columns of the *State Journal* the Republican party, its principles and candidates at the Fall election of 1866; that it was in consequence of this agreement, and for no other reason, that the notes were given; and the deponent does not remember whether they were given at his own room or at Senator Pomeroy's house; that he heard no more about this matter until after the meeting of the Republican State Convention for that year, held at Topeka, Kansas, about the first of September; that at that convention S. J. Crawford was nominated for Governor and the deponent for Congress, with a full Republican State ticket; that on my return to Lawrence, I think on the following evening, Geo. A. Reynolds and Milton W. Reynolds called at my residence on Tennessee street at a late hour in the evening, and desired to have a conversation with me in reference to the course of the *State Journal*; that they stated to me, that in consideration of the fact that Geo. A. Reynolds held the office of Seminole Indian Agent it would be more for their interest to sustain Mr. Johnson's administration, and secure the patronage and emoluments to the Indian agency, and perhaps other emoluments, than to support the Republican ticket; that they stated that it became necessary to decide this question before the issue of the next daily edition of the *State Journal* on the following morning, and they thought it would not be honorable to break the engagement with myself and Senator Pomeroy without notifying me of the fact, and consulting me in reference thereto. They stated to me, that inasmuch as there could be no doubt about the election of the Republican ticket, they supposed that myself and Senator Pomeroy would be willing to discontinue the arrangement heretofore made. I stated to them that while of course there was no doubt about the election of the Republican party and ticket, that I believed the administration of Mr. Johnson meant mischief to the country, and that while they might find it for their temporary pecuniary benefit to sustain the administration, in the long run they would not find it so, and that they would be liable to the charge of being inconsistent, vacillating and mercenary.

Both of the Messrs. Reynolds argued that they could not afford to relinquish the patronage of the Seminole Indian Agency, and that inasmuch as there was already one Republican paper in Lawrence—the Lawrence *Tribune*—and but few Democratic papers in the State, it was a better field for the *Journal* to support the Democratic ticket, and it was intimated to me that there were parties who would make it for their pecuniary interest to do so, to the extent at least of the amount of the notes which had been given by myself and Senator Pomeroy; and the conclusion of the whole matter was that they informed me before they left, that, taking all the circumstances into consideration, they thought it best for them to support the Democratic ticket. I remarked in substance to them that, of course, their doing so would relieve Senator Pomeroy and myself from all the obligations we were under; and to this intimation both Geo. A. Reynolds and Milton W. Reynolds gave their assent.

On the nomination of the Democratic ticket, the *State Journal* placed the said ticket at the head of its columns, and advocated its election, as the files of the paper will show. I did not remember anything more about this matter until I received a notice from Messrs. Riggs, Nevison & Foote, attorneys of Milton W. Reyrolds, calling upon me to pay the notes, and informing me that unless I should do so at an early day a suit would be brought against me.

A short time after receiving this notice, I met G. A. Reynolds near the store of Wm. E. Sutliff & Co , on Massachusetts street, in the city of Lawrence, when I said to him: George, I received notice the other day that you were going to sue those notes, and I said that if they did so I would be obliged to defend the suit; I proceeded to remind him of the conversation which took place at my house after the Republican Convention—which I have related—between myself and himself, and his brother, Milton W. Reynolds. He said, in reply, that he remembered the conversation very distinctly, and that I was right about it; that it must be a mistake on the part of "Milt," and that he would see that it was corrected so far as I was concerned. He said to me also, that the only object was to make Senator Pomeroy pony up; but that so far as I was concerned, he would see it, that I had no further trouble about the matter.

The notes were never presented to me, and never protested, and no claims were ever made upon me for their payment until I received the notice from Messrs. Riggs, Nevison & Foote, informing me that I would be sued unless I made the payment. As I was absent from Lawrence for most of the time, and as this matter had passed out of my mind until I got the notice from the attorneys of Reynolds that a suit was to be brought against me, I do not remember that I ever made any request for the surrender of these notes. I considered the matter entirely settled when the paper openly abandoned the Republican party.

SIDNEY CLARKE.

DISTRICT OF COLUMBIA, }
WASHINGTON COUNTY. } ss

I, Nicholas Callan, a Notary Public in and for the county and District aforesaid, do hereby certify that Samuel C. Pomeroy and Sidney Clarke were by me severally sworn to testify the truth, the whole truth, and nothing but the truth, and that the depositions by them, respectfully subscribed as above set forth, were reduced to writing by M. P. Callan, my clerk—who is not interested in the suit—in my presence and in the presence of the witnesses, respectfully; and were respectfully subscribed by said witnesses in my presence, and were taken at the time and place specified in the annexed notice; and that I am not counsel, attorney, or relative of either party, or otherwise interested in this suit.

[SEAL] N. CALLAN.
Notary Public.

STATE OF KANSAS, } ss.
DOUGLAS COUNTY. }

Milton W. Reynolds, plaintiff, *versus* Samuel C. Pomeroy and Sidney Clarke, defendants.

Deposition of sundry witnesses, taken before me, Geo. S. Hampton, a notary public, in and for Douglas county, State of Kansas, on the 7th day of January, A. D. 1870, between the hours of eight o'clock A. M. and six o'clock P. M., at the law office of Aiken & Barker, in the city of Lawrence, in said county, pursuant to the annexed notice, to be read in evidence on behalf of the defendants.

By consent of the attorneys for the parties, the taking of said depositions is adjourned until to-morrow morning at nine o'clock A. M., to be continued at the above mentioned place.

Pursuant to the above adjournment, the plaintiff appeared by W. W. Nevison, his attorney, and the defendants by Horton, Aiken & Barker, their attorneys, and the taking of said depositions was continued as follows:

George A. Reynolds of lawful age, being by me first duly examined, cautioned and solemnly sworn, deposeth and saith:

I reside in the city of Lawrence, State of Kansas, and know the parties to this suit.

In the month of March, 1866, my home was in Bourbon county, State of Kansas. I am the elder brother of Milton W. Reynolds, the plaintiff to this suit. I am the payee of the notes set up in plaintiff's petition to this suit. These notes were delivered to me in the city of Washington. I think they were delivered the day they are dated.

My recollection is that they were delivered to me in Mr. Clarke's room in the Metropolitan Hotel, or at the house of Senator Pomeroy on "H" street, in the city of Washington. Upon reflection, I think they were delivered at the Senator's house. Mr. Clarke, Mr. Pomeroy and myself, were present when the notes were executed and delivered. They were executed and delivered immediately.

Mr. Pomeroy wrote the notes and they both signed them,

In March 1866, Milton W. Reynolds was the editor of the *State Journal*, a newspaper published at Lawrence, Kansas, and had been for about one year previous. He continued to be the editor and publisher of that paper until about February, 1869, when it was merged in the Lawrence *Republican*.

Those notes were executed and delivered to me for the purpose as stated to me, by Mr. Pomeroy, to aid the Lawrence *Journal*.

There was other considerations for said notes. The considerations that M. W. Reynolds was to give for the notes, was that he should support Clarke and Pomeroy for re-election; one for the House of Representatives, and the other for the Senate. At this time S. C. Pomeroy was United States Senator, for Kansas; he was a candidate for re-election to that position, and the election was to take place in the Legislature in the succeeding winter.

At this time Sidney Clarke was Representative in Congress from Kansas, and was a candidate for re-election at the fall election in 1866.

There was no other consideration that I know of for the execution and delivery of these notes. There was, perhaps, one or two interviews in reference to this matter before the notes were given. M. W. Reynolds was not in Washington at the time the notes were given. I had no interest in the *Journal* further than this: I furnished M. W. Reynolds money to buy an interest in the paper when he started it, and induced him to come out here. He was engaged as an editor in Michigan on a salary.

The interest spoken of was purchased in the name of the plaintiff, and not in my name. I had no control over the *Journal* at the time the notes were given any more than one brother would have over another. I received these notes for M. W. Reynolds. After I received the notes, I forwarded them immediately by mail to my brother at Lawrence. I believed that I endorsed the notes to M. W. Reynolds before I forwarded them to him.

There was no consideration paid to me by M. W. Reynolds for the notes. They were taken by me for him, and they simply passed through my hands. I acted as his agent in receiving the notes.

I do not know of my own knowledge in reference to the payment of $250.00 on the notes. The plaintiff informed me that $250.00 had been paid on the notes. I had a conversation with Mr. Clarke in the fall of 1866, just previous to the election, in which I told him that I thought he ought to be released from any obligation on the two notes.

Q. State what was said by you in that conversation in reference to the plaintiff's fulfilling the agreement in reference to Mr. Clarke.

A. As near as I can remember the conversation now, I stated to Mr. Clarke that I thought he ought not to be held to pay his portion of the notes, for the reason that the paper was about to assume such a position that it could not be of any help to him. The paper did assume such a position that I thought it could not help him. At this time M. W. Reynolds was the sole editor of the *Journal*.

I have since that conversation, stated the same thing in substance to Mr. Clarke. The first convention was in the fall, just before the election, and after the first note became due. I am not positive that it was before the first note became due.

I knew James L. McDowell. He was a candidate for Governor of Kansas in the fall of 1866. The ticket upon which he ran was called either the conservative or democratic ticket. I do not remember which. It was in opposition to the Republican ticket. I think the *State Journal* supported that fall James L. McDowell for Governor and Charles W. Blair, of Fort Scott, for Congress. Blair ran on the conservative ticket and against Mr. Clarke. The plaintiff supported and advocated the election of these candidates through the *State Journal*.

Cross-Examined.

It was the understanding that M. W. Reynolds in consideration of these notes, should support Clarke and Pomeroy for re-election.

This is the understanding I had with Clarke and Pomeroy; after quite a lengthy conversation had with Mr. Clarke upon the subject of the proposed change of the position of *Journal* above referred to. Mr. Clarke said if the paper assumes the position talked of I presume you will not hold me on the note for any portion of it? I replied, certainly not. He then turned to my brother and said, "all right, go ahead, Milt." The plaintiff supported McDowell for Governor and Blair for Congress in the fall of 1866. These were the candidates. He supported the opposition ticket. M. W.

Reynolds was the owner of the notes sued upon on the 31st of July, 1869. I believe I had no interest in them, nor never had.

Re-Direct.

In the first conversation spoken of with Mr. Clarke, M. W. Reynolds, the plaintiff, was present. M. W. Reynolds was the owner of the notes at the date they were given. I expect to leave Lawrence about the 15th of January, 1870, and expect to be absent about three months. I am going to New York and Washington.

The candidates, J. L. McDowell and C. W. Blair, I presume, were not all the candidates the plaintiff supported on the opposition ticket in the fall of 1866.

Q. State whether or not the plaintiff, in the conversation between you and Mr. Clarke, at which time the plaintiff was present, consented that if the paper assumed a different attitude Mr. Clarke should be released from his portion of the notes.

(Objected to by plaintiff.)

A. I do not think he did in words. But my understanding was that his views and mine were in accord upon the subject.

(Signed,) GEO. A. REYNOLDS.

I, Geo. S. Hampton, a Notary Public in and for Douglas county, State of Kansas, do hereby certify that Geo. A. Reynolds was by me first duly sworn to testify the truth, the whole truth, and nothing but the truth, and the deposition by him, subscribed as above set forth, was reduced to writing by myself in the presence of the witness, and was subscribed by the said witness in my presence, and was taken at the time and placed in the annexed notice, specified; that I am not counsel, attorney, or relative of either party, or otherwise interested in the event of this suit; and commenced at the time in the notice specified and continued by adjournment from day to day as above stated.

In witness whereof I have hereunto set my hand and seal notorial this 8th day of January, A. D. 1870.

[SEAL]. (Signed,) GEO. S. HAMPTON.
Notary Public.

ELECTION OF UNITED STATES SENATOR.

The following is the vote of Senators and Representatives in the Senatorial election of 1871:

Gentlemen voting for Alexander Caldwell were:

Messrs. Haas, Hogeboom, Kellogg, McLellan, Miller, Sears, Van Doren and Wood.

Gentlemen voting for Sidney Clarke were:

Messrs. Logan, Price, Rockefeller, Vincent, Whitney and Worden.

Gentlemen voting for S. J. Crawford were:

Messrs. Cracraft, Fitzpatrick, Prescott, Stotler and Stover.

Mr. Bower voted for E. G. Ross.

Mr. Murdock voted for T. H. Walker.

Mr. Moore voted for W. R. Laughlin.

Mr. Snoddy voted for W. A. Phillips.

Mr. Topping voted for Jas. D. Snoddy.

Mr. Nelson voted for W. Shannon, sr.

Representatives voting for Mr. Caldwell were:

Messrs. Ashby, Babbitt, Bayers, Bennett, Burns, Butts, Cable, Cawker, Colley, Crook, Fenlon, Gandy, Higday, Howell, Kennady, Legate, Luce, T. H. Moore, McCartney, McLaughlin, Parker, Peckham, Pinkerton, Simons, Welch, Whittaker, A. C. Willams, J. S. Williams, W. Williams and Willetts.

Representatives voting for Mr. Crawford were:

Messrs. Bogart, Buzick, Campbell, Clapp, Friend, Hill, Hudson, Knowlton, Linn, Metcalf, Mowry, A. A. Moore, Olson, Osborn, Overstreet, Page, Phinney, Puffer, Redfield, J. M. Steele, Veale and S. M. Wood.

Representatives voting for Mr. Clarke were:

Messrs. Barnes, Benson, Bond, Fisher, Griffin, Ingle, Irwin, King, Manning, Mahr, Melville, Murphy, Reynolds, W. H. Smith, Snead, Speer, Strickler, Thompson, Van Natta, A. S. Wilson and J. C. Wilson.

Representatves voting for Mr. Ross were:

Messrs. Barber Haskell, D. B. Johnson, R. Johnson, McEckrom, Warner and Whistler.

Representatives voting for Mr. Snoddy were:

Messrs. Brice, Carpenter, Crocker, Green, Libby, Lindsay, Sells, Shattuck, H. B. Smith, Webb and Mr. Speaker SIMPSON.

Representatives voting for Mr. Fenlon were:

Messrs. Buttler and Churchill.

Representative Darling voted for Mr. Vaughan.

Representative Langdon voted for Mr. Laughlin.

Representative Morris voted for Mr. McVicar.

Representative C. S. Steel voted for Mr. Sells.

Representative G. W. Wood voted for Mr. Bennett.

AFTERNOON SESSION.

JANUARY 24, 1871, 2 O'CLOCK, P. M.

House met pursuant to adjournment.

Speaker in the chair.

The following members were present and answered to their names:

Messrs. Ashby, Babbitt, Barber, Bennett, Bogart, Brice, Burns, Buzick, Cable, Carpenter, Cawker, Campbell, Churchill, Clapp, Colley, Crook, Crocker, Fisher, Friend Gandy, Griffin, Haskell, Hill, Higday, Howell, Hudson, Ingle, Irwin D. B. Johnson, R. Johnson, Knowlton, Langdon, Legate, Metcalf, Mowry, Morris, T. H. Moore, McCartney, McEckron, McLaughlin, Olson, Page, Parker, Redfield, Reynolds, Sells,

Shattuck, Simons, Speer, J. M. Steele, Veale, Warner, J. C. Wilson, A. C. Williams, W. Williams, G. W. Wood, S. M. Wood and Mr. Speaker, SIMPSON.

Being a quorum of the House.

Senators voting for Mr. Caldwell were:

Senators Fitzpatrick, Haas, Hogeboom, Kellogg, Logan, McLellan, Miller, Murdock, Prescott, Price, Rockefeller, Sears, Van Doren, Vincent, Wood and Worden.

Representatives voting for Mr. Caldwell were:

Messrs. Ashby, Babbitt, Barnes, Bayers, Bennett, Benson, Bond, Burns, Butts, Butler, Cable, Cawker, Churchill, Clapp, Colley, Crook, Darling, Fenlon, Fisher, Friend, Gaudy, Green, Griffin, Higday, Howell, R. Johnson, Kennady, King, Legate, Lindsay, Luce, Manning, Mahr, Melville, Metcalf, Mowry, A. A. Moore, T. H. Moore, Murphy, McCartney, McEckron, McLaughlin, Oison, Page, Parker, Peckham, Phinney, Pinkerton, Puffer, Redfield Reynolds, Simons, W. H. Smith, Snead, Speer, C. S. Steel, J. M. Steele, Strickler, Thompson, Van Natta, Veale, Warner, Welch, Whittaker, Whistler, A. S. Wilson, J. C. Wilson, A. C. Williams, J. L. Williams, W. Williams and Willitts.

Senators voting for Mr. Crawford were:

Senators Bower, Cracraft, Moore, Snoddy, Stotler, Stover, Topping and Whitney.

Representatives voting for Mr. Crawford were:

Messrs. Barber, Bogart, Brice, Buzick, Carpenter, Campbell, Crocker, Haskell, Hill, Hudson, Ingle, Irwin, D. B. Johnson, Knowlton Langdon, Libby, Linn, Morris, Osborn, Overstreet, Sells, Shattuck, H. B. Smith, Webb, S. M. Wood, and Mr. Speaker, SIMPSON.

Senator Nelson voted for Mr. Shannon.

Representative G. W. Wood voted for Mr. Shannon.

TESTIMONY.

Joseph S. Wilson, of lawful age, being duly sworn, states: I am a member of the Legislature from Bourbon county; I board at Mr. Stevenson's; D. C. Finn, of Cherokee, boards at the same place. I think it was the day after the election that Finn showed several of us an envelope containing about seven dollars, and said that was all the money he had; a short time after that I saw a new pocket-book of his, which contained, I think, two (2) $500 bills and about $100 in small bills. This I saw. There was another roll of bills in a side pocket which I could not estimate. Finn stated to me that he had sold a farm in Missouri for $4,000, and received $50 down, and again he told me that it belonged to an estate and was in his hands. The members at the boarding house accused Finn of selling out and he never denied it. This was often charged against him by the boarders.

JOSEPH S. WILSON.

Sworn to before me and subscribed in my presence this 14th day of February, 1867.

B. F. SIMPSON,
Chairman.

STATE OF KANSAS, } ss.
SHAWNEE COUNTY. }

N. Green, of lawful age, being duly sworn, deposes and states: I am Lieutenant-Governor of Kansas. Was at Topeka during the Senatorial election. I had two conversations with Col. W. R. Davis, of Douglas; the first was at Mrs. Allen's, about the first of the session. I do not know R. M. Fish, of Shawnee county, except by reputation. I had another interview with Col. Davis at the Tefft House; this was a few days before the election. At this conversation there was little, if anything, said about the Senatorial election. There was some one in the room, who was a stranger to me; I do not know whether it was Fish or not. I never made a proposition to Col. Davis. on behalf of Gen. Pomeroy, or any one else, offering him a sum of money in connection with the Senatorial question, or for any other purpose. I was never authorized to do so by Senator Pomeroy. I never told Col. Davis that a sum of money was placed in my hands to pay over to him in case of his defeat, if he would form a combination with or would support General Pomeroy for the Senate. I have no personal knowledge that any member of the Legislature received money or other valuable consideration to influence their vote or action in the Senatorial election.

N. GREEN.

Sworn to before me and subscribed in my presence this 26th day of February, 1867.

B. F. SIMPSON,
Chairman.

R. M. Fish, of lawful age, being duly sworn, deposes and states: I am a resident of Topeka; was here during the Senatorial contest. I occupied room No. 11 at the Tefft House. Col. W. R. Davis, of Douglas county, who was a candidate for the Senate, was frequently in my room. On Friday, after the Legislature met, Col. Davis and myself were in the room, a person came in, who was introduced to me by the Colonel as Lieut. Gov. Green. I have seen the same person once presiding in the Senate. Green stated to Col. Davis that he (Green) came to him, authorized to speak for Gen. Pomeroy, and that the General had sent him, and desired that he (Gen. Pomeroy) and Col. Davis should form a combination and be elected to the United States Senate. Gov. Green told Col. Davis, in my presence, that if he (Davis) would form such a combination and was not elected, that there was an amount of money placed in his (Green's) hands, which he (Green) was to pay over to Davis in case of his defeat. I could not hear the amount stated, as Gov. Green spoke in a very low tone of voice when he named the amount. I know *now* what the amount was, but I obtained the knowledge by subsequent conversations with Col. Davis. There were other interviews between Gov. Green and Colonel Davis, but I do not know what passed. I retired from the room when Gov. Green came in.

R. M. FISH.

W. F. Travis, of lawful age, being duly sworn, deposes and states: I am a member of the Legislature, from Bourbon county; I am acquainted with D. C. Finn, of Cherokee county; I board at Mr. Stevenson's with Finn, Wilson and others.

The day before the election Mr. Finn showed me an envelope containing about $7, and said it was all the money he had. I heard Finn say the day after the election that he had sold a farm near Ball Town, in Vernon county, Missouri, for $4,000; afterwards I heard him say that he was Probate Judge of his county and had money belonging to heirs; I know of no money having been offered or received by any member of the Legislature for his vote. A short time after the vote I met Mr. Finn and told him that I thought, and everybody else thought, that he had sold out. He seemed uneasy, and stated that he had received a letter from his constituents instructing him to vote as he did. He showed me a letter—my recollection is that it was dated some ten or fifteen days before that. It was not a letter of instruction; it stated that "the introduction of the bill granting to settlers the right of homestead on the Neutral Land was a God send." I remarked to him that he ought to have changed his position some time ago, if the letter was the cause of his vote; he said the Sergeant-at-Arms gave it to him after we went into joint convention. The letter appeared to me to be an old one, or rather it looked as if it was pocket worn. D. C. Finn, up until about the time of his vote for Mr. Ross, was a warm supporter of Mr. Carney. I do not know that any other member of the Legislature received, or was offered money or other valuable consideration for his vote.

W. F. TRAVIS.

Sworn to before me and subscribed in my presence, this 19th day of February, 1867.

B. F. SIMPSON,
Chairman.

John D. Wells, of lawful age, being duly sworn, deposes and states: I am a member of the Legislature from Marshall county. On the day of the joint convention, and about 10 or 11 o'clock, as I was going up the steps that lead into the hall of the House of Representatives, and about half way up the steps, I met a young man whom I afterwards found out to be a Mr. Sells, who asked me to vote for Mr. Ross, and who told me that they lacked one or two votes, and that money was no object. He said this after he had followed me into the

House, and said that he was informed that I could be induced to vote for Mr. Ross. He inquired where my friend Mr, Vail was, and I pointed him out. He went to see Mr. Vail. and after some talk between them, Mr. Vail came to my seat, followed in a short time by Mr. Sells. Mr. Vail said to me that if I would vote for Ross I would make "my pile." I do not think this could have been over twenty minutes before the vote was taken. Mr. Sells then said I could fill up a blank check. I told him that I had voluntarily pledged myself to Gov. Carney, and that I considered my pledge worth more than money. I do not know that any other member has been offered money to vote.

JOHN D. WELLS.

Sworn to before me and subscribed in my presence this 17th day of February, 1867.

B. F. SIMPSON,
Chairman.

George D. Farr, of lawful age, being duly sworn, deposes and states: I am a resident of Topeka and am cashier of the National Bank; I was in the bank attending to business during the Senatorial election; there were not during the election, or before or after, checks presented by any member of the Legislature; some members have deposited money in the bank since they drew pay from the State, but not in large sums; not exceeding $200. No one of the Senatorial candidates had any considerable amount of money deposited in the bank during the Senatorial election. We cashed drafts for Mr. Pomeroy during the time he was here, not exceeding in the aggregate $4,000 or $5,000. We also cashed one draft for Mr. Carney; I think for $1,014. Two of Mr. Pomeroy's drafts were made payable to Mr. Lasher of the Capitol House. The others were drawn payable to Mr. Pomeroy himself. I have no personal knowledge of any member of the Legislature having been offered or having accepted a bribe to influence his vote on the Senatorial election.

GEO. D. FARR.

REPORT

Of the Committee appointed by the Senate of the Kansas Legislature of 1872, for the purpose of investigating certain charges against the Hon. Jairus Wood, of Doniphan county.

REPORT.

The following is the report of the Special Committee of Investigation to the Senate:

Mr. President: Your Committee, to whom was referred the subject of the above preamble and resolution, would respectfully submit that they have examined under oath all the witnesses whom they could learn, had or pretended to have any knowledge of the matter under investigation, or who could in any way throw any light thereon, and they unanimously find that there are no facts in the testimony justifying said charges against Senator Wood. But do find that an appointment to office, with a valuable consideration as security, for said appointment, was urged upon him by the friends of Sidney Clarke to influence his vote, but that he refused to allow his vote to be influenced by said offer. And the committee further beg leave to report the testimony in full, for the consideration of the Senate:

JOSIAH KELLOGG, *Chairman*,
JAS. McLELLAN,
E. H. TOPPING.

TESTIMONY.

Senator Wood having been sworn, testified as follows:

Q. Will you state any facts that you may know in relation to the charges of bribery and corruption against you in connection with the Senatorial election of 1871?

A. King and I roomed together during the Senatorial canvass of 1871, and in that time Mr. King asked me if I would not like the position of mail agent, held by neighbor Low, and I told him that I would. A few days afterwards he told me that I could have it, and that Mr. Clarke would give me the position, if I wanted it. At a still later period, he brought me a proposition in writing signed by parties—the conditions of which proposition were that the parties would be responsible for the appointment. My supposition was, (though Mr. King did not say so) that it was in consideration that I should support Mr. Clarke that they made me this proposition. When I told Mr. King that I considered there was no responsibility in that proposition, I did not intend by that remark to convey the idea to him that if there was any responsibility about it, that I would accept it; but I was afterwards satisfied that he placed that construction on my language from the fact that he brought me a different paper, which purported to be a responsible proposition. Afterwards, he came to me one night and said: "I have a certificate of deposit which, if you will accept of, is yours, provided Mr. Clarke fails to give you the appointment." I told him that I was surprised that one having known me so long and so intimately as he had, should have supposed my vote could be bought for money. I told him that my vote was not for sale for position or money, and further told him that Sidney Clarke and all his friends had not money enough to buy me. When he remarked that he had a certificate of deposit he took from his pocket an envelope which I supposed contained the certificate referred to. The envelope was not opened in my presence, and I never saw the contents. Mr. King then said to me that he would take it back to-morrow morning, and remarked that I need have no fear of his ever approaching me again on such a subject.

Q. Did any person offer you any consideration to influence your vote for any candidate for the position of United States Senator, other than the one mentioned above?

A. There never was any person made me any proposition, or offer of any kind, or description to vote for any other candidate than Sidney Clarke.

Q. Who were the parties whose names were signed to the proposition hereinbefore mentioned?

A. I paid little attention to it, and do not remember the names.

JAIRUS WOOD.

S. C. KING.

Having been sworn, testified as follows:

Q. Will you state any facts you may know which will sustain the charge of bribery and corruption against Senator Wood in connection with the Senatorial election of 1871?

A. I know of none.

Q. Were you a member of the House during the year of 1871?

A. I was from Atchison county.

Q. Were you frequently in Sidney Clarke's room?

A. Frequently.

Q. Do you know that Senator Wood was anxious to obtain money or other consideration for his vote for United States Senator?

A. I do not.

Q. Do you know that he ever offered his vote for money or other valuable consideration during that Senatorial election?

A. I don't know that he did.

Q. Did you ever tell any one that the vote of Senator Wood of the Doniphan county delegation could be influenced by money?

A. I did not.

Q. Did you ever tell any one that the vote of the Doniphan county delegation could be influenced by money?

A. No.

Q. Were you frequently in conversation with Senator Wood at that time?

A. Yes.

Q. Did Senator Wood ever give you to understand in any way that his vote could be influenced by money or other pecuniary consideration?

A. No.

Q. Did you, or do you know of any one else having offered Senator Wood, any money or other pecuniary consideration to influence his vote?

A. No.

Q. Did you or do you know of any one else having offered any consideration to Senator Wood to influence his vote in said election?

A. Sidney Clarke offered to procure for Dr. Wood the appointment as mail agent for his vote, which was refused by Dr. Wood.

Q. What assurance did Mr. Clarke or any of his friends offer Senator Wood as security that he should have said office of mail agent?

A. A check of $3,000 placed in my hand as trustee by Dan Adams conditioned verbally, that if Dr. Wood did not get the appointment in the time prescribed—being within three months—that I should draw the money and pay it over to Dr. Wood; otherwise the check to be returned if the appointment was made. I presented the proposition to Dr. Wood verbally, but he refused to entertain the proposition. I returned the check to Col. Abell, saying that I had failed in the negotiation.

Q. Do you know whether Mr. Clarke knew of the proposition stated by you as above?

A. Yes.

Q. Did Sidney Clarke know that you were authorized to make the proposition as above stated?

A. I refuse to answer the question.

The objection of the witness was submitted to the Senate, which body decided that the question should be answered, whereupon the witness appeared and answered as follows:

"I think he did."

The witness presented himself, and asked to explain his foregoing testimony, as follows:

"I was mistaken in regard to the check above stated. It was a certificate of deposit. I handed the said certificate, in a sealed envelope, to Col. Abell, with the request that he hand it back to Dan Adams, and to say that the negotiation had failed."

Q. Do you know of any one who professes to know any facts that would tend to show the truth of the charges made against Senator Wood.

A. I do not.

S. C. KING RE-CALLED.

Q. What do you know about Senator Wood having the certificate of deposit spoken of in his possession?

A. He never had it in his possession.

Q. Did you ever tell Mr. Dolan or any one else that Senator Wood had the certificate in his possession?

A. I never did.

Q. When you answered the question, "Did Sidney Clarke know that you were authorized to make the proposition as above stated," and you answered, "I think he did," did you refer to the mail agency, or to the certificate of deposit, or to both?

A. In giving that answer at that time "I did refer to both" My recollection is, that I mentioned the desired security to Mr. Clarke, who referred me to Col. Abell, and by him I was referred to D. M. Adams, who gave me the certificate of deposit; hence I could not testify that Mr. Clarke knew concerning the certificate; but from having had the conversation with him first I answered that I thought he "did know."

Q. Are we to understand that Mr. Wood stated to you that a money security would be desired by him ?

A. When I returned to Dr. Wood and stated to him that Mr. Clarke would procure me the mail agency, Dr. Wood stated to me that he would not take Mr. Clarke's word, but would like to have some security equivalent to the position for the time; he desired it.

Q. Did he state if that security was given he would then support Mr. Clarke?

A. He never did.

Q. Did you show Mr. Wood the certificate of deposit mentioned ?

A. I think not; but I am not clear on that point; but I do know that it was in an envelope, and never left my possession until I handed it back to Col. Abell.

Q. Did you endorse that check ?

A. I did not.

Q. Did Dr. Wood at any time say to you, that for any consideration he would vote for or support Mr. Clarke?

A. He did not.

T. J. DOLAN,

Having been sworn, testified as follows:

Q. Do you know Senator Wood ?

A. Yes, sir.

A. Do you know anything of his offering to sell his vote for money or other valuable consideration during the Senatorial election of 1871 ?

A. All I know, I learned from Samuel C. King.

Q. Do you know anything of the Doniphan county delegation offering to sell their votes at said election.

A. Not from my own personal knowledge ?

Q. What is the source of your information ?

A. What I have heard from other parties.

Q. Did you ever hear Wood say anything about the matter in question?

A. I never heard Wood say anything of it himself, but have heard Sam King, say that Wood was willing to compromise his vote, for certain considerations.

Q. What were the considerations?

A. The considerations were, as King informed me, that he (Senator Wood) would vote for Mr. Clarke, if he (Mr. Clarke,) would secure him the mail agency of the State of Kansas, but he wanted this appointment secured, and for that purpose Mr. King was to hold a certificate of deposit for $3,000, which was to be paid to Wood at the expiration of three months in case he did not receive said appointment.

A. Do you know whether Mr. Clarke had any information of the certificate of deposit mentioned by Mr. King?

A. I think not; my recollection is that I went with Mr. King to see Sidney Clarke, and stated that we could secure the Doniphan county delegation if he could give the appointment of mail agent. He said he thought he could, but would have to see Mr. Low before making the promise. Later on the same day he promised to give us the mail agency.

Q. Did Mr. Clarke understand that you wanted the mail agency to influence votes for him for United States Senator?

A. I think he understood by that appointment that the Doniphan delegation would vote for him.

Q. Was anything said to Mr. Clarke in regard to the certificate of deposit?

A. There was not.

Q. Was anything said to Mr. Clarke at any time in your presence previous to or during that election relative to said certificate of deposit?

A. There was nothing said in my presence relative to the certificate in substance, except that the appointment would have to be made, pledged our word and considered ourselves responsible for that appointment.

Q. Who do you mean when you say "we"?

A. I mean Mr. Clarke's friends, including myself.

Q. What were the grounds on which you considered yourselves responsible?

A. We considered ourselves personally bound to give that appointment as we had promised.

Q. To whom had you made that promise?

A. Mr. King reported that he had made that promise to Dr. Wood. I never made an individual promise to Dr. Wood; all my information relative to the promise being made, came from Mr. King, who was requested to confer with Dr. Wood.

Q Did Mr. King ever tell you that Senator Wood ever had the certificate of deposit spoken of in his possession?

A. I think not.

DANIEL M. ADAMS,

Having been sworn, testified as follows:

Q. What do you know of the alleged bribery of Senator Wood in the Senatorial election of 1871?

A. I don't know as I know anything of my own knowledge.

Q. Do you know of any one that claims to know that Senator Wood is guilty of the charge?

A. I do not.

Q. Do you know whether Senator Wood offered to sell his vote for money or other consideration at said election?

A. I do not.

Q. Did you ever tell anybody that you believed that the vote of Senator Wood could be influenced by money?

A. I cannot tell whether I ever made such a statement or not; but have heard such statements made?

Q. Did you know that Senator Wood's vote could be influenced by money?

A. I heard such talk and rumors quite often; but know nothing of their truth from my own knowledge, neither do I know from whom the rumors came.

Q. Did you ever tell Sidney Clarke that you believed the vote of Senator Wood of the Doniphan county delegation could be influenced by money?

A. I might have so stated, but I am not positive that I did, but I know that such statements were made and talked over in Mr. Clarke's rooms, and in his presence. If I did so state it was based on common rumor, and no personal knowledge.

Q. Where did you reside at that time?

A. In Topeka.

Q. Were you acquainted with Senator Wood at that time?

A. I never met Senator Wood until he came here last winter.

Q. Did you often talk with Senator Wood about the Senatorial election?

A. I think I had two or three little chats with him in Mr. Clarke's room in a general way.

Q. Did you have any talk with Senator Wood at that time about his vote for Senator?

A. I never did. We talked in a general way. I never talked alone with him.

Q. Did you receive any intimation from him that money would influence his vote?

A. I never did.

Q. Did you ever offer him money for his vote?

A. Never did; I am not in that business.

Q. Did any one professing to act for Senator Wood ever intimate that his vote could be influenced by money?

A. No.

Q. Did any one professing to act for the Doniphan county delegation ever intimate that the vote of that delegation could be influenced by money?

A. No, sir.

Q. Were you at that time in position to hear and know what was transpiring in reference to the Senatorial election?

A. No more than any other citizen in Topeka at that time.

Q. Did you have any conversation with Mr. King, of Atchison, in reference to Mr. Wood or the Doniphan delegation?

A. I do not do recollect that I had, except in a general way.

Q. Did you ever say to any one that Mr. Wood wanted $3,000 for his vote?

A. I don't think I did.

P. T ABELL,

Having been sworn, testified as follows:

Q. Did you see an article in the *Democratic Standard* of January 18th, 1872, concerning the bribery of certain members of the last Legislature?

A. I never saw the article; but I have heard its contents spoken of.

Q. State whether you know anything which will tend to substantiate those charges so far as Senator Wood is concerned?

A. Nothing whatever.

Q. Do you know anything that will tend to substantiate the charges made against the Doniphan county delegation as a whole?

A. I do not.

Q. Did you ever receive any proposition from Senator Wood or any one who claimed to act for him whereby he proposed to sell his vote for money or any other valuable consideration?

A. No proposition of that kind was ever made to me by him or any other person.

Q. Did you ever state to any one that the vote of the Doniphan county delegation could be procured by the use of money?

A. I have no recollection of telling any one so in direct terms; but I have no doubt but I said to Mr. Clarke and others, during the canvass, that it was reported that the Doniphan county delegation wanted money.

Q. Can you state any authority upon which you made a statement to Mr. Clarke or any one else in substance as above?

A. I cannot now give the names of any one who made such statements; but I know something of the kind was said by some one.

Q. Did you ever state to Mr. Clarke or any one elsethat you believed that the vote of Senator Wood or the Doniphan county delegation could be influenced by money?

A. I have no recollection of ever having made such statements to Mr. Clarke or any one else; but I know such opinions were expressed in Clarke's room and in his presence.

Q. Do you know anything of Senator Wood having offered his vote for $3,000 or any other sum?

A. I know nothing of anything of the sort.

Q. Do you know anything of any offer being made to Senator Wood or any of his friends of any sum of money or pecuniary consideration for the purpose of influencing his vote in the Senatorial election of 1871?

A. I do not.

Q. Do you know of Senator Wood having offered to vote for any Senator for money or other consideration?

A. I do not.

Q. Do you know of any one who claims to know of any matter which will serve to convict Senator Wood of the charges of corruption in the Senatorial election of 1871?

A. I do not.

F. P. BAKER,

Having been sworn, testified as follows:

Q. State what you know of the charges of bribery and corruption in relation to Senator Wood in the Senatorial election of 1871.

A. Nothing whatever.

Q. Do you know anything of the charges of bribery and corruption in which Senator Wood is connected with other parties in said contest?

A. Nothing whatever.

Q. Do you know any one who claims to know that Senator Wood in his connection with the Doniphan county delegation in that election, was guilty of the charges of bribery and corruption?

A. I have heard Tom Anderson say that $8,000 was divided between the seven members of the Doniphan county delegation and that one of the members did not get any of that amount.

T. J. ANDERSON,

Having been sworn, testified thus:

Q. Do you know anything about the truth of the charges of bribery and corruption as made against Senator Wood.?

A. I do not.

Q. Do you know anything of Senator Wood or the Doniphan county delegation having offered to sell their votes for United States Senator during the Senatorial election of 1871?

A. I do not.

Q. Did you ever state to any one that the Doniphan county delegation had sold out?

A. I never did.

Q. Did you ever have any conversation in the presence of F. P. Baker, in which you remarked that the Doniphan county delegation had sold out or offered to sell out for $8,000?

A. I have no recollection of any such conversation touching the Doniphan county delegation or Senator Wood.

Q. Did you ever make the remark in the presence of any one, that the Doniphan county delegation had sold out for $8,000, and that all but one had received their portion?

A. I have no recollection of ever having made any such statement.

Q. Do you know of any one who claims to know that Senator Wood sold, or offered to sell his vote during the Senatorial election of 1871?

A. I do not.

G. W. GLICK,

Having been sworn, testified as follows:

Q. Were you at Topeka during the Senatorial election of 1871?

A. Yes, sir.

Q. Do you know Senator Wood?

A. Yes, sir.

Q. Were you often in conversation with him during that time?

A. I think I met the Senator about the hotel. Do not remember of any extended conversation.

Q. Do you know of his having accepted money or other valuable consideration to influence his vote?

A. Of my own knowledge I know nothing at all of that kind.

Q. Do you know that he offered his vote for money or other valuable consideration?

A. No, sir.

Q. Do you know anything of any one else professing to act for Dr. Wood, having offered Wood's vote for money or other valuable consideration?

A. I do not.

Q. Do you know anything of any one having offered Senator Wood, or the Doniphan county delegation money or other valuable consideration for his or their votes?

A. No, sir.

Q. Do you know of any one who professes to know of Wood having offered his vote for money or other valuable consideration for his vote?

A. I do not.

SIDNEY CLARKE,

Having been sworn, testified thus:

Q. Did you see an article in the *Democratic Standard* of January 18, 1872, in relation to charges of bribery and corruption against members of the Legislature in the Senatorial election of 1871?

A. I did.

Q. Will you state any facts you may know which will sustain the charges as far as Senator Wood is concerned?

A. I have no personal knowledge on the subject only so far as it has been communicated to me by others, although I have a very decided opinion upon the matter.

Q. Can you give us the names of any persons who profess to know anything concerning the corruption of Senator Wood in the Senatorial election of 1871?

A. It was stated to me by various persons, among whom I remember the names of Hon. S. C. King, member of the House of Representatives from Atchison county, Col. Peter T. Abell and T. J. Dolan, that they believed that the vote of Senator Wood of the Doniphan county delegation could be influenced by money.

Q. Do you know of any one who claims to know anything concerning the bribery of Senator Wood in his vote for United States Senator in the Senatorial election of 1871?

A. The expressions which have been made to me by different parties have been generally of the nature of opinions. I do not know the source from which they obtained their opinions.

Q. Did you give N. Cree any authority upon which he might base the charges in the publication in the *Democratic Standard* of January 18, 1872, in relation to Senator Wood?

A. The subject of the Senatorial election has been the topic of conversation at different times since it occurred, and I have conversed with Mr. Cree upon the subject as I have with others. I do not now remember the precise date when these conversations took place.

Q. Did you or did you not give said N. Cree names of several members of the Legislature of 1871, among which were the name of Senator Wood, as having voted corruptly in the Senatorial election of 1871?

A. I gave him no list, but I talked with him about it as I would with any other person, and the name of Senator Wood was mentioned among others.

Q. Did you take a list of the members of the last Legislature, and name to Mr. Cree the members charged of being guilty of corruption?

A. At one of the conversations Mr. Cree took down a book containing the names of the members of the last Legislature, and referred to it in the conversation. He marked the names of different persons.

Q. Did he mark the name of Senator Wood on your suggestion?

A. The case of Senator Wood was spoken of, but I do not remember who first mentioned it. It might have been myself, Mr. Cree, or Mr. Shannon.

Q. Where was this?

A. It was in the *Democratic Standard* office. I also had a conversation with Mr. Cree and Mr. Shannon in Governor Shannon's office.

Q. Did you have a conversation at either of the above named places on or about the 15th of January, 1872?

A. I should think the conversation above referred to took place somewhere about that time.

Q. Did Mr. Cree give you to understand at that time that he intended to publish the names of those parties?

A. He said he intended to pitch into them.

Q. Did you give him the names of any persons by whom the charges might be proved?

A. In talking about the case of Senator Wood, the names of Col. Abell and Mr. King were mentioned as being posted in reference to the position which Senator Wood occupied. I mentioned their names.

Q. Do you know anything of Senator Wood having demanded money from any one for his vote for United States Senator?

A. I have no personal knowledge on the subject.

Q. Do you know of any one who claims to have personal knowledge of Senator Wood having demanded money for his vote for United States Senator in 1871?

A. Maj. Daniel M. Adams has given to me about the same expressions in reference to Mr. Wood as was given by Mr. King and others from Atchison.

Q. Did Daniel M. Adams or the other persons referred to say to you that Senator Wood offered to sell his vote for United States Senator?

A. On reflection, I state in answer to the question, that Maj. Daniel M. Adams and Mr. King both stated to me that this was the case. I cannot give their precise language; but the idea that Senator Wood wanted money for his vote was distinctly conveyed to me in several conversations.

Q. Did either of the persons referred to state to you that they had offered Senator Wood money for his vote?

A. They did not.

Q. Did they state that Senator Wood had authorized them to make any offer of his vote for money?

A. I do not remember that they stated that he had authorized them to offer his vote for money.

SIDNEY CLARKE RE-CALLED.

Upon his own request, Sidney Clarke was re-called and made the following statement:

"I have read Mr. S. C. King's testimony, and desire to say that he is mistaken in the supposition that I had any knowledge in reference to the certificate mentioned in his testimony. Since my attention has been called to the subject, I remember that Mr. King or some one else came to me with the statement that Senator Wood wished to obtain the position of mail agent, and wished that I should recommend him for the same in the event of my election. I stated, in reply in substance that the position was now held by Mr. Low, of Doniphan county, and that while I would not recommend that a friend be turned out of office to give place to another, I was willing to recommend Mr. Wood for the position he wanted provided Mr. Low, the incumbent, was willing to give his consent. My recollection is, that Mr. Low was consulted about the matter, and replies that if Senator Wood wanted the office he was willing that he should have it so far as he was concerned. I made no offer of money or other valuable consideration to Mr. Wood, neither did I authorize anybody else to do so."

WILSON SHANNON, JR.,

Having been sworn, testified as follows:

Q. Where do you reside?

A. Lawrence, Kansas.

Q. Are you one of the editors of the *Democratic Standard?*

A. I am President of the Kansas Democratic Publishing Company, publishers of the *Democratic Standard.*

Q. Do you know anything about the truth of the charges published in the *Democratic Standard* in relation to Senator Wood?

A. I do not.

Q. Have you ever heard of charges of bribery and corruption against Senator Wood in relation to the Senatorial election of 1871?

A. As a rumor I have heard of them.

Q. Can you mention any names of persons from whom you have heard these charges?

A. Mr. Glick, of Atchison, and Sidney Clarke, of Lawrence.

Q. When did you hear of these charges?

A. During the first week of the Legislature.

Q. Can you state on whose authority these charges were published in the *Democratic Standard?*

A. Not any more than I have stated.

Q. State if you were present at a conversation between Mr. N. Cree and Sidney Clarke?

A. I was.

Q. When was it?

A. It was about the 15th of January, 1872.

Q. State what was said about Senator Wood being connected with the Senatorial election of 1871?

A. Sidney Clarke said that the Doniphan county delegation had sold out in a body for $5,000 or $6,000.

Q. Did Mr. Clarke give you his authority for so stating?

A. I think that he gave Col. Abell as authority that evening.

Q. Will you state on whose information the article in the *Democratic Standard* of January 18, 1872, was published so far as Senator Wood is concerned?

A. As far as I know, Sidney Clarke was the authority.

NATHAN CREE,

Having been sworn, testified as follows:

Q. What is your present occupation?

A. I am editor of the *Democratic Standard*.

Q Can you give us any information in regard to the charges of bribery and corruption made against Senator Wood in connection with the Senatorial election of 1871?

A. I know nothing of my own personal knowledge.

Q. Do you know of any one that does know anything in regard to the matter in question?

A. Statements of certain facts have been made to me by parties who claimed to know certain things in relation to the subject of the investigation.

Q. Do those facts implicate Senator Wood in the Senatorial election of 1871?

A. They do.

Q. Who were the parties that made those statements of facts?

A. Sidney Clarke and F. P. Baker.

Q. Were the charges as published in the *Democratic Standard* January 18, 1872, against Senator Wood made by you on representations of those parties?

A. They were made on representations of Sidney Clarke.

Q. When were those representations made?

A. On January 16, 1872.

Q. Were those the only persons from whom you had heard charges against Senator Wood in this connection?

A. They were the only ones that made charges to me personally.

Q. Did you ever hear those charges from Sidney Clarke at any other time?

A. I never heard them prior to that time; but may have heard something said since.

Q. What were those statements made to you by Sidney Clarke?

A. I met Mr. Clarke in Lawrence post-office on the 16th day of January, I think. Mr. Clarke and myself are acquainted. I commenced a conversation with him, and the matter of Mr. Caldwell's election came up, and something was said about some articles that I had published in the *Democratic Standard* in relation to an investigation of the election of Mr. Caldwell. In the course of this conversation I told him the names of some members of the Legislature that had been given to me as members that were guilty of having been bribed in voting for United States Senator Caldwell, and I told him I thought I would publish them. I also told him my object was to bring the matter before the Legislature in such a manner that an investigation could not be avoided. Mr. Clarke said that if he had a list of the last winter's Legislature, he could point out about who sold their votes, and asked me if I had a list of them. I told him I did not have one of them, but that I could get one. He then asked me when I would be in my office. In reply I told him I would be in all afternoon. In the course of this conversation I told him I would like to get the names of the men who voted corruptly, and asked him if he would not assist me. He said he would; but could not go to my office then for it was almost his dinner hour; but that he would come after dinner. Towards night I met him again in the post-office, and he said he was coming to my office in a few moments. I told him I was going to Governor Shannon's office, and asked him to go; to which he replied that he would. I went to Shannon's office, and in a short time he came in. I had a list of the members of the last Legislature at that time. Wilson Shannon, jr., was also present. Mr. Clarke went over that list at Mr. Shannon's request and marked the names of those he knew or believed to have sold out on the occasion of the election of Senator Caldwell, and he marked some names, and among them that of Mr. Wood, and said he had sold out. He then stated that Mr. Wood wanted $3,000 for his vote last winter, and that Maj. Daniel M. Adams told him (Clarke) that Senator Wood wanted that sum from him

(Dan Adams) for voting for Clarke. I think that was all the conversation we had at that time in regard to Mr. Wood. The next day he (Clarke) called at the office, and said he wanted to know something about a letter from a gentleman in Lawrence, and asked if it had been published in the *Standard*; if not, he would have it published in the *Tribune*. I then referred to the conversation we had had on the previous day, and showed him an article I had written containing the names of persons who it was told to me had voted corruptly in the Senatorial election of 1871, and in that list was Senator Wood's name. I then asked him who knew anything about the facts, having determined not to publish the article unless he could give me the names of witnesses who could substantiate what he had asserted. He gave me, as parties who knew of Senator Wood's conduct last winter,—in regard to the Senatorial election—the names of Col. Abell and Dan Adams, and at the same time repeated what he had said the evening before, saying at the same time that Dan Adams would stand up to what he had said. Something being said in relation to an article that had appeared in the Augusta *Republican* about the Doniphan county delegation, he gave me the name of J. B. Davis, of Augusta; but did not say what he knew about the matter. I asked him if there could be any mistake about it as far as Senator Wood was concerned. To which he replied, no; that he was sure of it. That was all that was said about Mr. Wood.

NATHAN CREE RE-CALLED.

Mr. Cree recalled at his own request, after Sidney Clarke had testified.

I wish to state that Mr. Clarke did give me a list of the members, who he said sold out in the Senatorial election of 1871. He marked the names himself, among which was that of Senator Wood; first mentioning Senator Wood's name himself.

This was in Governor Shannon's office on the 16th day of January 1872. The next day in the office of the *Democratic Standard*, on being asked by me so to do, he gave me the names of several witnesses, in his own handwriting, who he said knew about these parties selling out, among them were the name if Major Dan Adams and Colonel Abell. [Here the witness presented a writing which he swore was that of Sidney Clarke containing the names of J. Wood and Colonel Abell and Dan Adams.] He also testified to me what he alleged Dan Adams had told him as to Senator Wood's offering to sell his vote for $3,000.

I asked him of there could be any mistake about the matter as far as Senator Wood was concerned, he asnswered, no, that there was no mistake about it at all; that Dan Adams had told him so, and that he knew he would stand up to it.

Q. Did Mr. Clarke make any arrangement to meet you for the purpose of giving you the list of those parties who he claimed had sold out?

A. Yes, he did; the writing which was had in accordance with previous arrangements was in Governor Shannon's office on the 16th day of January 1872; Mr. Clarke, also examined the proof in my office of the article entitled the "Caldwell Bribery," and pronounced it all right and correct.

INDEX.

Concurrent Resolution..

Report of Joint Committee..8, 9, 10

Special Report of Joint Committee..176, 177, 178

Special Report in Case of Hon. Jairus Wood.....................................283—304

Election United States Senator...278, 274, 275

Civil Action—Reynolds vs Pomeroy and Clarke....................................261—272

A.

Abell, P. T...124—182, 293, 294

Adams, D. M..135—149, 178—182, 291, 292

Anthony, D. R..74—79, 253

Anderson, T. J...295

Atherley F. A..235

B.

Baker, F. P...69—74, 294

Baker, H. D..175, 176

Banks, W. S..255—259

Bates, G. E..205, 206

Bond, Thos. L..58—66

C.

Chase, Enoch...178

Clarke, Sidney...80—48, 296, 297, 298, 299

Crawford, S. J..51, 52, 53, 54 2

Cree, Nathan....18, 19—24, 301, 304
Crozier, Robert.... 217—222

D.

Davis, J. B....248—249
Dolan, T. J....186—189, 289, 290
Drenning, T. H....100, 101

F.

Farr, Geo. D....279
Floyd, T. S....172, 173
Fish, R. M....277

G.

Glick, G. W.... 296
Greeno, H. S....11, 12, 13, 14, 24—28
Green, W.... 276, 277

H

Hammond, J....226, 227, 228
Hopkins, J....98, 99

J.

Jenkins, R. W....29, 30

K.

Kalloch, I. S....236—241
King, S. C....90—98, 286—289

L.

Lauter, J. T....215, 216, 217
Lindsay, John G....192—195
Linn, H. C....28, 29

M.

Manning, E. C....250, 251, 252
Macdonald, S. D....212

McDowell, James 112, 113
Melville, William 55, 56, 57, 58
Mobley, R. D. 209
Moses, Neal 243, 244
Morris, J. W. 82, 90
Mulvane, John R. .... 99, 2[illegible]
Murphy, Thomas 182, 183, 184

N.

Nevison, W. W. 48, 49, 50
Noble, George 152, 153, 154

O.

Osborn, Thomas A. 158–162

P.

Phinney, James 229, 230, 231
Prentis, N. L. 14, 15
Purcell, E. B. 221, 225, 226
Peckham, W. H. 207, 208, 209

R.

Raymond, W. G. 254, 255
Reynolds, R. J. 162–167
Russell, Edward 249, 250

S.

Sells, Elijah 196
Seip, Owen E. 189–192
Sharp, Isaac 210, 211
Shannon, Wilson, Jr. 244–21, 250, 251
Smith, J. E. 113–120
Smith, Jacob 200–204
Steele, J. M. 149–152
Stevens, James T. 133, 134, 135
Speer, J. L. 16, 17
Spriggs, William 242, 243, 244

T.

Thomas, Chester 174
Travis, W. F. 273

U.

Usher, John P 232, 233

V.

Van Doren, W. S. .... 79—82
Vincent, J. C. 213, 214, 215

W.

Webb, W. G. 222, 223, 224
Wells, John B 278, 279
Welsh, H. P. 121, 122, 123, 197, 198
Wilson, Joseph S. 276
Wheeler, Joshua 67, 68, 69
Wood, Jairus 285, 286
Wood, W. G .... 167—172

www.ingramcontent.com/pod-product-compliance
Lightning Source LLC
Chambersburg PA
CBHW031400270326
41929CB00010BA/1270

* 9 7 8 3 3 3 7 1 5 2 6 2 8 *